D1368176

Hiking the Triple Crown

Appalachian Trail

Pacific Crest Trail

Continental Divide Trail

HOW TO HIKE AMERICA'S LONGEST TRAILS

KAREN BERGER

THE
MOUNTAINEERS
BOOKS

Published by
The Mountaineers Books
1001 SW Klickitat Way, Suite 201
Seattle, WA 98134

© 2001 by Karen Berger

All rights reserved

First edition, 2001

No part of this book may be reproduced in any form, or by any electronic, mechanical, or other means, without permission in writing from the publisher.

Published simultaneously in Great Britain by Cordee, 3a DeMontfort Street, Leicester, England, LE1 7HD

Manufactured in the United States of America

Project Editor: Christine Ummel Hosler
Editor: Jane Crosen
Production Coordinator: Dottie Martin
Cover and book designer: Jennifer LaRock Shontz
Layout artist: Jennifer LaRock Shontz
Mapmaker: Jennifer LaRock Shontz
Photographers: Karen Berger and Daniel R. Smith

Front cover photographs: LEFT: *McAfees Knob in Virginia is one of the Appalachian Trail's famous beauty spots.* MIDDLE: *The hike around the shoulder of Mount Adams in southern Washington is one of the Pacific Crest Trail's highlights.* RIGHT: *The Anaconda-Pintlar Wilderness on the Continental Divide Trail.*
Back cover photograph: *The Glacier Peak Wilderness on the Pacific Crest Trail.*

Library of Congress Cataloging-in-Publication Data
Berger, Karen, 1959-
    Hiking the triple crown : how to hike America's longest trails :
Appalachian Trail, Pacific Crest Trail, Continental Divide Trail /
Karen Berger. — 1st ed.
        p.   cm.
Includes bibliographical references (p.) and index.
    ISBN 0-89886-760-6
1. Hiking—Appalachian Trail—Guidebooks. 2. Hiking—Pacific Coast
Trail—Guidebooks. 3. Hiking—Continental Divide National Scenic
Trail—Guidebooks. 4. Appalachian Trail—Guidebooks. 5. Pacific Coast
Trail—Guidebooks. 6. Continental Divide National Scenic Trail—
Guidebooks. I. Title.
    GV199.42.A68 B47 2001
    796.51'0973—dc21
                                                                00-012086

 Printed on recycled paper

Contents

Rae Lakes on the PCT
during snowmelt

Acknowledgments

I would like to thank the Appalachian Trail Conference, the Pacific Crest Trail Association, the Continental Divide Society, and the Continental Divide Trail Alliance for responding to inquiries and providing information and clarification. I also thank the many members of the AT, PCT, and CDT backcountry.net mailing lists who contributed tips and hints gleaned from their vast number of miles of hiking experience. And I thank Margaret Foster, formerly of The Mountaineers Books, for helping me conceive this project, and to Cassandra Conyers, Christine Hosler, and Jane Crosen for seeing it through.

Most of all, thanks to my husband, hiking partner, book reviewer, question answerer, trip planner, and occasional sherpa, Dan Smith, who hiked with me on all three trails, critiqued the manuscript, compiled the bibliography, and contributed some of his experiences and advice to this project.

This book is dedicated to Dan and to our many thousands of shared miles of wilderness adventure.

A view like this one from Stratton Mountain, Vermont, inspired Benton MacKaye to propose the Appalachian Trail.

Introduction

Some 80 years ago, so the story goes, a regional planner named Benton MacKaye sat atop Stratton Mountain in Vermont, looked over the endless green ridges, and envisioned a trail that would lead from mountaintop to mountaintop along the highest and wildest places remaining in the increasingly populated and industrialized East. And so he invented the idea of the Appalachian Trail.

Well, it makes a good tale. In truth, MacKaye was never able to say exactly when or where the idea came to him, only that it had been a long-held dream, which may have been born on a mountain in Vermont.

Nonetheless, the idea was real enough and in 1921, MacKaye published his article "An Appalachian Trail: A Project in Regional Planning" in the *Journal of the American Institute of Architects*.

"Let us assume the existence of a giant standing high on the skyline along these mountain ridges, his head just scraping the floating clouds," he wrote. "What would he see from this skyline as he strode along its length from north to south?"

MacKaye envisioned his giant starting at New Hampshire's Mount Washington, the highest peak in the Northeast. The giant would stride down through the Northwoods, step across to the Green Mountains and the Berkshires, then turn his head away from the "smoky beehive cities" of New York and New Jersey. As he crossed the Delaware Water Gap into Pennsylvania, he would see yet more smoke from the coal and iron industry, but also gentle green hills offering respite and rejuvenation. Continuing south, he would cross the Potomac and find himself in the still wild and primeval southern Appalachians, where he would reach his goal at Mount Mitchell, the South's highest peak.

"Life for two weeks on the mountaintop would show up many things about life during the other fifty weeks down below," MacKaye reflected—a sentiment echoed by many who have trod the long-distance trails his ideas helped to found.

MacKaye's ideas found ears ready to listen. Not far from his perch on Stratton Mountain, the Green Mountain Club had already formed. The first sections of Vermont's Long Trail, which would become America's first long-distance footpath and a key early section of the fledgling Appalachian Trail, had been cut nearly a decade before MacKaye published his article. By 1923, the first new section specifically built to be part of the AT was constructed in New York's Harriman State Park, and in 1925 the Appalachian Trail Conference was organized. On the other side of the country, a long-distance trail honoring Sierra Club founder and activist John Muir was underway in California's High

Sierra. State-long trails were being developed in Oregon and Washington, and hiking enthusiasts began talking about a Pacific Crest Trail. The idea of a trail along the Continental Divide was still many years away, yet even in that remote and wild region, seminal ideas of wilderness, land protection, and recreation were taking shape in the work of Aldo Leopold, who defined the concept of a wilderness as an area in which a person might take a two-week pack trip without crossing his own tracks. His ideas led to the establishment of the Gila Wilderness—and ultimately, the Wilderness Act, which protects so many of America's wild places.

But it wasn't until 1968 that the U.S. Congress finally passed the National Trails System Act. The AT and the PCT were the first to be designated as national scenic trails. In 1978, the CDT joined the fold. Later, five other scenic trails were added to the system, which also includes shorter national recreation trails and national historic trails. America's inventory of long-distance trails doesn't end there: it includes statewide trails, such as the Colorado and Arizona trails; regional trails, such as the Pacific Northwest Trail; the coast-to-coast American Discovery Trail; and even the International Appalachian Trail, which follows the Appalachian Mountains clear into Canada.

But of all these long-distance trails, it is the three great north-to-south trails—the so-called Triple Crown trails—that have captured the imagination of long-distance hikers and weekend backpackers alike. The Appalachian Trail (2167 miles long), the Pacific Crest Trail (2650 miles), and the Continental Divide Trail (approximately 3100 miles) are grand ideas. Each of them follows one of America's three great mountain systems; the variety of terrain and ecosystems represented in these trails is nothing short of mind-boggling. Think of America's classic landscapes. With few exceptions, you'll find them on the Triple Crown trails: Yellowstone, Yosemite, Shenandoah, Mount Rainier, and Great Smoky Mountains National Parks; the White Mountains, the Wind River Range, the Colorado Rockies, the Great Divide Basin, the Anza-Borrego Desert, the High Sierra, and the North Cascades. That's just the beginning of a list that encompasses many of America's national natural treasures.

Too, there is the idea of doing something big and grand; the ideal of being a hero in your own life. Like competing in the Olympics or playing on a major league baseball team, hiking a 2000- or 3000-mile trail is a massive achievement. Unlike the Olympics or pro sports, it is achievable by ordinary people. Anyone in reasonable health can hike a long trail. The key ingredient is desire.

Finally, there is the idea that Benton MacKaye understood so well—the need to get away from cities, industry, jobs, real life, pollution, hassle, schedules, traffic jams . . . all the ingredients of our "smoky beehive cities."

Interestingly, while Benton MacKaye invented the idea of thru-trails, he didn't invent the idea of thru-hikers. He didn't even consider it—unless you count the fictional giant in his article. In those early years, several people stated their intention to walk the entire Appalachian Trail, and a few actually attempted the journey. Among trail managers, the feat was thought to be impossible. Myron Avery, one of the AT's earliest leaders, who himself hiked the entire trail in sections, wrote a letter to a prospective thru-hiker stating why such a trip would be nearly impossible. ("Doing it all at one time would be a tremendous strain," he wrote.) Nonetheless, in 1948, a World War II veteran named Earl Shaffer hoisted his pack and started walking north. When he wrote to the Appalachian Trail Conference to announce his success—the first thru-hike on record—the reaction was skepticism. Not until Shaffer displayed his journals and slides were trail officials convinced that he had made the journey. (Although Shaffer was the first person known to have completed the AT, he may not have been the first to actually do it: In 1994, a former Boy Scout from Bronx, New York, informed the Appalachian Trail Conference that he had, in the company of five other Scouts, hiked the entire trail in 1936.)

In the following decades, a trickle of others found their way to the AT, some doing a one-direction thru-hike and others doing it in sections over a period of years. Perhaps the most famous end-to-ender was environmentalist, writer, outdoorsman, and Supreme Court Justice William O. Douglas, whose wilderness haunts also included many miles of what is now the Pacific Crest Trail in his native Washington.

In the 1970s, the interest in backpacking grew in tandem with the environmental movement. Thru-hikers, still a negligible minority on the Appalachian Trail, began to increase in number. As the interest in long-distance hiking caught on, other trails began to see scruffy, lean walkers arrive with goals thousands of miles away. And more and more people took to the long trails for hikes of a week, two weeks, a month, or more. Today, millions of people hike on America's long trails, whether they walk a few miles on a day hike or for a few months during the summer.

Benton MacKaye would be pleased to see that his idea of long-distance thru-trails has indeed sparked a "barbarian invasion."

WHY THIS BOOK

This is a how-to book for long-distance hikers—or for anyone planning extended travel on one of the jewels of the national scenic trails system: the Appalachian, Pacific Crest, and Continental Divide Trails.

In it, you'll find the information necessary for embarking on a long-distance hike—whether your definition of a long-distance hike is a two-week traverse of the John Muir Trail, a month-long crossing of Washington's PCT, a series of section hikes of the Appalachian Trail, or a thru-hike of the mighty Continental Divide.

To that end, the book begins with introductory chapters covering the basics of long-distance travel, including planning and food drops, gear and ultralight hiking, and health and safety. It then examines the three trails individually and describes the terrain, environment, and individual challenges of each. At the back of the book, you'll find a bibliography of references, a list of major resupply towns for all three trails, and contact information.

In more than 15,000 miles of backcountry travel, and having met many thousands of hikers, I've come to a few conclusions, which are reflected in this book and which I should state at the outset.

First, there is no single "right way" to backpack. This book will not give you a step-by-step blueprint; nor is it a one-size-fits-all manual for success. What works for one person might be disastrous for another. It's unreasonable to expect that a 20-year-old cross-country runner, a 40-year-old woman hiking with her dog, and a 60-year-old longtime woodsman are going to hike the same way. Long trails present different challenges to different hikers—each hiker will find different solutions.

There are, however, strategies that can increase your chances for success and enjoyment of your long-distance hike. When experienced thru-hikers have something resembling consensus on a certain issue, I'll stress it. I'll also report on interesting strategies I've observed other hikers use—both success-fully and unsuccessfully. I'll evaluate why something works for some hikers and not for others so that you can make your own decision on whether it'll work for you. Also scattered throughout the book are "helpful hints," many of them gleaned from observations on the trail or contributed by my fellow hikers.

The Colorado River has modest beginnings near Rocky Mountain National Park.

SHORT HIKES ON LONG TRAILS

Although this book focuses on long-distance backpacking, the majority of the people who hike on these three trails are hiking several miles, not several thousand. The Triple Crown trails offer hikers almost unlimited opportunities: a grand total of some 8000 miles of footpaths through many of America's most famous scenic locations.

Even if your ambitions are more modest than a thru-hike, you can learn and benefit from the skills long-distance hikers learn as they haul their packs up and down several thousand miles of trail and several hundred thousand feet of elevation gain. Thru-hikers learn to camp out in three weeks of steady rain, sleep cozily through a surprise blizzard, and cross snowmelt-swollen streams. From them, you'll learn skills that will make you a more confident hiker.

Each trail is divided into its major sections by chapter. For those readers who don't have the time or the inclination to tackle an entire long-distance trail, each chapter contains recommendations for shorter hikes (see the "Highlight Hikes" sidebars). Recommended hikes range in length from 30 miles to more than 200 miles and in difficulty from easy ambles to challenging scrambles; they will in-troduce you to some of each trail's most beautiful sections, from the Colorado Rockies to New Hampshire's White Mountains to Washington's North Cas-cades. For those planning to hike only some sections of a trail, or to hike a long trail in sections over a period of years, each chapter also includes seasonal in-formation to help you pick the best time of year to hike that part of the trail.

THE TRIPLE CROWN TRAILS

About all that can be said of the Triple Crown trails in one succinct sentence is that they are completely different from one another. Chapters 5 (on the Appalachian Trail), 10 (on the Pacific Crest Trail), and 15 (on the Continental Divide Trail) give overviews of each trail's character, challenges, and peculiarities. But it's worth summarizing some of their similarities and differences right at the beginning. These characteristics will affect which trail you choose, which gear you use, how much planning you do, and what challenges you will face.

Where They Go

The Appalachian Trail runs from Springer Mountain in Georgia to Katahdin in Maine through fourteen eastern states. The only East Coast states it doesn't cross are Florida, South Carolina, Delaware, and Rhode Island. Often called the "long green tunnel," the AT spends much of its time in temperate below-treeline forests. But whenever possible, it follows ridges in search of views. Its highest, most remote, and most scenic sections are in the southern Appalachians, particularly the Smokies and the Southern Balds, and in New Hampshire and Maine's above-treeline and wind-whipped mountains. Spring flowers and autumn foliage are highlights of a thru-hike.

The Pacific Crest Trail starts at the Mexican border about 50 miles east of San Diego and heads north over the jumbled mountain ranges of southern California, dividing its time between parched desert valleys, chaparral-covered hills, and the occasional snowy mountaintop. It then runs through the spectacularly scenic Sierra Nevada. In northern California, it enters the Cascades, then detours through the Klamath Mountains before rejoining the Cascades in Oregon and following them north to Manning Provincial Park in Canada.

The Continental Divide Trail follows the mighty watershed that separates America's waters. The Divide itself enters the U.S. in the boot-heel of New Mexico. Briefly in the Chihuahuan Desert, the CDT then climbs to the piñon-juniper zone, the dominant plant community on the New Mexico CDT. In the Gila National Forest and in northern New Mexico, the trail occasionally reaches elevations above 10,000 feet, and in Colorado it rises even higher, with an *average* elevation of more than 11,000 feet. The high, exposed ridges offer fantastic views of both the surrounding sea of mountains—and the approaching thunderstorms. In Wyoming, the CDT goes around the edge of the arid Great Divide Basin and through the Wind River Range and Yellowstone National Park. In Idaho and Montana, the CDT closely hugs the Divide before reaching its northern terminus at the U.S.–Canada border between Glacier National Park and Waterton Lakes National Park. The Divide itself continues north—to the Bering Strait!

Difficulty

The Appalachian Trail is usually considered the easiest, the Pacific Crest Trail more difficult, and the Continental Divide Trail most difficult. This corresponds with their length, the distance between resupply opportunities, and the navigational and backcountry skills required. However, all of the trails have their own challenges.

A couple of notes:

The well-marked AT goes through the most temperate climate and has a system of shelters spaced only a few miles apart. But although it requires the fewest backcountry skills, the AT is the most physically strenuous of the three trails, with by far the most difficult footway. AT hikers frequently use their hands to scramble up steep rocks and boulders. Sometimes they feel more like climbers than walkers, and as a result of the steep climbs and descents they have more knee problems than hikers on the other trails.

The PCT has the most challenging environment, ranging from scorching desert valleys in southern California, to ice-clogged passes in the Sierra Nevada, to early-winter storms in Washington's North Cascades. Navigational skills are useful when the trail is buried in snow; knowing how to use an ice ax is strongly recommended. Some stretches of trail require hikers to travel 30 miles or more between reliable water sources.

The CDT requires top-notch backcountry skills, especially navigation, along with the ability to carry large loads of water and food. You'll make your life easier if you can handle GPS as well as map and compass. Some cross-country travel is required, and you'll need ice ax skills either in Colorado or Montana.

Character

The Appalachian Trail is frequently called a "footpath in the wilderness." The truth is that there is relatively little wilderness left along the East Coast, especially by comparison to the great trails of the West. The AT might more accurately be called a "community in what's left of the wilderness," for the thru-hiking experience involves interactions with others, both hikers and residents of towns along the way. Sometimes the AT can seem like a traveling circus, and the social scene can be overwhelming. Traditional trail events and festivals, overcrowded lean-tos, and local residents who make a habit (or a business) of helping hikers all contribute to the AT's unique character. With the exception of Great Smoky Mountains National Park, where horses are permitted, the AT is open to foot traffic only.

The PCT is a "hiker's hike," no question about it. Much of the trail passes through large tracts of wilderness, including the High Sierra complex (the longest wilderness in the contiguous states) and the remote and rugged North Cascades. There are no shelters to congregate hikers together, and trail towns are farther apart with fewer hiker-oriented amenities. As more hikers take to the PCT, some AT-esque traditions are being established, such as an annual kick-off party. But for the most part, this is a wilderness hike. Bicycles are not currently permitted on any part of the PCT; however, stock use, including horses and llamas, is allowed.

The CDT is less easy to categorize. Much of it runs through high wilderness, but it also crosses multiple-use lands. The CDT shows hikers not only the space and scenery of the West, but also how this land is used—and sometimes, abused. You'll share plenty of water with cattle, see detritus from logging and mining, and ponder the fact that much of the water you see in rivers and cascades will never reach an ocean because it will be used up first. You'll also see evidence of those who came before. For decades, the Continental Divide was an obstacle in America's westward migration. The remains of mining camps, railroads, Native American settlements, and pioneer trails are all strewn along it, reminding us of our forebears who faced these mountains without the high-tech equipment we use today. Don't count on running into many people who know a lot about the CDT—it's still a new trail, and even the local rangers don't always know where it goes. The CDT is in places a multiple-recreation-use trail. Many of the sections in national forests are open to bicycles and even (sometimes) motorized vehicles. In wilderness areas, stock use is permitted, although trail conditions and altitude sometimes make it impractical.

Do any of them sound intriguing? Ready to take the first step? Come along! Like smelling more roses or spending more time with family, the decision to go on a long-distance hike is something that is never regretted.

A NOTE ABOUT SAFETY

Safety is an important concern in all outdoor activities. No guidebook can alert you to every hazard or anticipate the limitations of every reader. Therefore, the descriptions of roads, trails, routes, and natural features in this book are not representations that a particular place or excursion will be safe for your party. When you follow any of the routes described in this book, you assume responsibility for your own safety. Under normal conditions, such excursions require the usual attention to traffic, road and trail conditions, weather, terrain, the capabilities of your party, and other factors. Because many of the lands in this book are subject to development and/or change of ownership, conditions may have changed since this book was written that make your use of some of these routes unwise. Always check for current conditions, obey posted private property signs, and avoid confrontations with property owners or managers. Keeping informed on current conditions and exercising common sense are the keys to a safe, enjoyable outing.

—*The Mountaineers Books*

PART I

Long-Distance Hiking Basics

CHAPTER 1

Thru-hiking 101

Wake up, drink coffee, eat oatmeal, break camp.
Walk, walk, climb, walk, walk, descend, walk, climb.
Snack (energy bars, gorp), pump water, drink.
Walk, climb, walk, walk.
Eat lunch (peanut butter, gorp), pump water, drink.
Walk, climb, climb, walk, walk.
Eat dinner (ramen soup, macaroni and cheese), pump water, drink, write in journal.
Sleep.

Thru-hiking is a simple life, the daily routines as predictable as sunrise and sunset. But there is more:

Hear birds sing, frogs croak, rattlesnakes rattle, marmots whistle, pikas scream, elk bugle, wolves howl, coyotes call, woodpeckers hammer.

See deer and elk and mountain goats and bears. Also sunsets, mountain vistas, crystal tarns, endless views, snowy peaks.

Feel wind, rain, waterfalls, hot sweat turning cool on skin, mosquitoes biting, heat, and cold.

Smell flowers, rain-scented creosote, campfires, skunks, mushrooms, sweat.

Dream about pizza in town.

The next day: Do it again. And again, and again.

Welcome to the world of long-distance backpacking.

Previous page:
Trail like this, in northern California, gives the PCT the reputation for being "easy."

Ask any long-distance hiker about a thru-hike, and you're bound to hear certain things.

You'll hear about simplicity, about living life one day at a time with nothing to think about beyond the bare-bones necessities: eating, drinking, and deciding how many miles to walk before you sleep.

You'll hear about the challenge of living comfortably with only the contents of your pack and the sense of satisfaction of going one step farther than you thought you could.

You'll hear about trail magic: A couple of motorists stop to offer you a ride, and you end up spending the night in their home. You stumble exhausted into a town, to find yourself invited to the local church barbecue. You lose your pot-grabber, and someone gives you one at the next shelter.

You don't have to be a thru-hiker, of course, to experience the camaraderie of the trail, the pleasures of simplicity, and the self-confidence that comes with increased skills and experience. But the world of the long-distance hiker magnifies both the challenges and the achievements. Day after day, month after month, the long-distance hiker is immersed in nature. For many people, a 2000-mile thru-hike or a summer-long journey is a trip of a lifetime, a chance to ponder nature's marvels, an opportunity to slow down and reflect.

WHO ARE THE THRU-HIKERS?

Who sets out to walk a 2000- or 3000-mile trail? Rich people? Unemployed people? Super-athletes? Nature lovers? Earth mothers? Young guys trying to prove their manhood? Old guys trying to recover their boyhood?

And how do they afford it? Don't they have kids, bills, relationships, responsibilities?

In recent years, long-distance hiking has virtually exploded. A spring flood of thru-hikers arrives at the Appalachian Trail every March and April. Today, some 2700 people a year attempt an AT thru-hike. The Appalachian Trail Conference lists more than 5500 people as having completed the trail. Far fewer people attempt the Pacific Crest Trail and the Continental Divide, both of which are longer trails in more extreme environments, but traffic on those trails is growing too.

Perhaps the growth in long-distance hiking reflects our need to escape from city lives that have become ever more frenzied, as Benton MacKaye so astutely predicted. Perhaps it reflects the changing workplace, as more Americans change jobs and careers and have periods of "downtime" available for sabbatical adventures. Self-employment, flex time, and early retirement are also factors, as are

Crossing the Sierra during the snowmelt is one of the PCT's greatest and most rewarding challenges.

occasional economic downturns. Longtime AT watchers say the number of young hikers increases during a recession when jobs are hard to come by: "It's something to put on a résumé," several have said, while others prefer to spend part of a recession hiking in the hope that when they return, more jobs will be available. Others hike at times of change in their lives: to heal after a divorce or the death of a loved one. Whatever the reason, more and more people are seizing the moment to take a dream trip.

Perhaps the first thing you'll notice about thru-hikers is that underneath the trail dirt, they look pretty much like anybody else. Thru-hikers are not necessarily super-fit (although fitness certainly makes the trip easier, and they become fit during their journeys). Nor are they necessarily experienced hikers when they start. The youngest person to ever thru-hike the AT was 6 years old; the oldest was 80. My long-distance hiking friends include a respiratory therapist, a couple of firefighters, a lawyer, an optometrist, several students, a minister, a handyman, a nurse, a carpenter, a massage therapist, a writer, a couple of park rangers, a language teacher, a physician's assistant, several professors, a retired Marine Corps master sergeant, a few trail managers, and a whole lot of people about whose occupations I haven't the slightest idea. It's an elite crowd with no entry requirements save desire.

WHAT IT TAKES

Thru-hiking may be a grand adventure and a lifetime dream, but it is not easy—anything but. Despite the high hopes and grand ambition with which virtually all thru-hikers start their journeys, the dropout rate is extremely high. Appalachian Trail officials estimate that the dropout rate is 85 percent, and that of some 2700 starters, about *550 drop out in the first 30 miles!* On the PCT and the CDT, the percentage of finishers is higher, although far fewer hikers attempt those journeys. Also, the PCT and the CDT tend to attract more experienced hikers, many of whom have already completed the AT.

Thru-hikers leave the trail for a variety of reasons. Some run out of time; others run out of money. Some have family or career pressures back home; others get lonely or simply decide that they don't like hiking as much as they thought they would. Given that thru-hiking is an enormous commitment, it's useful to look at a few of the basic requirements before you sublet your apartment, sell your car, buy your gear, store your furniture, quit your job, put boots to trail, and start walking uphill.

Time Commitment

The first requirement for a thru-hike is time. An "average" thru-hike of a major trail takes between five and six months. True, trails have been done in less. A handful of lightning-fast hikers have raced through the AT in less than 60 days. On the other end of the spectrum are hikers who take seven months or more. For the vast majority of hikers, 60 days is unthinkable, and seven months is impractical. Indeed, on the western trails, a seven-month hike would force you to trudge through snow for weeks on end.

Nor will just any five- or six-month period suffice, especially on the CDT and the PCT, which have short snow-free windows. The AT's more temperate environment offers more flexibility in the scheduling department. But even there, northbounders need to reach New England before winter does (sometime in

> "Don't expect. Don't expect anything regarding comfort, weather, water, food, rest, etc. Most of all, don't expect to quit."
> —Mike Lowell

October). Katahdin "closes" sometime in mid-October, depending on snow conditions.

Trying to thru-hike without adequate time is like living under constant deadline pressure day after day. You'll want to be realistic about your schedule and what it means in terms of actual daily mileage. *And* you'll want to know what that actual daily mileage will mean to your particular body. During your planning, you may hear people throwing around phrases like "20 miles a day." But until you've walked a few 20-mile days, you won't know what it means for *you.* Unless you have reason to believe you are significantly faster or slower than average, it's a good idea to look at average thru-hiking timetables as a starting point.

Camping on sand or gravel, as in this high-country campsite in California's Sierra Nevada, minimizes impact.

What's average? Most AT hikers complete the trail in five-and-a-half to six months, with faster hikers doing it in four to four-and-a-half months, and slower hikers doing it in six to seven months. The five-and-a-half-to-six-month schedule assumes a daily average of 12–13 miles a day. This does not

account for short resupply days and rest days; the average mileage on the days you are actually walking will therefore be a bit longer.

On the PCT, most hikers aim for a five-month schedule, which translates to 17.8 miles a day (again, not counting rest days and resupplies). If you take 1 day off a week, you'd have to average nearly 21 miles a day the other 6.

On the CDT, the mileage requirements are even higher. Northbounders need to race winter to Montana; southbounders need to get out of Colorado before the snow settles in for good. Both have a maximum window of about five-and-a-half months—which works out to 18.8 miles a day (not counting rest days), assuming your CDT route runs the full 3100 miles (there are some shorter alternatives). If you take one day off a week, the mileage of your actual walking days increases to 22 miles a day. The higher your mileage, the better your chances of finishing.

These mileage requirements put stress on even the fittest hiker and are an excellent reason to consider hiking a long trail in sections over a series of years. Section hikers have the time and flexibility to slow down to smell roses and savor views.

Note also that all miles are not equal. The more rugged footway on the Appalachian Trail means that it takes more effort to do each mile. Most AT hikers find that they are able to do 30–50 percent more miles on the PCT and CDT, although CDT mileage can be slowed down by having to stop and navigate. Also, on both the CDT and the PCT there are sections where high mileages are easy to achieve (Oregon's PCT, most of New Mexico) and places where you'd almost have to be Superman to average 20-plus miles a day (the Colorado CDT, the PCT's High Sierra in snowmelt).

Money

The figure that's been bandied about for at least the last decade is that long-distance hiking costs about a dollar a mile, assuming that you have already bought and shipped much of your food and that you have most of your gear. It doesn't count transportation to and from the trailheads. Another figure you'll hear is $100 per food drop. Both figures are probably due for some inflation adjustment. Many hikers spend as much as two dollars a mile (or $200 per food drop), especially if they make frequent use of luxuries such as hotels and restaurants.

With most of your food and gear paid for, this money goes for hostels, campgrounds, or hotels in town, food in restaurants, minor gear replacement, laundry, and various miscellany (bug dope, camera batteries, shipping gear ahead or back home, a visit to a doctor, the occasional paid shuttle or taxi back to the trail)—all of which adds up astonishingly quickly. Couples and hiking partners can reduce some of the costs by sharing accommodations, transportation, and some equipment.

There are differences between the AT and the two western trails. The Appalachian Trail passes close to many towns, each of which offers temptation in

"The credit card I use on the trail is set up for automatic payment from my checking account. My utilities are paid the same way. My monthly income is deposited electronically, and I can bank by 800-number or computer (at a library) to move money from one account to another. This makes it easier on those at home, and you don't have to worry whether someone remembered to do your banking."
—Smith Edwards

the form of a restaurant meal, a real bed, a bath, and a day off. Given the social nature of the AT, many hikers spend more time and money than they had planned on little luxuries, especially in New England, where prices in quaint villages do the same thing as the trail's elevation—they rise. At the same time, the AT offers the disciplined hiker the chance to hike very cheaply, because many trail towns have inexpensive hiker hostels.

By contrast, on the big western trails there are far fewer trail towns, so you don't have as many opportunities to hop off the trail and splurge on a meal. There are also fewer facilities like hostels designed for hikers. On the PCT and the CDT, sleeping indoors generally means a motel—which means additional expense.

A word of warning: While it is possible to do a long trail on less than a dollar per mile, it does take a certain amount of discipline, especially if you gravitate toward social interaction and you hook up with other hikers on more generous budgets. The inevitable hardships on the trail make treats in town an important morale booster. If you don't have the funds to indulge, the sense of deprivation can rub off on your entire trail experience.

Fitness

By no means do you have to be a super-athlete to thru-hike the long trails. Long trails have been successfully thru-hiked by people of a wide range of ages, levels of fitness, and health, including (on the AT) a few handicapped people.

But at the same time it should be said that the fitter you are, the better you will enjoy your hike—especially for the first few hundred miles.

There's a lot of divergent thinking on the subject of pre-hike fitness. I have one friend who got ready for a PCT thru-hike by hiking a couple of hundred miles of the AT. Other people show up at trailheads with city-soft muscles and a plan to break in on the trail. Having done this once, I don't recommend it.

Despite its ruggedness, the Appalachian Trail is more forgiving of the unfit—if they start slowly. Campsites and shelters are spaced close together, allowing hikers the option of short days. PCT and CDT hikers face demanding conditions from the outset: long days, heavy packs, water sources spaced as much as 20 or more miles apart, and hot, dry weather (to which hikers are not yet acclimated). Southbounders on the western trails need to be in shape to tackle the snowbound mountains of the North Cascades or northern Rockies.

Desire and Attitude

There is no model for a successful thru-hiker.

People who have read every book available on the subject finish; so do people who show up at the start with no idea of what they are doing. People in great shape finish; so do people in not-so-great shape. People with money to pamper themselves in every hotel finish; so do impoverished hikers who rummage through hiker grab boxes. People with lightweight packs finish; so do people with traditional loads. People who have planned out every campsite

"Get in shape. I put on my hiking boots and hike with a pack that weighs about 45–50 pounds. I use a 4-mile loop trail in a nearby state park that has ups and downs that approximate wilderness trails. I also wear ankle weights."

—James Lynch III

and food drop finish; so do those who barely know where the trail goes next. Veteran thru-hikers finish; so do neophytes.

The least tangible requirements for finishing—desire and attitude—are perhaps the most important. Mental flexibility, patience, the ability to see a silver lining through a sky full of storm clouds are all important attributes of a successful thru-hiker. But perhaps most important of all is a love of hiking, which will help keep you walking when it's been raining for a week and mud covers every inch of trail. Before you commit to a thru-hike, spend some time in the woods. Be sure that this really is something you want to do.

Because here's the reality check and the unvarnished truth: A thru-hike is not always fun. Consider whether you love the *idea* of having thru-hiked or whether you love the *process* of hiking. If the former, you could be in trouble: It's no easy feat to walk 2000 or 3000 miles and climb several hundred thousand feet through heat waves, cold snaps, weeks of rain, blizzards, on ice slopes, through mud, and up rocks just for bragging rights. But if your motivation includes loving the outdoors and moving through it, slowing down to live at nature's pace, and taking the time to see the myriad wonders that unfold with the seasons, you're in for the trip of a lifetime.

THE THRU-HIKING COMMUNITY

The AT is by far the most social of the three trails. Some hikers are surprised to find that hiking the AT is at least as much a social experience as a wilderness experience. Northbound AT hikers starting in late March and early April can hardly avoid being swept into the social milieu; southbounders have a quieter time. Far fewer hikers attempt the PCT, but the shorter hiking season means that they tend to start at about the same time and travel at the same pace. That, and the fact that many PCT hikers are AT veterans, means that the PCT is an increasingly social trail. Northbound PCT hikers who want a more solitary experience can easily slip away from the crowd by starting a few days before or after the late-April kickoff party. Southbound PCTers and hikers on the CDT (no matter which direction they are hiking in) don't have to worry about crowds. To the contrary, most of those hikers will appreciate any occasional encounters with others.

Almost all thru-hikers you'll meet profess a love of the independence of the thru-hiking life. Like medieval pilgrims, thru-hikers travel outside the norms of society—they live outdoors making do with what they have, they don't work (at least, for the duration of their trip), they are transients, they form their own groups with habits and traditions.

So it's somewhat ironic that the thru-hiking community actually has a fair amount of unwritten rules, traditions, and protocols, along with a few "hot-button" issues that are guaranteed to spark lively debate whenever they are raised.

For example, in the early days of an AT hike, you probably won't be able to escape a conversation about whether you are a "purist"—someone who

"Join one of the long-distance hiking organizations and/or attend their gatherings. Most members of the Appalachian Long Distance Hikers Association (ALDHA) have hiked all of the AT. The American Long Distance Hiking Association West (ALDHA-West) is a good choice if you plan to hike the PCT or CDT."
—Roger Carpenter

believes that in order to claim to have hiked a trail, one must not deviate from the official route. On the PCT, you may be able to go a week or more before someone—usually an AT veteran—raises the question. On the CDT, the whole subject is generally regarded as ridiculous, because there's (a) no one to argue with and (b) no complete official route to either deviate from or be faithful to.

Reading the register in an AT shelter. These notebooks are communal diaries and message boards for the trail community.

The issue of being a "purist" is more complicated than you might think. Whether you're a thru-hiker or a section hiker, you'll have to make some ground-rule decisions: Do you follow every inch of the officially designated trail? On the AT, if you take a side trail into a shelter, must you go back the way you came—or is it okay to take a different side trail back to the AT? Do you have to carry your pack every inch of the way—even if someone offers to drive it to the next hostel for you? Is a hiker who sleeps in comfy hotels whenever possible less of a purist than a hiker who always camps out? Do thru-hikers who "flip-flop" (change directions) compromise the purity of their hikes? Do section hikers have to do the trail in order, each year picking up where they left off the year before, or can they simply hike wherever or whenever they want to? The short answer is, of course, that it's completely up to you. There are myriad reasons for deviating from the trail or from your original plan. Women hiking alone might be well advised to take shortcuts from the trail into town when such options eliminate the need to hitchhike. Section hikers might opt to do each section of trail in its optimum season, rather than in geographic order. Slower hikers worried about encountering foul weather in late fall in New England might take the pressure off (and reduce the risk of hypothermia or falling on ice) by flip-flopping. Several years ago there was an alternate route on the PCT, which was no shorter or easier than the official route and not much different in character. It led to a backcountry hostel that offered hikers a pleasant afternoon's respite, conversation, cold drinks, and snacks. Some hikers passed it up in the name of "purism." Would you?

The phrase "Hike your own hike" runs like a mantra through the thru-hiking community. Nonetheless, you'll meet your share of people who think their way is a better way or (worse) the only way. You'll also meet some people whose idea of thru-hiking involves hitchhiking (called "yellow-blazing," after the yellow line in the middle of the highway). When they show up at a hostel before you, courtesy of their thumbs and a set of wheels, you may find your tolerance tested as you hear them holding court as "thru-hikers." What sounds petty when you're reading about it in your living room can become passionate when you're arguing about it in a trail shelter.

Other hot-button issues include the use of cell phones and other kinds of technology, like mini-computers and communications devices. Cell phones destroy the illusion of being removed from the rest of the world, especially when the person next to you in a shelter is talking with his stockbroker. Some hikers don't *want* to hear the latest news, even if it's available through a communications device someone else is carrying. Personally, I'd rather not know what the Dow Jones is doing in the middle of a hike. Finally, the clickety-click of keyboards pattering on and on at a shelter can drown out the sounds of chirping birds and babbling brooks. On the other hand, cell phones can give hikers, especially women traveling alone, a sense of security. Today's esthetic suggests that hikers keep their use of technology discreet.

As in any undertaking that involves others, the rules of the trail are constantly changing. But one thing has remained constant: purists or non-purists, techno-geeks or technophobes, some of the hikers you meet will become some of your closest friends. In fact, most thru-hikers, when asked about their experiences, talk about the people they met on the trail.

Some of the people who may most influence your hike—and play a large role in your memories of it—are not hikers at all. In fact, one of the most interesting intersections along the trails is the meeting between the mobile and transient thru-hikers and the small and stable rural communities through which they pass. The result is something hikers call "trail magic." Along the AT, long-standing traditions of hospitality have been established; as the PCT has become more popular in recent years, "trail magic" traditions have also taken root. And even on the remote CDT, hikers are likely to be welcomed by people in small towns and ranches along the way.

Sometimes this hospitality takes the form of an organized party for whatever thru-hikers happen by. Sometimes it's a plate of cookies left for hikers on a resident's porch or a basket of fruit placed on the side of the trail. Sometimes it's an entire town turning out for a celebration of hiking. And sometimes it's a passing stranger stopping to chat with a thru-hiker and ending up taking him or her home for a day of rest. Trail magic, hikers come to think, is the habit of the trail to provide wonderful surprises round every corner. The people who interact with, host, help, and entertain hikers are called "trail angels."

Dogs

Whether or not to take your dog on a long trail is an important decision—and a controversial one. Thru-hiking is hard on everybody—including dogs. The trail can damage their feet, and they can develop dysplasia—as well as suffer from the same aches and pains, cold, heat, and dehydration as us humans. If you take your dog, you will have to be as attentive to his health as you are to your own.

You'll also have to cope with more difficulties: Hitching to town, staying in hotels, and eating in restaurants will all be more of a challenge. Dogs are not permitted on some parts of the trails, including most of the national parks. Not all your fellow hikers will be glad to see your pet, especially if your dog is rambunctious and overly friendly in a crowded shelter, if your dog is aggressive toward other hikers (and their dogs), or if your dog charges pell-mell into the only spring for miles around. Dogs also chase after wildlife, so your chances of seeing any is much reduced. The ATC distributes information on long-distance hiking with dogs.

Nonetheless, many hikers enjoy traveling a long trail with their dog. Dog packs are available so your pooch can carry his own load.

Minimum-Impact Issues

Thru-hikers are a large and visible group, especially on the AT during the main hiking season. In most instances, the relationship between hikers and residents of trail towns is positive, but it can be overwhelming for non-hikers to encounter a large group of bearded, dirty, smelly thru-hikers. Another potential problem is that, as with all groups, the thru-hiking community includes its share of welchers, mooches, and occasional petty criminals who steal from other hikers, don't pay bills in town, or simply feel that they are entitled to special treatment because of their grand odyssey. In recent years, some much-needed services in trail towns have been closed due to irresponsible hiker behavior. Please be aware of the sometimes delicate relationship between the stable, often conservative, rural townspeople and the rollicking, rambunctious thru-hikers. People will judge other thru-hikers by your behavior.

When camping above treeline, as here, near Washington's Glacier Peak, stay off the fragile grasses.

On the trail, always practice minimum-impact hiking. Try to leave no trace of your passage and your campsites. Standard techniques include carrying a small plastic trowel to bury all human waste in cat holes at least 6 inches deep; packing out all trash (yours, as well as other trash you happen upon); camping no closer than 200 feet from streams, rivers, and springs; traveling single-file in small groups; staying on the trail (do not cut switchbacks); and limiting fires to small cook-fires in existing fire rings. For more information, contact "Leave No Trace" at 800-332-4100, *www.LNT.org*.

CHAPTER 2

Food and Planning

Planning a multimonth hike can seem overwhelming, with an endless list of tasks that grows ever longer. Most of us don't have the slightest idea of what we'll be eating a week from next Tuesday, but when planning a long-distance hike, it's not unusual to buy food you'll be eating six months from now. Where will you resupply? How often will you take breaks? Where will you get money? What will you do with your pet, your house, your car, your furniture? Section hikers don't have to deal with these "trip of a lifetime" issues, but they have their own planning concerns, which mostly revolve around transportation. It's not unusual for a section hiker to put 10,000 or more miles on a car while driving to and from trailheads!

There are as many ways to hike a trail as there are ways to live a life. Some people plan every detail; some hike on the fly, going as far as their fancy takes them. Some methodically buy and ship their food in advance; others rummage through "hiker boxes," living on what's been left behind by others. Some organize their resupplies in such detail that they not only know the exact flavor of noodle soup they'll be eating five months down the road, they also know when they'll be getting new socks, mosquito repellent, and sunscreen. Others plan to buy those items en route. Some buy backup gear and organize it carefully; others follow the "cross that bridge when I come to it" philosophy.

Long-distance hiking accommodates both kinds of philosophies. Whichever kind of planner you are (or aren't), this chapter addresses the major planning concerns that you'll need to deal with—either before or during your hike.

PLANNING RESOURCES

Times have changed since Earl Shaffer took to the AT with little more than a road map. Today, there is a veritable library of information about the Appalachian Trail and a growing collection of references

The AT is well marked with white painted blazes and frequent signage.

about the PCT and the CDT, as well (see Appendix 1, "Recommended Reading"). Most of these resources are readily available through the trail organizations, whose contact information is found in Appendix 2.

Trail resources fall into several categories. Some hikers use all of them; some only use one or two. It's helpful to know what kinds of information are available.

Guidebooks

Guidebooks describe the trail in detail: where the trail goes, where the campsites are, where the water sources are, and where roads and trailheads are. They also include information about elevation changes, mileage between points, local regulations, resupply opportunities, and challenges and dangers. Some discuss the plants, animals, and historic features you are likely to see. Guidebooks are useful both during the planning process and on the trail.

Maps

Which kind of map you take will depend on your hiking style, the particular trail, and your map skills. Some hikers prefer maps over guidebooks because the information is more objective (assuming you know how to use a map). Even guidebook authors sometimes get stymied trying to give good directions!

But maps, too, have their downside. Many of them are out of date. You'll often find dozens of roads on the ground that don't show up on any of the maps. Or trails will be marked on maps, but won't show up on the ground because they've been abandoned by land managers and reclaimed by the forest.

Note that maps are increasingly available on the Internet. New sites spring up almost daily. It's easy to get current recommendations from people who participate in hiker-oriented electronic mailing lists (see "Internet Resources," later in this chapter).

Here are the different kinds of maps you'll have to work with.

Maps in guidebooks. Most guidebooks on the Triple Crown trails (and most other trails) contain at least rudimentary maps. Sometimes these are "strip" maps, so-called because they only show a small amount of the land on either side of a trail. On the AT and the PCT, guidebook maps are usually adequate. But if you are hiking in winter (when deep snow may make the trail difficult to find), if the trail is closed due to a forest fire, or if you need to find a way out because someone in your party has an injury, strip maps may not have enough information.

USGS maps. USGS topographical maps at a scale of 1:24,000 are not necessary for the AT and the PCT. The AT is thoroughly marked with its white blazes. Although the PCT is not as frequently blazed, with few exceptions it is easy enough to follow. However, hikers expecting to cope with snow-covered trails (usually in the High Sierra or the North Cascades) should consider carrying topos. Unfortunately, many USGS maps are badly out of date and don't show the correct route of the trails—not to mention roads, powerlines, and

> "Tear guidebooks into sections that correspond with your planned resupplies (a few pages are a lot lighter than a whole book). It's a good idea to bind the torn-out pages together with tape, or you'll be constantly fussing around with which page you're on."
> —Dan Smith

other man-made landmarks. They do, however, show geographical features such as mountains and water sources. CDT hikers should consider using USGS maps for cross-country segments—they will allow you to pick a better route because they give more detail.

Profile maps. Profile maps aren't really maps at all; they are graphs that show relative elevation gain and loss, usually with campsites, major road crossings, and water sources noted. Currently, good profile maps are only available for the AT. Some hikers like knowing where the steep climbs are. (For me, there's nothing worse than a surprise 2000-foot climb when I'm worn out at the end of a long day!) Other hikers would rather not spend all day dreading the next big climb.

Forest Service maps. Usually at a scale of about 1:100,000 or 1:135,000, Forest Service maps show land ownership (including private in-holdings), roads, rivers, springs (approximate locations only), and mountains, but they do not usually contain topographic information. Many Forest Service maps contain only a small fraction of the roads in the forest, making it difficult to navigate—and difficult to choose the right route. Forest Service maps are recommended for the CDT. They can also be useful on the PCT, especially if you have to hike off-trail to resupply. The Pacific Crest Trail Association also sells extremely good overview maps of Oregon and Washington (but not California).

BLM maps. Bureau of Land Management maps do contain some topographic information, but their small scale (usually about 1:135,000) makes them difficult to read. Some hikers use them for going cross-country, but they don't show all the trails, minor roads, and water sources. If you depend on them, you may find yourself frustrated at the lack of detail and the missing information.

Wilderness area and national park maps. Trails in most wilderness areas and national parks tend to be much better maintained than those in multiple-use national forests, so you don't need detailed topos. Maps on a scale of 1:50,000 or 1:65,000 give adequate information. (Note: Because of wilderness policy, trails in wilderness areas may be less well marked. However, they are generally well mapped and often well maintained.)

Commercial maps. Commercially produced maps are available for many key areas, especially national parks and popular recreation areas, usually at a scale of 1:50,000–1:65,000. Many are waterproof and contain information of interest to outdoorspeople (such as locations of ranger stations and campgrounds).

Data Books

These handy booklets, available for the AT and the PCT, contain summary information about the mileage between and the elevation of various points, with special attention to campsites, water sources, and resupplies. They are invaluable in planning and can also help you keep track of your distance as you are hiking. (The Continental Divide Trail Society guidebooks by Jim Wolf contain summary information about mileage and elevation at the beginning of each section.)

> "Always carry the next section of the guidebook rather than rely on your resupply. If your parcel is not received, you can still get to the next drop."
> —William Jennings

Town Guides

Also called "thru-hiker guides" or "companions," town guides (available for the AT and the PCT) give information on resupply stops near the trails, including information about services such as email, ATMs, laundry, hostels, restaurants, post offices, etc. Some contain maps of trail towns—handy when you're trying to get a lot of errands done. They are useful in the planning process because they contain information on what supplies are available in which towns.

Planning Workbooks

For the uber-planner, two workbooks are available for the AT, so you can write out every night's dinner and every town stop's budget. Most hikers find that this level of planning is too cumbersome or that they never stick to plans made in such detail. But some like the security of a complete plan.

Trail Narratives

If you like to read about where you're going before you get there, a plethora of trail narratives (listed under "Journeys" in Appendix 1) can feed your imagination. Many hikers find that these books help them know what to expect and keep them motivated and excited about their upcoming trip.

Interpretive Guides

These books discuss the geology, natural history, plant life, or historic sites along the various trails. Some focus on single topics, such as flowers or geology. Others are more general. Many of these guides also contain practical information.

Internet Resources

One of the fastest-growing sources of information on long-distance hiking is the Internet. All of the trail organizations involved in the AT, PCT, and CDT have websites (see Appendix 2), and there are also a number of dot-com outdoor sites and personal interest sites, including exhaustive trip journals. Mailing "e-lists" and discussion groups such as those found at GORP.com help hikers connect with each other and share information. Caution: Internet information is only as good as its source.

Videos

How-to videos are available from the major trail clubs (see Appendix 2) which address such issues as lightweight hiking or long-distance hiking on particular trails.

Other Literature

And that's not all! Also available are guides for women and videos about seniors, literary anthologies, cookbooks, and even children's guides.

GETTING THERE AND AWAY

Dealing with transportation logistics to and from trailheads is one of the necessary evils of the planning process. Very few trailheads are accessible via public transportation (although there is an "Appalachian Trail" train stop an hour from New York City!). Hikers use a variety of different strategies to get to and from trailheads. For short-term hikes, some arrange car shuttles or pick-ups with the help of cooperative friends. Others take public transportation to the town nearest the trail, then spring for a taxi or pay someone local for a ride to a trailhead. (If you don't see a taxi listed in a local phone book, ask around at a gas station.) Some hiking clubs will also help with transportation logistics; the Appalachian Trail Conference, for instance, keeps a list of people who provide shuttling services. Hitchhiking is a last resort that many hikers have to use simply because many trail locations are just too remote. (See Chapter 3 for some commonsense precautions.)

For thru-hikers, the termini are located as follows.

Appalachian Trail

Southern terminus. Springer Mountain is in Amicalola Falls State Park near Dahlonega, Georgia, about 70 miles northwest of Atlanta. The nearest major airport is in Atlanta; the nearest Greyhound station and Amtrak stations are in Gainesville, about 40 miles from Springer Mountain. From Gainesville, a taxi to Springer costs about $50. Shuttles may also be available; check with the ATC for people currently offering this service.

Northern terminus. The AT's official northern terminus is at Baxter Peak, on Mount Katahdin in Baxter State Park, in north-central Maine. The nearest airport and Greyhound station are in Bangor, Maine. The nearest town is Millinocket. Cyr Buslines (207-827-2335) serves northern Maine, but goes only as far as Medway. From Medway, a taxi ride to Millinocket costs approximately $8; to Katahdin Stream Campground, the tab will run about $40. Check with the ATC to see whether anyone is currently offering shuttle services.

The International Appalachian Trail, which will extend the AT north along the Appalachian Mountains into Canada, and the Benton MacKaye and Pinhoti Trails, which extend to the southern end of the Appalachian chain in Alabama, have alternate termini. (See "The International Appalachian Trail/ Eastern Continental Trail" in Chapter 5.)

Pacific Crest Trail

Southern terminus. Campo, California, is about 50 miles east of San Diego, which has the nearest major airport. From San Diego, the trailhead is accessible by taxi (for the well-heeled) or by public transportation. Take County Bus 894 from the El Cajon Transit Center in San Diego. The bus runs once a day. For more information and reservations (which are recommended; tell them you're traveling with a pack), call Southwest Rural County Transit System (619-478-5874).

The plaque at Springer Mountain, Georgia— the AT's southern terminus—and the very first white blaze

Northern terminus. The northern terminus is officially at the U.S.–Canada border where the PCT crosses into Canada just south of Manning Provincial Park in British Columbia. From the border, it's another 7 miles to park headquarters and a road. A Greyhound bus stops at the park and provides service to Vancouver or Osoyoos (from which you can connect to an Empire Bus line to Ellensberg, Washington). Canadian Greyhound: 1-800-661-8747.

Continental Divide Trail

Southern terminus. Greyhound stops at Deming, New Mexico, about 30 straight road miles from the Mexican border at Columbus, and at Lordsburg, about 60 miles from the border at Antelope Wells. There is no public transportation to Columbus or to Antelope Wells. The nearest major airport is in El Paso, Texas.

Northern terminus. The nearest American airports are located in Kalispell and Great Falls, Montana. Canadian airports are located at Calgary and Lethbridge, Alberta. Greyhound bus service is available to Pincher Creek, and an affiliated service (403-627-5205) offers a shuttle to Waterton Lakes National Park. Amtrak stops in East Glacier Park and Whitefish, Montana.

RESUPPLY

Planning a thru-hike can seem overwhelming. Cutting the chore down to a manageable size requires changing the way you think about it. Rather than looking at a thru-hike as one unbroken multi-thousand-mile-long journey, divide it into smaller chunks. After all, it's not really such a big deal to plan a one-week hike, is it?

Remember: You're not going into a vast wilderness for six months (never mind what you tell your friends or what your family thinks!). On the AT, you're almost never that far from a road; and even on the CDT, hikers rarely need to carry more than 7 or 8 days' worth of food.

For most hikers, the foundation of a thru-hiking schedule is the series of town stops, where you will resupply, do laundry, get clean, eat a meal, and perhaps take a rest. Think of each town stop as the starting point or ending point of a shorter hike. When you think of a thru-hike as a series of short jaunts from one mail drop to the next, planning becomes a lot less overwhelming—and hiking does, too!

There's no need to overcomplicate the issue of planning. How much planning you do boils down to personal preference. If you're the planful type, *The Thru-hikers Planning Guide* by multi-time AT thru-hiker Dan "Wingfoot" Bruce has pages and pages of forms where you can write down every noodles-and-sauce dinner you'll eat for the next five or six months. If you're more spontaneous, you may be satisfied with sending only a few food drops to key towns and winging it the rest of the way.

There are two ways to resupply: Either send yourself prepackaged supplies which you have bought and boxed ahead of time, or buy supplies as you go. Most hikers do some combination, shipping food to smaller towns where there may not be a large selection of foods appropriate for hikers and buying food in larger towns with reliable supplies. On some trails, towns are so far away that hikers resupply at backwoods lodges or small businesses near the trail. Because businesses frequently change owners and policies, information about these resupplies is quickly outdated. The town guides (mentioned above) are frequently revised and contain the most current information on these options for the AT and the PCT. For the CDT, the best source of current information is the Continental Divide Trail Society.

Not all resupply towns offer all the services and luxuries you may need, but you'll have plenty of opportunities to buy most supplies en route. So when you're deciding how much planning to do, consider the following questions:

- Does planning make you feel more secure? Are you the kind of person who makes reservations six months in advance, or the kind who wanders into town hoping to find a place to stay?
- If you're more spontaneous, how do you cope when things go wrong—like when it's raining and there are no rooms in town and you're not going to get that hot shower you were looking forward to? Are you willing to cope with the consequences of not having a plan? What if the only store in town has run out of lunch food, and you have to live on beef jerky and beer nuts for the next 100 miles? Is that part of the adventure or a massive pain in the neck?
- How important is spontaneity to you? Will your experience be compromised by always having to stay on schedule?
- What is your partner's perspective? If one partner is planful and the other is spontaneous, you can have serious compatibility problems.

Identifying Resupply Stations

Typically, hikers carry between 4 and 6 days' worth of food at a time. (More than that starts getting too heavy; less than that, and you'll spend all your time running into and out of towns, which takes time, gets expensive, and interferes with the rhythm of a thru-hike.) Whether you are a thru-hiker or a section hiker, if you'll be out for more than 4 days, you'll need to consider how to resupply.

The first step is to identify the resupply stations that are on or very close to the trail. Then identify other towns where you can stop at 4- to 6-day intervals. You'll need to guess your daily mileage in order to know how many miles you'll be able to cover in that amount of time. On the AT, most hikers groan at having to carry food for 100 miles. (The so-called "Hundred-Mile Wilderness" in Maine is the longest stretch between resupplies on the AT.) On the PCT, most hikers easily handle the 147 miles between Cascade Locks and White Pass in Washington, but balk at the 200 miles between road crossings in the Sierra Nevada.

Resupplying on the PCT in Oregon means stopping in a backwoods lodge; towns are too far away.

Recommended resupply stations and mileage information for all three trails are listed in Appendix 3, "Mail Drops."

Resupplying via Mail Drops

Prepurchasing and prepacking all of your food is an enormous investment in time. Is it worth it?

Advantages of sending mail drops

- Everything is already bought and divided into the right portions.
- You can send yourself food you've dehydrated, which saves money and improves nutrition.
- Shopping at home offers more variety than is available in small towns along the trail.
- You can save money by buying food in bulk quantities from warehouse-type discount stores or by special-ordering in large quantities from outdoor suppliers. (Prices in small towns and resort area can be exorbitant.)
- You can add to the variety of your trail diet by buying from specialty stores like health-food coops and ethnic groceries. On the trail, small towns and lodges may have extremely limited supplies.

- You aren't dependent on supplies in small towns. Early in the AT thru-hiking season, the hiker ahead of you might have bought the last mac-and-cheese dinner or jar of peanut butter.
- Resupplying as you go can be a hassle: You have to use your rest time to buy, repackage, and pack your food.
- Planning and sending mail drops ahead eliminates one variable in planning: how much money you'll need to budget for what you'll need to spend on the trail—most of your expenses for food, gear, and supplies having already been taken care of in advance.

Disadvantages of mail drops
- You might get bored with items you bought six months ago or develop cravings for food you didn't pack.
- Mailing expenses can be high.
- Packages occasionally get lost.
- You lose spontaneity because you have to stick to a schedule, especially when long weekends are approaching. (You'll need to get to the post office before it closes for the weekend.)
- It's an awful lot of work!

WHAT TO EAT

Put a vegetarian and a meat-and-potatoes guy in a room. You don't expect consensus on what to eat, do you? Don't expect to find it on the trail, either.

What you will find is a lot of conversation about food, because the way to a hiker's heart is definitely through his or her stomach.

If you already have quite a bit of backpacking experience, you know whether you are a fussy (but well-fed) gourmet, or whether your idea of haute cuisine involves pouring boiling water over some dried flakes of (presumably) food. You know whether you snack all day, or whether you prefer more formal breakfasts, lunches, and dinners.

But food planning is a little different for long-distance hikers. Appetites are larger. Nutritional needs are more important. Here are a few factors to consider.

Nutrition and Variety
Hikers need not only quantity but quality. Unfortunately, it's not as easy to plan for good nutrition on the trail as it is at home. Quick-cooking foods are less nutritious than their longer-cooking counterparts (which take time, attention, and fuel). The amount of fresh foods you can carry is limited because of weight and spoilage. At the same time, your body is working at maximum capacity: It needs good fuel, and if it doesn't get it, you might turn into a tired, cranky hiker.

The first strategy: Go for variety. There's no reason to subsist on the same

> "When packing a mail drop, include a list of what gear and supplies you've put into the next couple of mail drops. That way, if you're running out of something, you'll know if a replacement is coming in the next mail drop—or if you should go ahead and buy it at the next opportunity."
> —Roxanne Everett

> "The one thing that stands out in my mind is the right food. I read all the hype about carrying 6000 calories a day and eating corn pasta for every meal. The thing to remember is: Take food that appeals to you. If it doesn't, it has zero caloric value because you won't eat it."
> —Dick E. Bird

five meals over and over again—especially if those meals are prepackaged noodles-and-sauce dinners that vary only in the flavor of the cheese and the shape of the noodle.

There are several types of foods available.

Standard packaged foods. Readily available packaged foods like macaroni-and-cheese, noodles-and-sauce dinners, and quick-cooking rice dinners are all found in supermarkets and grocery stores in trail towns. You can vary the flavor (and add a little zest) by adding a little real cheese, hot sauce, Parmesan, or freeze-dried veggies.

You can also concoct your own lightweight recipes from foods like instant mashed potatoes, stove-top stuffing, couscous, instant rice, and quick-cooking pasta (the thinner, the better.) In recent years, corn pasta has been highly touted as an "energy food," but many hikers can't stand it after a while (it has a chewy, some would say gluey, texture), and it ends up filling hiker boxes from one end of a long trail to the other.

You can add tomato paste (available in cans or tubes), pesto, cheese, sausage, cans of tuna, salmon, or chicken, veggies, and gravy mixes.

Some examples:

- One package of stove-top stuffing, one small can of chicken, freeze-dried peas, mushroom gravy mix. Serves two.
- One package of mac-and-cheese, one small can of tuna, Parmesan cheese, extra "real" cheese left over from lunch, freeze-dried beans. Serves two.

Home-dehydrated foods. If you can cook it, you can dehydrate it; there are excellent cookbooks available to show you how.

The advantage to dehydrating: You'll be able to eat as well in the woods as you do at home. You can make meals as tasty, as nutritious, and as varied as you like.

The key issue for long-distance hikers is quantity (more on this later in the chapter). You're going to eat a lot of food in five or six months: Preparing and dehydrating 150 or so dinners is no mean feat.

You'll also have to experiment with how much food you need for a meal. A big portion of robust stew can be dehydrated, but when you reconstitute it later, it might seem a little smaller. Be generous with portions.

Foods from ethnic groceries and health-food stores. Another way to introduce variety into your diet is through ethnic and health foods. At some ethnic groceries, you'll find dried whole milk (difficult to find in American supermarkets). You'll also find different flavors of old standbys like Oriental noodle soups. In health-food stores, you'll find bins of different quick-cooking grains, great-tasting instant soups, miso soup, as well as just-add-water hummus, tabbouleh, refried beans, and black bean dip—a great way to spice up your lunches, which, let's face it, can otherwise be rather boring.

Canned foods. True ultralight hikers eschew cans. But some small cans actually make good additions to a backpacking diet. In addition to the cans of tuna and chicken mentioned above, small cans of sardines or smoked oysters

"Potatoes make a great alternative to rice and noodles. They keep extremely well, so they can be mailed in parcels."
—Brian Robinson

make a nice treat at lunch. Foods like canned chili or ravioli are not such a good idea; you can get those same meals in much lighter freeze-dried form. If you do use cans, remember that you'll have to carry them out.

Freeze-dried foods. Freeze-dried foods are lightweight and offer a variety of different flavors, which you'll definitely appreciate if you've been having a series of noodles-and-sauce meals. Freeze-dried foods are easy to prepare. Be sure to read the labels, though, as some are easier than others. The downside is that, after a while, even a variety of flavors of freeze-dried food starts to taste the same. Some hikers feel that they don't get enough fuel from a steady diet of freeze-dried meals. And finally, there's the expense: Freeze-dried meals aren't cheap and can set you back five dollars or more per dinner.

Wild foods. Forget about it! Sure, you might occasionally catch a fish (on the AT, that means fourteen fishing licenses!). If (and only if) you're an expert on wild mushrooms, you might find a few to flavor a sauce. Ramps (wild onions) in the southern Appalachians can add bite to soups and meals. Few hikers can resist a bush full of plump, ripe huckleberries. And yes, fiddlehead ferns (when young), daylilies, dandelions, and wild carrots are all edible. But really, after a 20-mile day, are you going to have the energy to forage? Don't expect a garden of edible plants to be growing right outside the shelter. Wild foods are a fun novelty menu item, but they're not sustenance for thru-hikers. You have too much walking to do.

Food for Lunch

Some hikers snack continuously all day; others like to sit down for a midday meal. Few hikers actually cook lunch on the trail because of the fuss and the extra fuel they'd have to carry. Crackers are compact, and generally manage to hold together if left in their cardboard containers. Cheese lasts an astonishingly long time, even in hot weather, as does sausage (and, of course, beef, turkey, or chicken jerky). Peanut butter is another standby. You'll also see pita bread and bagels on the trail, as well as tortilla wraps. Make a burrito with instant refried beans, instant rice (you can cook it up the night before), cheese, and hot sauce.

Quantity

Thru-hikers' appetites are legendary. Surveys indicate that thru-hikers burn between 4000 and 6000 calories per day—far more than they can carry. Numbers vary according to your metabolism, mileage, the weather (cold-weather hikers need extra calories), and exertion. Figure about 2 pounds of hiking-suitable lightweight food per person per day.

Here are three daily menus from one of my food drops. It seems to me that my husband and I carry a little more food than most hikers, but both of us lose weight over a long hike. In cold weather or when doing mega-mileage, we might need (or want) a little more. Unless noted "shared," the quantities cited are per person.

> "I put my food in three different bags: Breakfast, Lunch & Snacks, Dinner. When I leave in the morning, I put the lunch/snack bag at the top of the pack, and I don't have to dig through the whole pack to get my munchies."
> —K. A. "Goose" Cutshall

Menu 1

Breakfast
2 packages of instant oatmeal
Dried milk
Coffee (optional; we actually stopped using coffee
    a couple of years ago while hiking the PCT
    because caffeine is a diuretic; we never resumed
    the habit)

Midmorning Snack
Handful of gorp
Dried fruit
Power bar
Flavored drink

Lunch
2 ounces of cheese
A few crackers
1 energy bar

Afternoon Snack
Two cereal, power, or chocolate bars

Dinner
Cup of instant soup
(Shared) 2 packages of noodles-and-sauce dinner
    with a little extra parmesan cheese, dried milk,
    clarified butter (optional; can be bought from
    backcountry food suppliers in plastic packets)
    and 2 ounces of freeze-dried vegetables

Dessert
Chocolate bar
Hot tea

Menu 2

Breakfast
3 ounces of cold cereal with dried milk and raisins

Midmorning Snack
2 cereal bars
Handful of gorp

Lunch
Peanut butter and crackers

Afternoon Snack
2 energy, power, or cereal bars
Handful of dried fruit

Dinner
Cup of instant soup
1 freeze-dried dinner
(Note: Most freeze-dried dinners say something like
    two 8-ounce servings. For thru-hikers, that
    means one meal.)

Dessert
Fruit bar

Menu 3

Breakfast
3 cereal bars

Midmorning Snack
Mixed nuts
Fruit leather

Lunch
Small can of sardines (shared), 1–2 ounces of
    cheese, crackers

Afternoon Snack
2 Snickers bars

Dinner
Miso soup
(Shared) ½ pound spaghetti, 6-ounce can of tomato
    paste, packet of sauce mix, and Parmesan
    cheese

Dessert
Chocolate bar

For more ideas, go to your local outfitter, where you'll find a selection of outdoor cookbooks. Or watch what other hikers are making.

Shopping Mistakes

After all the work of doing your food drops, you may find that your tastes change during a thru-hike. Many hikers develop cravings for something new and different, but when they get to town, their food drop is waiting with the same old stuff in it. Leave some meals out—so that if you get bored or want to test a recipe you've learned from a hiking friend, you can try something new.

Another problem: Beginning thru-hikers sometimes make assumptions that turn out to be false. One common mistake is buying far too much of a food that's new to you, especially if it's been touted by hikers in publications and workshops as the newest miracle food. (Fruitcake was popular on the AT for some years for this reason; corn pasta has similarly had its day on the PCT.) You'll see evidence of people's shopping mistakes in all the hiker grab boxes found in hostels and other hiker gathering points along major trails. Another, less common occurrence: Some hikers decide on the trail that rather than fuss with cooking, they'd prefer to just eat cold food all the time. More than one former thru-hiker has an attic filled with unused backpacking food.

Hikers sometimes plan a little too ambitiously. At some outdoor schools, participants learn to bake fresh bread in the backcountry. Outdoor cookbooks suggest a whole smorgasbord of delicious options. But before you invest in extra cooking utensils and complicated ingredients, consider that thru-hikers tend to do bigger miles and hike through worse weather than weekend hikers. (After all, a weekend hiker can bail out on a hike on a rainy Saturday; a thru-hiker just keeps going.) Most long-distance hikers quickly decide that simplicity is a key ingredient of the perfect backcountry meal. A just-add-water meal can be a real blessing at the end of a tough day in bad weather. If you get bored with simple food, you can always get more ambitious later in your hike.

"I packed with a gourmet type last year who insisted that we buy a bag of nitrogen-packed salad. To my amazement, I sat up near Silver Pass enjoying a large green salad before dinner. The total weight is a few ounces, and the nitrogen pack keeps the greens fresh. We had it for two days."
—Pete Asprey

PUTTING IT ALL TOGETHER

Make a Schedule

To pack your boxes, you need to know how many days it will take to go from one food drop to the next. To find this answer, simply divide the mileage between towns by your anticipated daily mileage.

A few words about calculating mileage: You'll probably find that your mileage varies considerably due to changes in your fitness, changes in the terrain and difficulty of the trail, and other factors, such as water availability. We have already taken a quick look at estimating mileage in Chapter 1, in the section "Time Commitment." Chapters 5 through 19 cover specific issues on the three trails that will influence your mileage in particular sections. (An example would be that on New England's AT, most hikers' mileage drops drastically because of trail difficulty.) Regarding fitness, unless you're in top shape to start, plan modest mileage for the first month. Average hikers find 10 miles a day (or even less) more than enough at the start of the AT. It's harder for PCT and CDT hikers to start slow because they have to factor in water availability (see Chapters 5, 6, 10, and 11).

It's not necessary to know every single campsite to figure out how many meals you need to pack in a resupply box. You just have to know how many days it's going to take you to walk from point A to point B. The data books can easily help you calculate the mileage between any two points.

CDT hikers should note that there are sometimes several alternate routes, which influences the mileage between resupplies. Choosing a route for the CDT is discussed in Chapters 15 through 19; it's an added step in the planning process that you'll need to do before you can pack your mail drops.

Repackaging food in zipper-lock bags helps prevent spills and spoilage.

Make a Food List

For each food drop, start a list. At the top of the list, write down the number of the mail drop, the date you expect to be there, the "mail-by date," the starting and ending towns, the miles, and the number of days you expect it to take. Then write down the number of breakfasts, snacks, lunches, dinners, desserts, soups, and drinks you plan to take. The following example, for the PCT, assumes that you'll leave Mount Laguna, California, in the morning after breakfast and that you expect to arrive in Warner Springs before lunch. Let's assume you plan to stay in the Mount Laguna lodge and cook your own breakfast from fresh store-bought food. And let's assume you plan to arrive at Warner Springs in time for lunch at the restaurant there. Your list, then, would read as follows:

PCT Mail Drop #1: Ship to Mount Laguna
Mail by April 15
Expect arrival: May 2
Mount Laguna–Warner Springs
40 miles, 3 days

Standard items
Dried milk
Parmesan cheese
Clarified butter
Louisiana hot sauce
Spice kit

Meal	Number needed
Breakfasts	2
Snacks	3 days
Lunches	2
Dinners	2
Desserts	2
Soups	2
Drinks	3 days

Make a similar list for all your food drops. (I find it most helpful to keep the list with the actual box.) Here's the beauty of this plan: Once you have your lists, you can start buying and packing piecemeal. If you buy 20 noodles-and-sauce dinners at a discount superstore, you can divide them up among the boxes, then keep count of how many dinners you've put in each box. The next time you go to the store, you might buy masses of different soups—you simply divide them up and check off how many soups you've put in each box. By spreading out the food over lots of different food drops, you'll give yourself a menu with more variety. And, with your list right there, it's easy to keep track of what you've already packed and what you still need to buy.

Many hikers find that they buy too much, and end up either shipping unused food home (at the cost of postage) or giving it away. There are two reasons: First, with dreams of pizza and an all-you-can-eat buffet luring you on, you may speed up and get to town earlier than you had anticipated. Second, on the AT and in some places on the other two trails, there are more opportunities to get food along the way than you might anticipate. Some hikers ship one or two meals less than they think they'll need, especially when resupplying in larger towns. If you find you have meals left over from the last food drop, you can use those. If you need more food, you can easily buy a meal or two in a local grocery.

If you want to plan down to the last detail, you might also note information about stores, cafés, and other sources of food that are near the trail. This info is available in the town guides for the PCT and the AT. (On the more remote CDT, the issue is just about moot.) If one of the guides tells you that there is an RV campground ½ mile from the trail that serves burgers, you might consider leaving out a meal and planning to eat there instead. But for many people, trying to factor in every hamburger stand overcomplicates the planning

> "Tip for cooking pasta: Use thin pasta and pour just enough water over it to cover it. Let the water come to a full boil for a good solid minute with the lid on. Shut the stove off. There is enough stored heat in the water to continue cooking the pasta that it will be done in five minutes."
> —Gary Greaser and Sharon Burrer

process. The worst thing that will happen if you skip this step is that you might carry an extra meal a few miles too far.

Finally, once you have your food bought and listed, note what you still need to buy en route. Perhaps you put in one dinner too few because you think you might like to try something new down the road. Make a note of it. Same goes for foods that you can't buy in advance, like sausage, cheese, and fresh fruit.

Gear Resupply

Mail drops can also be used to send yourself gear that may be used up during a hike. If you are planning to use mail drops, you should plan to also use them to resupply yourself with items that may be difficult to find on the trail:

- Gear that wears out, such as hiking socks.
- Consumables such as sun lotion or bug repellent. (While these items may be available in some towns, they may not come in appropriate sizes or containers. You could get stuck lugging an 8-ounce spray can of bug goop instead of a 2-ounce container.)
- Replacement notebooks for your journal.
- Maps and guidebook sections for the next section of trail.
- Film (especially if you are picky about what you use).

Another consideration is seasonal gear. As the seasons wear on or the elevations change, you may find yourself wanting to send home that extra-warm sleeping bag you've been sweating in, add a couple of layers of warm fleece, swap sneakers for boots, get rid of an ice ax, or switch from a tarp to a tent. So even if you don't use mail drops for food, you'll probably find yourself using at least a few post offices for swapping equipment and for receiving things like new guidebooks. (After all, you don't want to be carrying the guidebook for New Hampshire when you're hiking in Georgia!)

Before you leave, make a stack of gear you think you might need later in the hike. You'll need to enlist a friend to send you this gear when you ask for it. If the person isn't a hiker, be sure to label your equipment so you get what you asked for. It also helps for both you and your friend to have on hand a list of mail-drop addresses (you can photocopy the addresses listed in Appendix 3).

Finally, some hikers use "floater" boxes to ship ahead gear that they don't need at the moment but may need a little later in the hike. For example, in a stretch of desert trail in the dry season, you might forgo your raingear, but you'll want it back before you climb into the next mountain range. Floater boxes can also contain treats for town, such as clean clothes or personal toiletries. Floater boxes are most useful for sending things a short distance ahead. If you think you won't need a particular piece of gear for several months, it's better to ship it to a friend at home so it's not sitting in a post office (where it might get lost or where the postmaster might think it's abandoned and return it to the sender).

Packing and Sending Food Drops

There's no magic to packing food boxes, although it helps if you have some space to work with. Get a bunch of sturdy boxes. I usually beg empty boxes from a local liquor store, because they are sturdy. Book boxes are another good choice.

Remove excess packaging, but leave enough to keep the food from being squashed. Include a supply of zipper-lock bags so you can repackage the food for backpacking. In addition, I recommend throwing in some rubber bands: The channels in zipper-lock bags frequently get gummed up with milk powder, grated cheese, and other foods. Wrapping a rubber band around a bag prevents spills if the zipper-lock comes undone.

The address should say:

Your name
c/o General Delivery
Hikertown, USA, 12345

Important note: *Never* send a mail drop to a post office via UPS or any other private delivery service. They will not deliver it, and the post office will not accept it. Same goes for a post office box address. You must use the postal service. Over long distances, priority mail gets there in 2 to 3 days and usually costs only a nickel more than fourth class. Over shorter distances, fourth class is much cheaper, but can take *two weeks* or more to get there. Be sure your mail-drop sender knows the "mail-by" dates for each package. When you calculate the "mail-by" date, give yourself some leeway and expect that you'll pick up speed and get there a little early. There's nothing worse than arriving at a resupply to find that your mail drop hasn't gotten there yet.

Sometimes you may need to use UPS. Many western lodges that hold packages on the PCT and CDT require you to use UPS or another private delivery service because they don't get postal delivery. If you're planning on arriving in a town on a long weekend, and have made reservations at a motel, you might use UPS to send the mail drop and avoid the hassle of having to race to the post office before it closes for 2 or 3 days. Clearly mark the boxes "via UPS" and make sure you've noted how the package is to be shipped on your master address list.

Make a Last-Minute Checklist

Once I showed up for a hike without the hipbelt for my pack. Another time, I pulled out my stove in the middle of Shenandoah National Park (no fires allowed) to find that I'd forgotten the pump. Now I keep a list of all my gear, down to boots, shoelaces, and the buckles on my pack.

THE HOME FRONT

Another issue you'll need to deal with is the home front. This is definitely a case of "less is more." People who have the least complicated lives will have

> "Give your food plan a trial run before you hike. Try to eat and cook out of your pack for 3 days while you're still home. How much fuel did you use? What kitchen gear did you need? How much water did you need? What did you run out of, have too much of, want more of, or not use at all? This exercise will give you a reality check on just how little (or how much) you need to carry."
> —John "T. J." Gordon

the easiest time getting away for six months. Are you a recent college graduate whose possessions fit into the back of your car? You might be able to store your stuff in your parents' basement, toss the keys to your jalopy to a younger sibling, and stride out the door. On the other hand, if you are a forty-something professional with a mortgage and kids, disengaging for six months is going to become a major project in and of itself.

The best strategy is to keep a running "to do" list broken into time blocks. What needs to be done six months before you leave? Four months before you leave? Two months before you leave?

Here are some examples of issues to consider; the time frame and how you handle them will depend on your own particular circumstances.

Houses and Apartments
- Find a tenant or a house sitter, or arrange to end your lease.
- If you have a tenant, draw up an agreement and agree on a process for paying rent.
- Make a list of key contact people. (Who does your tenant call if the roof caves in? Do you have a trusted friend who can check your property every once in a while?)
- If necessary, make arrangements to store your possessions—and don't forget to budget for it.
- If you don't already have a home security system, consider installing one for both protection and peace of mind while you're away from home.

Financial and Legal
- How will your bills be paid? (Some options: prepay your credit cards, have an accounting or banking service pay bills, entrust the task to a friend.)
- How will your mail be forwarded, and who will look out for important notices, such as a summons for jury duty, a tax notice, or problem mail? (For example, what if the phone company erroneously bills you for $400 calls to Turkistan?)
- If you use professionals (lawyers, accountants, and bankers), make sure they have a contact person. You may need to draw up a power of attorney.
- Arrange for health insurance.
- Check with your insurance agent: Some people have had difficulty getting car insurance reinstated after they cancel it for a thru-hike.
- Warning: A car that's not used for six months can develop serious problems. You can't just park it in a driveway and walk away. Put it on blocks for proper storage, sell it, or entrust it to someone. If you don't want the legal liability for a car you're not going to be driving, sell your car to a *very* trusted friend and then buy it back after the hike.
- How will you get money on the trail? Data books tell which towns have banks and ATMs. Some hikers carry a stash of traveler's checks just in case.

- If you plan to use credit card cash advances, be aware that they come with exorbitant interest rates, and the finance charges often carry over to your other purchases. You could prepay a certain amount on a credit card, and then you won't have to pay the finance charge for advances up to that amount.

Family and Friends
- Who will be your main contact at home?
- Have you prepared a mail-drop schedule for family and friends?
- Will you use email to keep in touch?
- Will you have a website for your hike? (This is an increasingly popular way to share a thru-hike with friends and relatives.)
- How and where will your mail be forwarded?
- Will you invite your friends to participate in some way in your hike? Before you do, consider that most "normal" people cannot keep up with thru-hikers. If you invite friends to join you, plan shorter days.
- If you are leaving your spouse or children at home, how will you involve them in your hike?
- Who is going to send your food drops? (Be very, very nice to this person.)
- Who is going to have access to any backup gear in case something breaks?
- Do you have a telephone calling card? Check the rates carefully; some plans are more expensive than others.

CHAPTER 3

Health and Safety

Hikers out for a few miles or a few days rarely worry about the long-term effects of hiking on their health. Quite the contrary: Walking is one of the best low-impact exercises around, and who could argue that a day in the fresh air of the great outdoors expands your lungs, works your muscles, and relaxes your mind?

But for long-distance hikers, the situation is more complicated. Long-distance hikers face physical challenges day after day, with little time to recover in between. The feat of completing the Appalachian Trail is equivalent to 82 marathons and 380 trips up and down the Empire State Building—while carrying an average of 25 to 45 pounds on uneven terrain through sometimes vile weather. The wear and tear on the body is enormous.

Hardly anyone is going to complete a thru-hike without some aches and pains along the way. Health and safety problems can be minimized with pre-hike physical fitness training, a little knowledge about first aid, common sense, and, perhaps most important, paying attention to your body and fixing little problems before they turn into big ones.

FIRST STEP: FIRST AID

Your safety is your responsibility, and the first way to ensure that you'll know what to do if something happens is to take a first-aid class. If you took a class a few years back or if your certification has expired, retake it. You'll be surprised at how much you've forgotten.

A basic first-aid class covers wounds, broken bones, burns, and mouth-to-mouth resuscitation—along with accidents you're less likely to need to know about (poisons, seizures, etc.). CPR training is not included in a basic first-aid class, but it's a useful skill to have. The American Red Cross offers courses in both. The only problem with these classes is that they assume the injury takes place in the "real" world, where you can call for help—in fact, calling for help is the first thing they teach you to do. In the backcountry, however, calling for help may not be possible, even if you happen to be carrying a cell phone.

In a wilderness first-aid class, instructors understand that in the backcountry, help may be far away. Wilderness first-aid classes focus on the injuries you're more likely to encounter, including climate-induced problems like hypothermia and dehydration. They'll also cover planning an evacuation and signaling for help.

First-Aid Kits

Commercial first-aid kits are a starting point, but only a starting point. Most thru-hikers start with more first-aid equipment than they need and leave out some of the things they do need. No standard first-aid kit list I'm aware of contains hydrocortisone, but I won't go on even an overnight hike without it. (Among other things, it relieves itching from insect bites, heat rashes, and poison ivy.) On the other hand, for many years I've lugged miles of gauze and various-size bandages hither and yon—and have never once needed them. At the end of the hike, they're dirty and I throw them out, only to buy more for the next hike.

New Hampshire's steep trails and rocky footway can put pressure on joints and muscles.

Your first-aid kit should have a few standard items. Most thru-hikers' first-aid kits fit in a zipper-lock plastic bag.

- Ibuprofen
- Other meds: medication for giardiasis and poison ivy; prescription painkillers, antihistamines, antibiotics (talk to your doctor)
- A few Band-Aids (various sizes)
- A few bandages (various sizes)
- Blister kit (Second Skin dressing, moleskin, a needle)
- Small amount of alcohol for disinfecting
- 1-inch-wide roll of athletic tape
- Antibiotic ointment (½ ounce)
- Tweezers and scissors (found on many army knives)
- Topical antihistamine (calamine lotion, Benadryl, or hydrocortisone)
- Ace bandage (not all hikers carry this)
- Small stash of medicine in case you get a cold (not all hikers carry this).

Cell Phones

Most people don't take cell phones on a thru-hike—to the contrary, you'll hear a lot of scoffing at the idea. But many day-hikers and overnight hikers use them, and on a well-traveled section of trail, if you need to call out in an emergency, there may be someone with a phone who is willing to help you.

Be aware that carrying a cell phone is not a cure-all. First of all, conditions in the outdoors, especially rain and battery-killing cold, are hostile to delicate electronic equipment. Second, a fall that smashes

"Even the lightest commercial first-aid kit weighs almost a pound. Be judicious about what you take."

—James Lynch III

your knee can just as easily smash your phone. Third, many sections of trail (especially in the West) are not within line of sight of a cell tower, so cell phones don't work. And fourth, many 911 services are tied in to local phone systems; the 911 service area may not extend to the backcountry. In some areas, you may need to call a different number to get help in the backcountry. This is something to check before you go.

ON THE TRAIL: INJURIES AND IRRITATIONS

Aches and Pains

Aches and pains on a long-distance hike range from stiffness that tells you you've had a good workout to down-and-dirty pain that tells you that you've done yourself injury. The better shape you're in before the hike, the better you'll feel in those early "break-in" days.

So what do you do to get in shape? Some hiking experts suggest walking with a pack for as many miles as you can fit into your schedule. Taking practice hikes and day hikes with your gear is an excellent idea, because it strengthens the very muscles you'll be using and familiarizes you with your gear.

Many hikers have successfully and painlessly begun a thru-hike simply by working out beforehand. Anything that works your legs, heart, and lungs will help you on the trail. Running, using stair climbers and treadmills, walking, swimming, climbing up and down flights of stairs, and aerobics classes are all good ways to get creaky office-bound muscles moving again.

Even with pre-hike training, however, the relentless demands of a long-distance hike can lead to more serious problems, when twinges turn into pain. Here again, a little prevention can make all the difference.

Sore knees. Long trails can be hellish on knees—especially the Appalachian Trail, with its steeper ups and downs. If your knees are getting a little creaky, give them extra attention in your pre-hike workouts, strengthening supporting muscles (quads, hamstrings, and calves). On the trail, use two trekking poles to take some of the pressure off your knees. Note: There is a difference between ski poles and trekking poles. To some, trekking poles may seem like an expensive waste of money, but if you're coping with knee problems, their shock-absorbing springs might be the solution you've been looking for.

Stress fractures. Stress fractures are fine breaks in bones, usually in the foot. They are caused by carrying too much weight for too many miles, and by the time you have one, your hike is over. Most of the hikers I've seen with stress fractures have been wearing extremely lightweight footwear and doing big mileage.

Numbness in feet. Some hikers report numbness. Sometimes this can be alleviated by changing shoes, lacing the shoe differently, reducing the pack weight, or wearing supporting insoles or orthotics.

Lost toenails. This is more of a problem on the AT than on the other trails because of the AT's much steeper grades. On long descents, the toes are pushed

"On the trail, aches and pains are my friends. The real enemy is an injury that could end my hike. Pain is an early-warning system. I neither mask it nor curse it."

—Brian Robinson

against the front of the boot, and the nails can bruise and eventually fall off. The problem can be prevented with footwear that fits properly (with extra room around your toes so they don't jam against the boot on downhills) and insoles to keep your foot in place. Once the toenail starts falling off, cover it with tape or a Band-Aid so it doesn't rip off before the new nail is in place underneath.

Blisters

Nothing—not rain, not mosquitoes, not cold, not heat, not even that irritating thru-hiker who keeps following you from shelter to shelter—can derail a thru-hike as fast as a niggling little blister that grows and breaks and hurts so much that it's the only thing you can think of step after miserable step.

You may think I exaggerate, especially if you've had a couple of blisters on a weekend hike. Here's the difference: A weekend hike ends after a weekend. A long-distance hike keeps going on—blisters or not. What starts as an innocuous hot spot can actually end a hike. This is no joke. I've seen hikers with blisters on blisters, raw open wounds, infections, and even gangrene.

But blisters are highly, if not completely, preventable. I didn't get one on the entire Appalachian Trail.

Double-check the boot fit. Make sure that your toes don't hit the tip of the boot when you're going downhill. There should be enough room at the back so that if you push your foot forward in the shoe, you can barely fit a finger between your heel and the boot. And the heel should not slide up more than about ½ inch when you are walking up a ramp. (Most outfitters have ramps to help in fitting boots.) If you're a beginning backpacker and you're not used to the feel of hiking boots, wear them at home for a couple of days for several hours to be sure they are comfortable. If you wear them at home and they don't feel right, you can take them back to the store for exchange.

Break in your boots. This is usually as much of an issue of toughening your feet as softening your boots, and it's best done before you get on the trail. I like to walk about 50 miles in new boots before I hit the trail (which is great exercise, too). If you're starting your thru-hike with a pair of trustworthy broken-in boots, they need to be reintroduced to your feet if you've been sitting around all winter.

Get the right socks. First rule: Avoid all cotton. Cotton absorbs sweat and dries slowly; that keeps moisture right up against your skin and causes blisters. Wicking socks—polypropylene or nylon—are a much better choice. Wear them under a pair of wool or wool-and-nylon blend outer socks. Wicking socks are less abrasive, plus they move moisture away from your feet. Another option: Try the new Teflon socks. This slippery material reduces friction between sock and foot; tests have shown that it reduces blisters, too.

Take it easy. Limit your early mileage, and keep your pack as light as possible.

Air out your feet. During breaks, take off your boots, and air out your feet and socks, especially if your feet have been sweating.

"Check your feet every hour. This means stopping, taking off the pack, sitting down, taking off shoes and socks, and giving yourself a foot massage for a couple of minutes. Then put on a different pair of socks. Rotate socks throughout the hiking day."
—Jeffrey Olson

"I wear my socks (both liners and outer socks) inside out; this keeps the sewn line in the toe of the sock away from my toes and helps avoid friction and blisters."
—Gary Greaser

Pre-treat trouble spots. Put a piece of moleskin on known blister trouble spots before you start walking.

Don't wait. The second you feel the slightest hint of something rubbing in your shoe, STOP WALKING! Find the problem and stop it. It could be something so small as a speck of sand. Treat a hot spot with moleskin or Second Skin (a dressing available from Spenco). I recommend using white athletic tape instead of the tape that comes in the package, which doesn't adhere nearly as well.

Altitude Sickness

Altitude sickness can be a problem on the PCT and the CDT, each of which frequently climbs higher than 12,000 feet and sometimes above 13,000 feet. Thru-hikers have plenty of time to acclimate; however, it's not uncommon for them to be wheezing and out of breath when they first hit the high country.

Weekenders, section hikers, and people coming directly from sea level are much more at risk. When going to elevations above 10,000 feet, take time to acclimate and try to limit your net elevation gain to 1000 feet per day. Early symptoms of altitude sickness include shortness of breath, nausea, and headaches. The best thing to do is slow down, enjoy the scenery—and not gain any more elevation until you are feeling better. Most people can acclimate to the elevations on the Triple Crown trails if they take enough time. The preventative drug Diamox can be helpful (consult your physician). Finally, be sure to drink enough water. Dehydration (see the next section) will make altitude sickness even worse.

More severe symptoms include disorientation, vomiting, a rapid pulse, cyanosis (bluish coloring of the skin), ragged breathing, and white or bloody sputum. Do not ignore these symptoms; the result can be fatal pulmonary or cerebral edemas. If you have severe symptoms, you must descend immediately.

Heat and Cold

Dehydration and Heat Exhaustion

If you're wondering what's so bad about being a little thirsty, it's probably an indication that you've so far been fortunate enough not to be hiking uphill in a blazing sun with 5 miles to go to the next water and half a cup left in your canteen. The feeling that your mouth is full of spiderwebs and choking dust is unforgettable.

Dehydration and heat exhaustion (or worse, heat stroke) occur when your body can no longer deal with being hot and thirsty. Thru-hikers are more at risk because we're used to discomfort, and we're used to pushing ourselves.

Warning: Dehydration can be fatal. Every year, illegal aliens die from dehydration and heat stroke while trying to cross the deserts of southern California. Thru-hikers are more fortunate: We have maps and guidebooks, a

> "Foot care is critical. At the first sign of a problem, I stop and find a solution. Even if the only solution is to rest 15 minutes every hour, that's much more efficient than having to recuperate for days."
> —Brian Robinson

clear trail to follow, and information about water sources, and we don't have to fear knocking on someone's door or flagging down a car at a road crossing. Still, many thru-hikers have had close calls.

Heat-related problems occur on all three trails. June temperatures in the Middle Atlantic States can be 100 degrees, with humidity of 90 percent or more. But by the time most AT hikers get that far, they are fit, well acclimated, and have a good idea of how much water they need. In the southern drylands of the PCT or CDT, even experienced long-distance hikers are usually not acclimated and frequently underestimate the amount of water they need.

Symptoms of dehydration and heat exhaustion include nausea, headaches, fatigue, and dizziness. Treatment includes shade, rest, drinking water, and immersing yourself in cold water.

Heat stroke is much more serious. It occurs when the body has overheated so badly that it just shuts down. Victims will have dry skin (they are no longer sweating) and a high temperature. Treatment must be immediate. Try to find some shade, and cool off the victim. It's best to use wet towels (or whatever you have available: T-shirts, bandannas) rather than immersion, which can cause shock. In desert environments, where there isn't likely to be much shade or water, prevention is the best treatment. Pay attention to how you're feeling, slow down, take rests, and if necessary, wait until it's cooler to hike.

Preventing heat stroke and dehydration requires pacing yourself, taking cool-down breaks, and drinking enough. For more information, see "Water Strategies" in Chapter 11.

Hyponatremia

This exotic-sounding affliction occurs when your body has excreted so much salt and other electrolytes (like potassium) that it can no longer process and use the water you are drinking. A severe case of hyponatremia can cause kidney failure. Usually hikers get enough salt from food to replace electrolytes lost to sweat. However, when hiking hard and long in hot weather, you may need electrolyte replenishment. Eating foods such as gorp (with banana chips for potassium, raisins for sugars, and salted nuts for sodium), drinking diluted electrolyte-replacement drinks (Gatorade is available in powdered form), and eating salty soups at night can all help keep your electrolytes in check. Sipping water with sugar and salt added to it is an effective field treatment.

Chafing and Heat Rashes

Chafing occurs most commonly between the thighs or around the groin. Heat rashes can occur anywhere, but tend to happen when the skin is constantly hot, wet, and irritated, as it can be if a pack doesn't ride properly and traps sweat against the back (one reason why many hot-weather hikers prefer external-frame packs to internal-frame packs).

Chafing can be prevented by a thoughtful choice of clothing: If you have thighs that rub together, wear biking shorts. Look for wicking fabrics, not cotton.

Climbing out of Lehigh Gap in Pennsylvania: Take lots of water on a hot day.

Don't assume that you won't get a chafing rash simply because you never have in the past. In extremely hot weather, you may be much more susceptible. Some hikers use cornstarch or petroleum jelly to reduce chafing.

Both heat rashes and chafing can be treated with hydrocortisone.

Sunburn

Sunscreen is important for all hikers, but especially for those on the PCT and CDT. Northbounders have southern California's and New Mexico's desert sun to contend with; southbounders have the high-altitude glare off snowy slopes. Use sunscreen with an SPF of at least 15, and pile it on. A sun hat with a wide brim can help prevent sunburn. Some hikers wear bandannas desert-sheik style, hanging down from their hats to cover their necks and ears.

Another kind of sunburn is snow-blindness, when the glare of the sun burns the retinas, causing temporary blindness and excruciating pain. Hikers on the western trails can encounter snow almost anywhere: Always carry sunglasses with side flaps and UV protection.

Hypothermia

Thru-hikers are less at risk for hypothermia than for heat exhaustion, but the risk does exist, particularly at the bookends of the season and in high (and wet) mountains. Specific locations and seasons (Georgia in March, Washington and Montana in October, the High Sierra in early June, the White Mountains of New Hampshire anytime) are discussed in the appropriate chapters.

Hypothermia occurs when the body's core temperature drops and the body can no longer warm itself. Symptoms include uncontrollable and prolonged shivering, pale coloring, low blood pressure and pulse, errors in judgment, and slurred speech. As the condition worsens, there may be other, more dramatic symptoms: spastic, uncontrollable shivering, erratic behavior, wild energy bursts, and violent reactions.

As with all backcountry problems, prevention is better than treatment, and prevention begins with having the right clothing and gear to keep you warm. Ultralight hikers carrying minimal clothing are especially vulnerable to hypothermia.

If you find yourself chilled, stop the exposure, either by adding layers or putting up your tent and crawling inside. Reduce further heat loss by sitting on a foam pad or air mattress and by changing out of wet clothes. Hot soup or a hot drink can help tremendously; the leftovers can be used as a hot-water bottle.

WATER-BORNE ILLNESSES

Giardia and *Cryptosporidium*

Water-borne illnesses such as giardiasis, caused by the protozoan *Giardia lamblia*, and cryptosporidiosis, caused by the microscopic parasite *Cryptosporidium*, can cause severe intestinal distress. Of the two, *Giardia* is more common, although *Cryptosporidium* is sometimes found in areas where grazing is permitted. Both illnesses can be treated with drugs.

Water filters are an essential piece of gear on all the Triple Crown trails.

There are three ways to purify water: water filters, boiling, and iodine. Iodine is not effective against *Cryptosporidium*, however, and doctors discourage using it for long periods of time (like a whole thru-hike!). Most hikers use a combination of methods. Whichever method you prefer, you should take a filter in all dryland and desert areas and in places where livestock grazing is permitted, because if the only water source is a cattle-fouled puddle, you'll definitely want to filter it before you drink it. Given the rise of *Giardia* in the backcountry, it is wise to treat all "wild" water.

Other Intestinal Problems

When water is in short supply, personal hygiene may not be the first priority for thru-hikers. But many intestinal ailments can be traced not to a polluted water source, but to bad hygiene. Wash your hands before eating, don't share utensils and dishes with other hikers, and clean your pots thoroughly.

POISONOUS PLANTS AND ANIMALS

Rattlesnakes

There are four kinds of venomous snakes in the United States, but on the Triple Crown trails you are likely to encounter only copperheads and rattlesnakes. I've seen rattlesnakes on all three of the Triple Crown trails, from Pennsylvania forests to southern California deserts. I've seen copperheads on the Appalachian Trail. Coral snakes and water moccasins, the other two North American venomous snakes, don't consider Triple Crown trails to be prime habitat.

There are several different species of rattlesnake in North America, but regardless of the species, your experience will probably be the same. You will be walking along minding your own business when a sudden sharp rattle blasts you into full alert.

If you hear a rattle, move away from it as quickly as possible, then look for the snake so that you can walk around it. Rattlesnakes often hide beneath bushes or boulders and are superbly camouflaged. In the evening, they are often found sunning themselves along trails. In thick chaparral on the PCT, walking around snakes may not be possible. Trouble is, in hot weather, snakes are often torpid and they'd rather sit there and rattle than slither away. You might have to convince them to move by throwing rocks from a safe distance. Use small rocks; the point is to get the snake to move, not to kill it.

Like rattlesnakes, copperheads are pit vipers with wedge-shaped heads and pits under their eyes. They are easily identified by their coloring: copper-brown and gold, arranged in an hourglass pattern. Copperheads do not rattle, so chance encounters with them are far more dangerous. Never put your hands on rocky ledges where you can't see them. If you're stepping among rocks and boulders in snake country, use your hiking stick as a snake detector. Don't step *over* obstacles; instead, step *on* them and look down to see what you're stepping into: for example, rather than stepping over a log (where you can't see where you're putting your foot), step on the log and look down.

In the unlikely event that you are bitten, try to stay calm. Remember that only about half of venomous snakes inject venom when they bite, and that snakebites are almost never fatal to healthy adults. Treat for shock by elevating the legs (where most snakebites occur). In a hot environment, try to crawl into some shade (or make some with a tarp) and drink plenty of water.

This situation proves the value of carrying a map that covers more than just the trail. The best treatment for snakebite is to get to a doctor, and a good map will help you plot a route. While snakes can and do occasionally venture into the type of high country that is usually set aside as remote wilderness, they like arid areas even more. On the Triple Crown trails, most prime snake territory is also laced with roads. Even if you've been walking for several days since your last resupply, there are usually side trails that can quickly take you back to civilization.

Do not use snakebite kits. Medical experts say that they promote the spread of the venom and infections. Instead, splint the injured limb, and slowly walk out.

Poison Ivy and Poison Oak

Poison ivy is endemic on the AT from Georgia through Vermont. Poison oak is common on the PCT, especially in southern California, where it is one of the predominant plants in the chaparral community. With the exception of parts of New Mexico, neither is much of a problem along the CDT.

The ingredient in poison ivy and poison oak that causes all the trouble is urushiol; most people are allergic to it. If you're not, don't go swaggering about; many hikers develop an allergy with exposure.

Poison oak and poison ivy are easily recognizable because their leaves grow in triads. Poison oak leaves are smaller and rounder than poison ivy leaves. Unfortunately, both AT and PCT northbounders typically start their hikes before the leaves have sprouted. All parts of both poison ivy and poison oak are toxic, including stems, roots, and the bare vines, so you should be familiar with what they look like.

Poison oak is a shrub with fine thin long branches that look a little like super-skinny deer antlers. They grow out and then, near the ends, turn up, toward the sun. Look for the dried and shriveled remains of last season's white berries, which are very small and grow together in groups.

Poison ivy can be a shrub, a ground cover, or a vine. Its branches curve up the same way that poison oak branches do. When growing as a vine, poison ivy can be as thick as your wrist. The vine is covered with reddish-brown hairs that attach to a tree.

If you know you're allergic, talk to your physician about getting a prescription of prednisone, used to treat the rash. An antihistamine cream may help relieve the itch. Several anti-ivy solutions on the market are also effective. Some of them can be applied before anticipated exposure, but for thru-hikers, that's impractical—you'd be constantly adding the caustic soap to layers of grime, mosquito repellent, sunscreen, and sweat. But if you know you've touched poison ivy or if a rash starts to develop, lotions like Ivy-Out can work after the fact.

Wearing long pants or gaiters in areas infested with poison ivy also helps, but you can contact poison ivy from clothing and gear. Washing them with water deactivates the urushiol.

Stinging Nettles
You'll learn to recognize stinging nettles (most common on the AT). The sharp, stinging pain usually lasts a few minutes and is well worth avoiding, although it doesn't have any long-lasting side effects. Trail maintainers usually cut nettles back, but they can grow quickly. Sometimes you'll have no choice but to wade through a patch. Your best option is to put on long pants or gaiters.

Creepers, Crawlers, Biters, and Stingers
Different hikers are differently sensitive to mosquito bites and blackfly bites. Some calamine lotion or hydrocortisone is a good thing to keep in your first-aid kit.

There is a real danger, especially along the Appalachian Trail, of picking up deer ticks, which carry Lyme disease and erlichiosis. Ticks are also common in some sections of southern California and along the Hat Creek Rim in northern California. A bite from an infected tick sometimes produces a red "bulls-eye" rash. Both diseases can be treated with antibiotics, but they can be difficult to diagnose and can lead to serious long-term complications. A vaccine is now available for Lyme disease, although it is not 100 percent effective.

In tick country, wear light-colored clothing. Clothes washed in Permethrin, an insecticide, can repel ticks. Try to bathe as frequently as possible, and give yourself a full-body check. (With the help of a partner, you can be more thorough.) Ticks like to burrow into warm, sweaty skin—very often under the waistband of your shorts or in your socks.

Removing ticks isn't easy. The folk remedies we all know about—smothering them with Vaseline or gas, putting the hot tip of a match on them—work better in theory than in practice. To extract a tick, gently grab it with tweezers as close to the skin as possible, then pull (don't twist) firmly and gently. Disinfect the bite. If you know you have been bitten, you might want to be checked for Lyme disease.

Mosquitoes aren't usually dangerous, except in the northeastern United States, where they have recently begun spreading the West Nile virus. In study after study, DEET comes out on top of surveys as the best preventive. It is not necessary to use 100 percent DEET.

Blackflies are another misery inducer. On the Triple Crown trails, they are mostly a problem for AT southbounders starting in New England in June. Head nets and loose-fitting clothing are the best defense. Northwoods folks swore by Avon's Skin-so-Soft lotion for so many years that the Avon Company finally developed a plant-based insect repellent that has a loyal following, especially as a blackfly repellent.

Spiders also pack a nasty bite. Look for them in old buildings and outhouses. Scorpions are desert residents that come around at night. They may take shelter from the morning sun in your shoes, so be sure to shake out your footwear before putting it on.

If you are allergic to bee stings, you should have a prescription bee-sting treatment kit from your doctor.

FIRE

Forest fires are potentially a danger or, at the very least, an impediment on all three trails. Areas may be closed due to fire danger or active fires, or the trail may be full of blow-downs from recent fires.

Fire is a part of forest ecosystems. Land-management agencies try to manage fire danger by setting and controlling limited fires when conditions are right. Sometimes these supposedly controlled burns get out of control and spread. Some fires are started by lightning strikes. But in most instances, fires are started by careless humans: by runaway campfires, by not-quite-put-out cigarettes, by arson, or even, if conditions are dry enough, by sparks from a chain saw. Most of these fires are quickly put out, but sometimes many thousands of acres (and miles of trail) are burned. On all three of the national scenic trails, especially in the West, you will walk through many acres of forest and scrub in various stages of recovering from burns. Some of the scars are fresh, others have started to heal. A number of burns on both the PCT and CDT, especially in California and Montana, were caused by fires in the summer of 2000, which has been called the worst fire season in 50 years.

At Colorado's high elevations, many hikers find themselves out of breath and more tired than usual.

During dry spells and when traveling in dry country, be scrupulously careful with anything that could potentially set a fire. Refrain from making campfires; if you do make campfires (or cook on a wood-burning stove), be sure the embers are cold to the touch before you leave the area.

The PCTA and the ATC (see Appendix 2) are reliable sources of information about current trail conditions; on the CDT, trail condition information is a little harder to come by and may require a call to the local land-management agency.

Usually, if you are walking toward a fire zone, you will learn about the danger far in advance from other hikers and from land-management personnel. You may be required to leave the area. Often, rangers will post instructions and directions at trail junctions. Wildfires are generally visible from several or more miles away, so you should have plenty of warning. If you see one, the best thing you can do is retreat. If possible, try to put a ridge between yourself and the fire. While fires race uphill with ease, they rarely drop down the other side of a drainage.

But retreat is only an option if you have enough time. The Federal Emergency Management Agency cautions that you cannot outrun a fire and recommends the following steps if you are caught in one:

- Crouch in a pond or river.
- Cover your head and upper body with wet clothing.
- If water is not around, look for shelter in a cleared area or among a bed of rocks.
- Lie flat and cover your body with wet clothing or soil.
- Breathe the air close to the ground through a wet cloth to avoid scorching your lungs or inhaling smoke.
- Take care when reentering a burned wildland area. Hot spots can flare up without warning.

PERSONAL SAFETY

Stranger Danger

Long-distance trails are probably one of the safest places you can be, but societal ills sometimes intrude. A few commonsense tips can reduce your chances of trouble. (See also the section on "Safety" in Chapter 8.)

- Don't travel alone. There is safety in numbers.
- Don't tell strangers where you plan to camp.
- If strangers make you uneasy, indicate that you have a partner just ahead or behind (even if you don't).
- Check out the people in a lean-to or at a campsite before you decide to stop there. Solo women thru-hikers will often tell people they haven't decided whether to stop for the night. After a little conversation, they can make the call with more confidence. If you're the first one into a lean-to, you may want to sit there without unpacking until others arrive and you can check out your potential roommates.
- On the AT, problems often occur in lean-tos close to or readily accessible by roads—sometimes via side trails thru-hikers aren't aware of. A drunken mob of good ole boys with guns is usually a good reason to move on—although you might be surprised when a group of rough-looking characters turns out to be fascinated with your story and invites you to participate in the barbecue they've brought along!

Hitchhiking

While all three trails occasionally go into or through small towns, hikers need to resupply far more often than on-trail facilities allow. Hitchhiking, therefore, is often part of the long-trail experience.

Don't hitch for a ride; beg. Standing out in the middle of the road leaves you vulnerable to anyone who happens to pull over—and many hikers have hair-raising stories about their hitches. But at a trailhead, you may be able to strike up a conversation with day hikers who might be interested in your journey. After you and the driver have a few minutes to size each other up, you can ask for a ride to town.

When you're coming out of town, you may be able to arrange a ride from someone you've met. Or ask in a motel, hostel, or café whether there's someone who might be willing to drive you back to the trail. You'll be surprised at how many people are willing to help out, especially if you offer to pay for gas. Some towns have taxi services.

If you do hitch, the safest ride is in the back of a pickup truck. Drivers of pickup trucks—the more beat-up, the better—are often willing to lend a ride. Unfortunately, it is now illegal in some states for passengers to ride in the back of pickup trucks.

Be watchful over your gear, and keep in as much physical contact with it as possible. If you and your gear have to be separated, be sure to keep your important papers—money and ID—and any expensive camera equipment on you.

CHAPTER 4
Thinking About Gear

Get a group of thru-hikers together, and there's a good chance the conversation will turn to gear. Join an Internet chat-room or subscribe to an e-list, and you'll learn ten ways to make a homemade stove. Thru-hikers sometimes seem obsessed with their equipment: what they're using, how it's working, what broke, which manufacturers are helpful to long-distance hikers, and (perhaps most important) how much it all weighs.

Two factors affect how thru-hikers think about and use gear, and as a prospective long-distance hiker, you should start thinking about them, too.

First of all, gear must be rugged enough to withstand months of abuse. No matter how carefully you treat your gear, mishaps happen, and it's a major pain to deal with equipment failure on the trail. My own experience includes delaminating boot soles (two different models, three times), broken tent poles, broken tent zippers, ripped sleeping bags, a snapped pack buckle, snapped-in-half walking sticks (the high-tech expensive kind), holes in air mattresses, and a succession of hiccuping stoves.

Manufacturers frequently offer lifetime guarantees on their products. However, you don't only want a product with a good guarantee—you want a product that isn't going to *need* a guarantee. After all, a guarantee doesn't, in the end, help that much when your stove breaks in the middle of a week of rain. The manufacturer might be willing to send you a replacement—but you've still got to get through the stoveless days between the breakdown and the next town, then wait for the new stove to arrive.

How do you learn about durability? One way is to talk to other hikers, either in person or via the Internet. Another is to choose products with an eye to potential problems. Look for simple designs (fewer seams to split, fewer features to fail). Buy from manufacturers with a reputation for quality customer service—and from stores with good return policies.

In order to produce products that warrant a lifetime guarantee, manufacturers use stronger materials that can withstand more abuse. The problem with that? Stronger often means heavier, which brings us to factor number two.

Thru-hikers want the lightest weight gear possible. This is a no-brainer. Hikers with lighter packs can go faster more comfortably with less wear and tear on their bodies. However, some lightweight gear may not be rugged enough to stand up to a thru-hike. And some ultralight strategies may not work, or may even be dangerous, in certain environments or conditions.

And so begins the endless conundrum of the thru-hiker: finding gear that

will meet the challenges of the environment where it is being used, that will survive the journey, and that will weigh in at the lowest poundage.

You might as well learn one thing now: There are no right answers. No one has a lock on the best way to backpack. Grandma Gatewood, the famous three-time AT thru-hiker, hiked with a duffel bag slung over her shoulder and a shower curtain for shelter. People have hiked in sandals and sneakers; they've slept in hammocks and bivvy sacks; they've carried full-fledged expedition packs and homemade sacks, leaned on high-tech hiking poles and sticks picked up off the ground. Your ideas about gear may change over time to reflect your increased experience or changes in the way you like to hike. The point of this chapter is to help you choose the gear that fits *your* hiking style, experience, and personality—at the lightest weight possible.

Much of the credit for the current trend to lightweight backpacking goes to Ray Jardine, who promotes a big-mileage, lightweight hiking style, most recently in his book *Beyond Backpacking*. The growing number of thru-hikers has also led to more discussion about various techniques in both old-fashioned venues such as trail festivals and gatherings and new media like the Internet. Want to find out how to make your own tent-cum-poncho? Want to turn an empty can of cat food into a stove? Join an e-list and ask the question; you may get five designs sent back in the click of a mouse.

Manufacturers, too, have stepped into the act. The introduction and development of ever lighter and stronger materials has enabled manufacturers to design amazingly lightweight gear. Materials like Spectra—used in satellite tethers and bulletproof vests—are being turned into lightweight backpacks. It is not unusual for today's long-distance hikers to have base pack weights of 15–18 pounds. (Note: Base pack weight does not include food and water, which vary from trip to trip.) With a 5-day supply of food and 2 liters of water, that makes for a total pack weight of 29–32 pounds—far lighter than what most thru-hikers carried a decade ago.

Today there are really three different styles of long-distance backpacking, assuming a basic level of skill. (I'm not counting those unfortunate folks who show up at the beginning of the Appalachian Trail with scuba tanks or a Russian army helmet—and no, I am not making that up!)

Traditionalists carry the standard gear you might find in your basic outfitting store. Usually, their base pack weight will be in the 20- to 25-pound range for temperate three-season hiking; some hikers carry more.

Lightweight hikers shave pounds off their pack weight by modifying their gear, doing without, or buying the most lightweight or stripped-down models available (a 20-degree sleeping bag that weighs less than 2 pounds, titanium pots that shave ounces off the weight of a steel cook set, photon lights rather than flashlights, a tarp instead of a tent, a closed-cell-foam sleeping pad instead of an air mattress). They know exactly how much fuel their stove requires to cook a certain number of meals, and they take precisely that much and not a teaspoon more. Figure their base weight in the 15- to 20-pound range. Most

"Not all pack loads are created equal. A pound of water may be gone in a couple hours. A pound of food may be gone in a couple days. But a pound of gear is carried for the duration."

—Brian Robinson

Previous page:
Using trekking poles helps hikers keep their balance when rock-hopping across streams.

hikers can, with a little trial and error, get down to this base pack weight without risking their safety or sacrificing too much comfort.

Ultralight hikers are easy to spot: they are the ones who sleep on a foam pad the size of a doormat, sew their own sleeping sacks, and carry packs that don't even have a hipbelt. Figure their base weight on the 10- to 15-pound range, with the occasional extremist carrying even less.

Note: These weights are given for solo hikers. The pack weight of people sharing gear with hiking partners will be a couple of pounds lighter.

ULTRALIGHT BACKPACKING

A 10-pound pack? It sounds so seductive.

But before you ditch your tent for a tarp and your boots for sneakers and succumb to the allure of "fast-packing" fleet-footed and unencumbered through the wilderness, you need to carefully evaluate both your skills and your style. A word of warning: Without strong wilderness skills and good physical fitness, not to mention common sense, ultralight hikers may be risking their safety, especially at the edges of the hiking season or in high mountains.

There's nothing new about ultralight hiking. In his 1984 *Complete Walker III*, Colin Fletcher ruminated that, "if you never attempt more than weekends in smiling or familiar country and hug frequented trails or always have companions to bail you out of trouble, and if you so choose, you can ride the New Wave [of ultralight hiking]. But if you know you may find yourself alone in a mountain storm, three days from roadhead, then false weight-economy could prove fatal, and you had better forget the gossamer game and lean heavily toward Old Wave ruggedness."

True, we've got some lighter options nowadays. The "gossamer game" doesn't always compromise our safety—but sometimes it can. In general, I cast my vote with Fletcher. I've been too many places where I needed to use absolutely everything in my pack to stay warm and dry (and many of those places have been on the Triple Crown trails). And I've seen too many people carted out of the mountains on stretchers.

Going Ultralight: Is It Right for You?

Going light means being more responsible. You can't afford to take chances because you don't have a pack bulging with everything you might need for every contingency. If you only have one layer of warm clothing and a tarp, you need to be more careful about letting yourself get wet and cold. Ultralight hikers need to be more respectful of what the weather can do and more careful of how and where they make camp.

Going light means being more flexible. You need to be willing to change your hiking and camping plans if the weather is threatening.

Going light means going without. Most people find that thru-hiking is hard, and they are grateful for some creature comforts at the end of the day. It

> "I carry a gallon milk jug with the top cut out so it makes a bowl. It weighs almost nothing and comes in handy for all kinds of things such as scooping water, and washing socks and underwear in (not all in the same basin or trip)."
> —Carolyn Eddy

Above treeline in the White Mountains, storms can come in quickly; ultralight hiking gear may not be sufficient.

takes a great deal of mental fortitude (and maybe a little self-deception) to convince yourself that you are as comfortable lying in a tight little bivvy as you would be in a more spacious tent, especially if bugs or bad weather drive you "indoors" for extended periods of time. Also note that other hikers are not going to appreciate it if you constantly borrow their gear to make up for what you don't have.

Going light means being strong. Ultralight hikers often take the attitude that they'll outrun the weather. It's very true that even in our most remote wildernesses, there are very few places that are more than 30 or 40 miles from what we so mistakenly call "civilization." But can you do a 40-mile day if that's what it takes to get you out of trouble? What if there is 2 feet of snow on the ground?

Personal Weight and Fitness

Before starting to slice tags off your gear or the spare pouches off your pack, remember that the biggest weight savings of all might be to jettison the spare pounds you may be carrying around on your own body. Unless you are at your optimum weight (or unless you are actually underweight), the most effective thing you can do to give your heart, lungs, and legs a break is to reduce the amount of weight they have to carry. This is especially important for those hikers planning to wear running shoes, because lightweight footwear demands a lightweight load.

> "Following a hike, always make note of what you used and what you didn't. Consider leaving things in the latter category home the next time."
> —James Lynch III

LIGHTENING THE LOAD

So, down to nuts and bolts. A few commonsense strategies can help you turn pounds back into ounces:

- **Modify your gear** by getting rid of features you seldom use.
- **Do without.** Forgo all those backcountry espresso machines, cake-baking gizmos, collapsible chairs, portable saws, nesting pots, and towels—just some examples of items that are sometimes seen at the beginnings of long trails but almost never at the end.
- **Downgrade.** Take the absolute minimum required for your safety and comfort. Reevaluate your definition of comfort.
- **Make your own gear.** Need ideas? Some talented do-it-yourselfers display their designs at hiker gatherings. You can't always get a true reading of how good the gear is, though, because people can be understandably and inordinately proud of their accomplishments.
- **Buy light.** Never buy an item of backpacking gear without checking its weight and the weight of alternatives. *Backpacker* magazine's annual gear guide has manufacturers' weights for everything from tents to trekking poles. Double-check the weights yourself—too often, manufacturers understate the weight of a piece of gear.
- **Double up.** Look for equipment that does double duty.
- **Keep up with new technology.** Manufacturers are using lighter and lighter materials. These can be costly, but the weight savings on a few key items alone can add up to several pounds without sacrificing performance, safety, or comfort.

So, let's look at the major gear categories and see how these principles can be used to reduce pack weight. The first thing you'll probably realize is that I didn't start with the biggest and heaviest items—packs and boots, which are what most hikers look at when trying to lower their pack weight. True, you can shave whole pounds—not mere ounces—off each of these. But attractive as the weight savings may be, boots and packs are the *last* things to consider when thinking about your weight-paring strategies. That's because before you can decide *how* to carry your load—i.e., what kind of backpack and footwear to use—you need to know *how much* of a load you'll be carrying.

Tents

Adequate shelter can be provided by a 10-pound four-season tent big enough for three people, gear, and maybe even a dog. Or it can (usually) be provided by a simple 1½-pound tarp. But before you rush out to buy a tarp, consider the kind of shelter in the context of the environment in which you plan to hike. Chiefly, you will need protection from wind, rain, and bugs—and sometimes, from the sun. Tarps are good shademakers, they are usually (if well pitched) adequate against rain, but they aren't so good in a windstorm, and they are useless against bugs, unless you rig up a bug screen. Other kinds of shelters

> "Don't take a whole book to read. It weighs a good half-pound. You'll do less reading than you think; take just a few pages if you must."
>
> —James Lynch III

> "I carried a tent on the AT and a tarp on the PCT. On the entire PCT, I set the tarp up perhaps 10–15 times. I slept out on the ground, and it was wonderful to have the star-filled sky as my roof. Setting up the tarp was no slower than erecting my tent. And bugs were not a problem with a 6-ounce bug bivvy protecting me."
>
> —Stephen Martin

include bivvies, one-person tents, free-standing tents, tents with large vestibules and tents with no vestibules, tarp-tents, and (primarily on the AT) lean-tos.

Sleeping Bags

The main debate in sleeping bags is down versus synthetic. With innovations in technology continuing to make the formerly impossible merely run-of-the-mill, synthetic bags are now almost as light, although still not as compressible, as down. But the very lightest high-tech (and, not incidentally, most expensive) bags on the market continue to be made of down. You can compare weights and prices in the annual *Backpacker* magazine *Gear Guide*, which comes out in February.

A couple of thoughts: Synthetic bags can provide insulation even when wet; down bags can't. With proper care, this shouldn't be a problem. But it is something to think about, if, for instance, you're taking a tarp on the PCT in Washington in September.

Some hikers have been successful in making bags, half bags, or quilts that have minimal fill beneath the body (the idea being that smushed fill underneath you doesn't help keep you warm, so why carry its extra weight?). One popular design is a sort of modified elephant foot, with a bottom that encloses the feet and legs and a coverlet that goes over your trunk and shoulders. Some couples successfully share a coverlet. New patterns and fabrics, each lighter than the last, are constantly being developed. Ray Jardine's *Beyond Backpacking* contains information about making your own gear. Whether these ideas work for you will depend on whether you are a warm sleeper or a cold sleeper. On all three trails, temperatures can dip into the 20s or lower, and some hikers find that they need to be fully enclosed in a bag to stay warm.

> "The advantages of a wood-burning stove are: no fuel to carry, no fuel to run out of, and no fuel to buy."
>
> —David Cossa

Sleeping Pad

Choosing a lightweight half-length closed-cell-foam mattress instead of a cushy body-length air mattress is a lightweight strategy that can save you as much as a pound. You'll carry less weight during the day—but you might not sleep as well at night. The extreme ultralight strategy is to eschew sleeping pads altogether and sleep in carefully chosen campsites with lots of soft forest duff. Some people choose sites where they can easily dig a depression for their hips, which is *not* an acceptable minimum-impact practice. Note that some of the new ultralight packs use closed-cell-foam pads as part of the framesheet—a great way for a piece of gear to do double duty, night and day!

However, the thinner the pad, the less flexibility you'll have at the end of the day (unless you're the type who can sleep on a log). This is especially true in high mountains and deserts, where the ground is often hard and gravelly. Comfort might also be an issue on the hard wood floors of an AT shelter. While a hiker using an air mattress can sleep almost anywhere, the hiker with a closed-cell-foam pad needs to be a little pickier. There's also the issue of heat conduction. Cold ground conducts heat away from the body. You could make up some of the difference with clothing, but clothing doesn't prevent conduction as well as a sleeping pad does. Over time, you may find that the lack of good sleep affects how you feel during the day.

Stoves

Gourmet hikers look for stoves that simmer. Just-add-water short-order chefs look for fuel economy. People who travel in remote areas where it's difficult to buy camping fuel want stoves that can burn auto fuel. Canister stoves have their own cheering section. And everyone wants a lightweight stove that burns reliably and fast.

For shaving weight, propane-butane stoves are lighter than traditional gas stoves with full fuel bottles. The wood-burning Zzip stove is, at 8 ounces, less than a third of the weight of a traditional white gas stove with a small fuel bottle. Homemade hobo stoves burning either wood, alcohol, or Esbit tabs weigh only ounces—but may take much longer to boil water than you are willing to wait.

Clothing and Raingear

In other venues, clothing may be a matter of fashion. For thru-hikers, it's all about function. The standard uniform for most thru-hiking conditions is a pair of shorts and a T-shirt. (Note that many hikers prefer synthetic shirts to cotton, because they wick moisture better and dry faster.) In colder temperatures, some hikers wear polypropylene underlayers, wind- or water-resistant overlayers, or a fleece jacket.

Even if you wear a different outfit every day of the week while at home, on the trail you'll probably decide that you can get by with an extremely limited wardrobe: two pairs of shorts and two T-shirts (at the most), plus a few layers of warmer clothes, depending on the temperatures you expect to encounter. As you hike through the seasons, you'll probably send home some of your warmer layers, and then arrange for them to be sent back to you later in the hike as autumn temperatures start to drop. You also may need to account for changes in elevation or bug season, which may require an extra layer of clothing. You may find that your shorts and T-shirts don't last the entire trip. You can either plan ahead to replace them or plan to buy new clothes at outfitters along the way. You'll find a few outfitters on or near all three of the Triple Crown trails.

Most thru-hikers do laundry whenever they stop in town to resupply, generally once every five to seven days. Be careful of commercial dryers: some of them can be too hot for fussy fabrics, especially polypropylene and wool. Many hikers also wash out (or at least rinse out) their socks every night on the trail, or whenever possible, which helps prevent blisters and makes the socks last longer. Some hikers also rinse out the clothes they've been wearing, although you'll want to be sure they have plenty of time to dry. If you use soap, be sure to dispose of the waste water at least 200 feet from a water source.

Having been caught short a few times (this ultralight stuff is very seductive!),

> "Gear can change with the seasons. I love using a homemade alcohol burner to cook in warmer parts of any trail, but still enjoy the heat output of a gas 'blowtorch' in colder snowy sections. Down is still my choice of sleeping bag, even though I live in the shadow of the Olympics (keep your powder, or in this case, down dry). One-man tents are nice in the desert but come up short in rainy North Cascades. I own two different types and rotate ahead as needed."
> —Monte Eugene Dodge

Hiking in winter requires lots of layers—even in the southern states.

I've become a big believer in adequate clothing, which I define as one more layer than the average conditions require. I always take some sort of rain jacket, although in desert and dryland areas that "rain" jacket might be a lightweight, not entirely waterproof jacket that can act as a wind barrier or as an extra layer at night, when temperatures drop. Lightweight nylon wind pants are a good idea on trails where rain and cold are exceptions rather than the rule. Above treeline, especially in mountains with reputations for stormy weather, I take rain pants and a good rain jacket. Ponchos are an excellent lightweight option in temperate climates: They provide both rain protection (for you and your pack) and superb breathability, although in windy weather, you might have to tie them around your waist with a bit of parachute cord.

Packs

Once you've reduced the weight of what you'll actually be carrying in your pack, it's time to think about how you can comfortably tote it all.

It's impossible to make sweeping pronouncements about packs. People are built differently, and they respond differently to the day-after-day pressure of weight on the back. Some people say that a 7-pound pack is simply 5 pounds heavier than a 2-pound pack. Others would rather carry 27 pounds in a comfortable pack than 22 pounds in a sack that hangs from their shoulders.

A few observations:

Thru-hikers carry packs without a lot of time off for their bodies to recover. A pack that felt fine on day 1 might feel like a sack of poorly packed potatoes on day 42. Some of the lightest packs on the market are actually designed for mountaineering; the manufacturers' reps stress that they are not intended to be used day after day for months on end. (The assumption is that a mountaineer may be willing to trade comfort for speed for a couple of days, but that a thru-hiker would develop pain after constant daily use.)

Remember: No matter how low you get your pack weight, water still weighs 2 pounds a quart and food still weighs approximately 2 pounds per day. If you're hiking for 6 days between resupplies and there are dry stretches where you need to carry a gallon of water, we're talking 20 pounds in food and water. Even if you've managed to get the weight of your equipment down to a scant 15 pounds, you'll still be carrying a 35-pound pack (at least for a couple of days).

It is possible to shave some weight off your pack by getting rid of extraneous features. Don't need the side pockets? Take them off. Don't need that top compartment and the crampon guard? Get rid of them. What about those straps you've carried a gazillion miles and never used? Cut them off (but leave enough webbing to sew them back on if you find a use for them later).

Boots

As with packs, once you know the total weight of what you'll be carrying, you can address the most important issue of all: footwear. It's not an exaggeration to say that the entire pleasure of your hike depends on your decision.

I have seen people hike the entire PCT wearing sandals. I have seen people hike the AT in sneakers. I have seen 5-pound clodhoppers and 1-pound trekking

External-frame backpacks are a good choice for easy, well-graded trails.

shoes. I myself have worn all of the above. And I still don't know what makes the ideal trail shoe—although I do have a good idea of what works for me.

Beware of anyone trying to talk you into doing what *they* do. People starting in sneakers will switch to boots; people starting in boots will switch to sneakers. There is no right answer.

The old saying has it that 1 pound on your feet equals 5 pounds on your back. Obviously, you want the lightest footwear possible. Some hikers find that hiking in sneakers allows you to go faster with less effort because you don't have to carry all that extra weight. Others succumb to stress fractures and other foot problems.

There are two things to consider when you think about footwear: your own personal feet and ankles, and the terrain. Chapters 5, 10, and 15 discuss footwear in terms of the terrain found on the three trails.

Below are some considerations that pertain to your feet. Answer the following questions:

1. Is your base pack weight below 18 pounds?
2. Have you ever had a stress fracture?
3. Do you have strong ankles?
4. Are you overweight?
5. Do you have a good sense of balance?
6. Are you well above average in height and weight?
7. Are you in good overall physical condition?
8. Do you have any preexisting foot problems such as heel spurs or fallen arches?
9. Do your feet often blister even if your boots are properly broken in?
10. Are you a clumsy smash-and-stomp sort of hiker?

Give yourself one point for every odd-numbered "yes" answer. Give yourself one point for every even numbered "no" answer. The more points you have, the more suited you are for wearing sneakers. If you scored a measly two or three points, stick with boots—especially on those sections of the various trails (discussed in each chapter) that are harder on the feet, including most of the AT, the Colorado CDT, the California High Sierra, and northern Washington. If you scored four to six points, you might be able to wear sneakers, especially on gentle terrain. If you racked up seven or more points, it's up to you.

Blow-outs, Replacements, and Lifetime Guarantees

First, a reality check: When manufacturers advertise lifetime guarantees, it's not the lifetime of a thru-hiker they're thinking about! Indeed, a thru-hike puts a lifetime's worth of normal use on a piece of gear.

Most gear—never mind that it's named the "Everest," the "K2," or even the "thru-hiker"—is not designed with thru-hikers in mind. Face it, we're not a big enough market. Manufacturers do know, however, that having thru-hikers use

> "Hiking with an umbrella makes me a lot happier. There's no rain on my face, so I can see better. I'm not sweltering in a jacket. I can hear better because I'm not wearing a hood. I can turn my head easier without the hood, too. Hiking in the rain is almost pleasant, and hiking in the Pacific Northwest you either learn to live with rainy hikes or stay indoors much of the year."
>
> —Steve Fox

> "Umbrellas—ha ha ha! Wind and brush rip them apart in hours."
>
> —David Cossa

a product is the best kind of advertising there is. I can't count the number of boots, packs, and hiking sticks I've "sold" to friends and folks I've met on trails.

High-end manufacturers offer excellent customer service. The usual process is for manufacturers to request that the faulty item be either shipped back to the company or brought to a nearby retailer that carries that brand. (The first option is far preferable for thru-hikers on foot because the "nearest" retailer may be many miles away.) After the manufacturer or retailer evaluates the problem, they may replace the equipment, repair it for free, or charge to repair it.

Of course a thru-hiker doesn't have the time to sit around while the manufacturer evaluates and repairs the product. So, often, a manufacturer will send a loaner or a whole new item to a stranded thru-hiker. As you might imagine, there have been abuses. Some hikers try to get replacements for packs that were used since God was a child or boots that have been resoled three times. As a result, many manufacturers require a credit card number if they send you new equipment to ensure that you do in fact send the old gear back to them and that the gear you send back is truly defective and not beaten to a pulp. Carry the phone numbers of major gear manufacturers in your address book.

Boots require a separate notation: Almost no one hikes a long trail in one pair of boots. Expect sneakers to last about 700 miles, lightweight boots to last about 1000 miles, and heavyweight full-grain leather boots to last 1600 miles. Buy two pairs before the start of your hike and break them both in. Try on the second pair with extra insoles and extra-thick socks. Most hikers find that their feet expand a little on the trail, so the backup boots should be a bit loose. Store the boots at home with your mail drops so that when your first pair starts to wear out, you can request that your mail-drop person send you replacements. If your feet don't expand, you can wear them with the inserts and thick socks; if they do expand, you can take out the inserts and wear thinner socks.

PART II
Appalachian Trail

Above treeline in Maine, the weather can turn suddenly. Good raingear and a warm layer are a "must" even in midsummer.

CHAPTER 5

The Long Green Tunnel

t's commonly thought that the Appalachian Trail follows an old Indian route along the ridges of the Appalachian Mountains. Truth is, Native Americans had far too much woods sense to make these steep mountains a travel-way, with gentler valleys so close at hand. Nor is the AT a pioneer path. The pioneers trended toward the west, across the mountains, not along them.

Indeed, when Benton MacKaye came up with his idea of linking the highest mountain in the South with the highest peak in the North, few trails existed along the ridgelines in between. The AT is almost wholly the work of volunteers, who built it for the sole purpose of recreation.

CHARACTER OF THE TRAIL

Of the three trails, the Appalachian Trail is the most temperate, staying largely below treeline. Elevations range from near sea level at the Bear Mountain Bridge in New York to 6642 feet at Clingmans Dome in the Great Smoky Mountains. In the South, the trail frequently climbs above 5000 feet. That altitude is not technically above treeline, but many of the mountains are "balds," so called because they are, in fact, treeless. (Given the latitude, natural treeline in the southern Appalachians would be above 7000 feet, but there are no mountains that high. North Carolina's 6684-foot Mount Mitchell, which, ironically, is *not* on the Appalachian Trail, is the highest mountain east of the Mississippi River. The trail was routed away from Mount Mitchell to take advantage of the greater recreational opportunities in the Great Smoky Mountains.) Scientists debate the reasons the Southern Balds are bald—theories include Indian fires, grazing, and high wind—but no one knows for sure. Their appearance, however, is that of high western mountains, with wide open spaces, big skies, and long views.

New Hampshire and Maine offer stretches of true above-treeline travel in the alpine-arctic zone. But by far the majority of the AT runs through hardwood forests—hence its nickname, "the long green tunnel." It is ironic, then, that this temperate, low-elevation trail boasts some of the toughest climbs and most knee-wrenching descents in the entire national scenic trails system.

CHALLENGES OF THE TRAIL

The elevations seem modest—4000, 5000 feet. I keep remembering my friend Sandy, who lives in Colorado. "I'd have to dig a well to get to that elevation,"

Following page:
Largely in the Temperate Zone, the AT is sometimes called "the long green tunnel."

she snorted, when I described the AT. (That, I might add, was *before* she joined me for a stretch in modest, "flat" Virginia. Limping around after the hike, she admitted, "I just couldn't imagine how *anything* at those elevations could be that hard.")

True, the AT has the most temperate weather of any of the long trails.

True, the AT's highest points are less than half the elevation of the high points on the western trails.

True, the distances between towns are short, there are shelters on the way, there is less exposure to lightning and weather, and the climate allows a more leisurely pace.

But the AT is not an easy trail. As many unprepared hikers learn to their dismay, this is no mere walk in the woods. The AT gets the prize as the most underestimated trail in America.

The facts:

The AT's footway is the most difficult of the three trails—steeper, rockier, muddier, and ornerier. Parts of the AT eschew switchbacks, especially in Maine, where the trail builders' battle cry seems to be "Damn the contour lines and full-speed uphill." AT hikers all too often "hike" on all fours—pulling themselves up with their arms and clinging to branches, rocks, roots, and vines to help them keep their balance. Some parts of the trail in New England are so boulder-choked and precipitous that the hiking resembles climbing more than walking, and a pace of 1 mile an hour is something to brag about. For hikers, aches and pains and blisters are exacerbated by the difficulty of the footway and the steep climbs and descents. Knee problems are common.

Nor, it should be added, is the weather along the AT always as temperate and gentle as postcards of shady green forests would have you believe. Summer temperatures and humidity can be brutal for weeks on end. Early-spring snow-storms—even in Georgia—can stop hikers in their tracks. New Hampshire's Mount Washington might rise to a "mere" (by western standards) 6288 feet, but it lays claim to some of the harshest weather ever recorded. In 1937, an anemometer on the summit recorded a wind speed of an astonishing 231 miles per hour—the highest wind speed on record anywhere on Earth. And while it's true that Mount Washington's wind speeds have never since come close to that astonishing force, it's also true that they exceed hurricane strength 120 days a year.

A COMMUNITY IN THE WILDERNESS

Unless you were to hike in the dead of winter (and perhaps not even then), it would be difficult to thru-hike the AT without experiencing its traditions, fellowship, and overwhelming sense of community. Misanthropes would be well advised to choose another path!

Several factors contribute to the social nature of the AT.

First: Sheer numbers. In 2000, the ATC estimated that 2700 people set out with the intention of hiking the entire Appalachian Trail. Most of them start northbound from Georgia in the spring. On popular starting dates—like March 20 (the first day of spring) and April 1 (is this therefore a fool's mission?)—you might run into 100 or more hikers atop Springer Mountain.

Second, the trail has more than 250 shelters, which act as magnets, especially in bad weather. Ranging from simple wooden lean-tos with a floor, a roof, and three walls to complicated rustic showpieces with sleeping lofts, picnic tables, benches, and chairs, shelters give the AT a unique social character. Some sleep four, some sleep twenty; outside are inevitably well-used campsites. Usually built near reliable water sources and spaced, on average, less than 10 miles apart, shelters make logical daily goals. They are noted on maps and in guidebooks.

Third, traditions have grown up around the AT. Events such as church pot-luck suppers and festivals in trail towns enhance the sense of community. During the main thru-hiking season, it sometimes seems a miracle any hikers make any forward progress, with all the temptations to stop for yet another impromptu gathering at a former thru-hiker's house or a full-fledged festival. Each year, some thru-hikers quickly become ex-thru-hikers, but stay around in order to participate in the fun.

This sense of community surprises many hikers, who expected more solitude and less company. But friendships often become one of the most important parts of an AT thru-hike, an intrinsic part of the magic of the trail.

Trail Names

If you interact with other hikers, somewhere in the first couple of hundred miles you will probably pick up a trail name. Like CB handles, trail names are nicknames that reveal something about your life philosophy, work, hiking style, personality, favorite food, injuries, alter ego, or habits. Creativity abounds. Tradition has it that you are supposed to "find" your trail name on the trail, not decide on it beforehand.

LONG-DISTANCE CONSIDERATIONS

Which Way?

Despite the fact that the Appalachian Trail is officially described as going from Maine to Georgia, most hikers blithely ignore the description and walk from Georgia to Maine. According to the Appalachian Trail Conference, more than 90 percent of hikers are northbounders, most of them starting between March 15 and April 15.

Several factors encourage a northbound hike.

A northbound hike maximizes the chance of good weather. That doesn't mean that a northbounder arrives in each place along the trail during the optimal season, but it does mean that he or she avoids blackflies in New England, minimizes time spent in below-freezing temperatures, walks among the glorious wildflowers of the southern Appalachians during their peak

"Expect the unexpected on an AT thru-hike. There are lots of information sources and lots of people to tell you what to expect, but things often turn out differently. You might hear that 'the Smokies are always jam-packed,' and then you'll get there during a lull and be by yourself for three days. Or you might hear stories about how bad the rocks are in Pennsylvania and worry about them for 500 miles, only to find that they aren't so bad."

—Dan Smith

Walking with spring: Leaves and flowers unfold during the long Appalachian spring.

bloom, and summers farther north where temperatures are at least a little cooler.

However, it's not all clear sailing.

In late March or early April, when most northbound hikers start their journeys, the high country of the southern Appalachians is still brown and wintry. Snowstorms are not unheard of (especially in March). Temperatures frequently plummet below 20 degrees and sometimes hover around 0. By mid- to late April, spring, already well established in the valleys, starts to creep up the hillsides. Now, in the words of Earl Shaffer, the hike becomes a walk with spring.

Summer catches most hikers somewhere in Pennsylvania, New Jersey, or New York. Heat waves of 95- to 100-degree weather coupled with 95- to 100-percent humidity typically start in July, but can catch you by surprise in mid-June. Continuing north, you finally escape into the cooler climes of New England. If you take the full six months, you'll finish your hike in a blaze of fall foliage and arrive at Katahdin just as winter is blowing its first snowy breaths across the high peaks.

By contrast, the typical southbound hiker starts in June during blackfly season in Maine, heads south into summer heat, and arrives in Virginia just as the springs are starting to dry up. Finishing is then a race with cold weather in October, November, and December.

Starting northbound is easier. Starting in Georgia is easier than starting in Maine. A Maine start forces hikers immediately to confront New England's famously difficult footway, with its diabolical, boulder-strewn climbs that go straight up and down slopes that most sensible people would agree are far too steep for walking.

The thru-hiking community goes north. Finally, there is the lemming syndrome. If everybody does it that way, and everybody knows that everybody does it that way, then there must be a reason—so everybody does it that way. To put a more positive spin on it, part of the AT experience is the interaction with other hikers. If you hike with the flow, the hostels will be open, festivals will be going on, and you will experience the whole gamut of trail community. If that doesn't appeal to you—after all, not everyone's idea of a wilderness trip includes sleeping in a shelter with twenty snoring strangers or partying at every road crossing—go southbound or start earlier. In recent years, many hikers have found that a February (or even January) start lets them experience some of the trail camaraderie without the feeling of social claustrophobia. Warning:

"EVERYTHING went into zipper-locks—food, clothing, everything!"
—K. A. "Goose" Cutshall

January and February starts should be undertaken only by hikers experienced in and prepared for winter conditions. You *will* be snowed on.

A note for southbounders: All of the above notwithstanding, some hikers prefer to go southbound. A southbound hike has a more independent wilderness character, without the inevitable petty social conflicts of a northbound hike. There's less competition for shelter space and supplies in town. If you don't mind cold weather, one attractive option is to start in midsummer (after the blackflies) and head south through the fall. You'll still have to deal with dry stretches on the Southern ridges, but "walking with fall" through the Appalachians would put an end to the business of a long green tunnel!

The International Appalachian Trail/Eastern Continental Trail

Maybe a walk of almost 2200 miles isn't quite enough for you. In that case, you might consider extending your trip on the Appalachian Trail by adding on one (or all!) of a system of connector trails. In recent years, trail advocates have begun working on an International Appalachian Trail (also called the Sentier Appalaches International in Canada) to connect the AT to the true northern terminus of the Appalachian Mountains at Cap Gaspé, Canada. South of Springer Mountain, the Benton MacKaye and Pinhoti Trails extend to the southern end of the Appalachian chain in Alabama. The total mileage is some 3200 miles.

Still not enough for you? From Alabama you can skip over to the Florida Trail and tack on a road walk through the Florida Keys to Key West. That brings the total to a whopping 4400 miles.

One caveat: Much of the route both north and south of the official Appalachian Trail (including large sections of the Florida Trail) is still on roads or not yet completely marked, mapped, described in guidebooks, and blazed. A trip of that magnitude requires both mental and physical fortitude; it also requires navigation skills, patience, and a tolerance for roads—not every hiker's cup of tea. Nonetheless, some stalwart folks have already made the journey. For more information—or to travel the route vicariously—check out the book *10 Million Steps* by Eb Eberhart.

Resupplies

Resupplying is easier on the Appalachian Trail than on any other major trail. Frequent road crossings make it convenient to hop off the trail and into town. The average AT hiker doesn't carry more than about 5 days' worth of food—and it is possible to carry much less. Sometimes, especially in the Middle Atlantic States, there are chances to resupply almost every day.

Frequent road crossings also make it possible to almost "day-hike" the AT with a support vehicle—ideal for people who would like to involve spouses or children in their trip.

In addition, an informal system of hostels and B&Bs exists on some sections of trail. Proprietors will "slackpack" your gear to the B&B or a nearby road

> "The *Data Book* and some of the planning guides list dozens of possible mail drops on the AT. Some are much more convenient to the trail, offer better chances for getting rides, and have more services. Don't just choose a mail drop based on the mileage you'd ideally like to do. First check the annually updated *Thru-Hiker's Companion* to be sure the town has the services you need. Some towns near the trail (like Bastian, Virginia) have little more than a post office. Others (like Montebello, Virginia) require long, steep detours from the trail with no hope of a ride. It might be better to walk another 20 miles to a bigger, better-supplied town."
>
> —Dan Smith

crossing or give you rides to town to resupply. These trailside services change from year to year. The annually updated *Thru-hikers Companion* (published by the Appalachian Trail Conference) contains current information.

Planning Resources

Of the three trails, the AT has far and away the most planning resources, maps, guidebooks, narrative accounts, and interpretive guides. A selection is recommended in Appendix 1. In addition, links from the ATC website (*www.appalachiantrail.org*) will take you to related sites and the ATC's online store.

Permits and Regulations

AT hikers can either sleep in shelters or camp out almost anywhere they like as long as they follow applicable regulations. These may vary according to season and locale; check the ATC website, *www.appalchiantrail.org*, for current information.

Permits are required in Great Smoky Mountains and Shenandoah National Parks. For thru-hikers, forms are available at the trailhead when you enter the park. You simply fill them out, note that you are a thru-hiker, and walk on. Baxter State Park in Maine has strict camping regulations, but provides a walk-in site for thru-hikers.

In addition to permits, hikers should take note of regulations regarding camping and fires, which are restricted in some areas, including New Jersey, New York, and Connecticut. For current fire regulations, check the ATC website.

For more on camping accommodations, see "Shelters" and "Tents, Tarps, and Bivvies" later in this chapter.

Finding Your Way

Blazed with white paint strips 2 inches wide and 6 inches long, the AT is so well mapped, well marked, and well described in guidebooks (see Appendix 1) that many thru-hikers return from their hike and don't know how to use a compass because they never had to! Blazes—on trees, cairns, rocks, boulders, highway signs, trail signs, and occasionally, the sides of buildings—are usually in sight of each other. Two blazes together indicate a change of direction. No blazes in sight is a pretty reliable sign you've lost the trail (except in some wilderness areas, where a more minimalist trailblazing approach prevails).

The AT is the best marked of the Triple Crown trails.

SHELTERS

Not everyone's idea of nirvana is a shelter filled with snoring strangers and food-raiding mice. Being part of a community may not be what you went into the woods for—not to mention the group of camp kids that straggles in at sunset or that obnoxious hiker you can't seem to shake.

But say what you will, shelters are a key part of the AT experience—and it's guaranteed that at least on one rainy night along the way, you'll find yourself grateful for the accommodations they provide.

Shelter Etiquette and Traditions

Except in the national parks, there aren't any hard and fast rules regarding shelter use. But there are a few traditions of which hikers should be aware.

- **First-come, first-served.** Some thru-hikers like to think that shelters are "reserved" for them or that they have priority over other hikers. Not so.
- **Don't race ahead and "claim" space** for your ten new buddies. It's excusable to claim space for one hiking partner with whom you're sharing gear. But when you start reserving space for your whole trail family, you start irritating everyone else.

A typical AT shelter. More than 250 of these lean-tos, which operate on a first-come, first-served basis, are found along the AT.

- **There's no rule against groups** using shelters, and most shelters are too small to accommodate both groups and other hikers. If you arrive at the shelter after a group sets up shop, that's your hard luck.
- **Carry some sort of tarp or tent.** Even if you plan to stay in shelters, you can't count on space being available, especially during the main thru-hiking season. It's considered bad form to arrive at a jam-packed shelter after dark and announce that since you're not carrying a tent, everybody has to make room for you.
- **But speaking of making room . . .** An old thru-hiker saying has it that "The shelter is full when everyone who needs shelter is inside." With the ever-increasing number of thru-hikers, this isn't quite true anymore. I once saw thirty-eight people in and around a shelter built for eight, and no amount of good will and space-sharing would have gotten them all inside. These days, it's not unusual for fifty or more people to start an AT thru-hike on the same day—and all those people may be vying for shelter space. In bad weather, it's common etiquette to at least try to offer space to late arrivals, even if it means squeezing together more than you would like. Also, there may not be room in the shelter for everyone to sleep, but people tenting nearby may want to cook under a roof if it's raining. Be gracious and make room.
- **Quiet hours are dusk until dawn.** If you arrive in the middle of the night, don't turn on your camping stove and treat everyone to the sounds of dinner preparation—put up your tent outside, instead. And if you *must*, for whatever demented reason, get going at 4:30 A.M., do it quietly.
- **Bring ear-plugs.** People snore. People zip and unzip their bags all night. Despite the above protocol, people do show up at midnight and turn on their camping stoves. People get up before dawn and do the same.
- **A shelter is not a doghouse.** People have priority, including people who hate dogs and want you to keep yours outside. Even if your pooch wouldn't hurt a fly, it may become territorial around a shelter (barking at new arrivals). Some people are allergic to or afraid of dogs or simply don't want a wet dog walking on their sleeping bag and sniffing around their food. Ask if people have any objections before bringing your dog into a shelter, and be prepared to put up your tent.
- **Tents in shelters.** It used to be that only true die-hards camped in winter, and you could pitch your free-standing tent inside a shelter for additional warmth. These days, more people are hiking earlier in the season, so putting up a shelter in a tent is decidedly uncool: You're taking up more space than you need, plus it's hardly a welcoming sight for the hiker who comes in after you.
- **Registers.** Notebooks in shelters serve as communal diaries and message boards. Many hikers carry a blank notebook, hoping to leave it in a shelter that doesn't have one or a shelter in which the old notebook is full. The tradition is to carry the old register out and mail it to the person whose

name is in the front of the book. You leave a blank register with your name in it and hope that someone will return it to you when it's full. Entries in registers range from poems to trail conditions to moans and groans to info about the best pizza in the next town. Trail registers make coveted souvenirs.

- **Commercial announcements.** Thru-hikers form a small tight-knit community, and, like any small tight-knit community, molehills quickly become mountains. There's a definite feeling against commercial activities on trails—including notices left in shelters.
- **Electronic devices and cell phones.** Most hikers go to the woods to leave behind the noise and confusion of everyday life and prefer that shelters and other places where hikers congregate are free of cell phone conversations, the click-click-click of computers, or someone else's favorite rock band. Be discreet in your use of technology.

> "Hike your own hike. The trail experience is more mental than physical, as your body will strengthen along the way."
> —Tom Caggiano

Shelters and Wild Animals

You're never exactly alone in a shelter, even if there are no other hikers. Among the company you keep may be (in order of probability) mice, chipmunks, raccoons, skunks, birds, porcupines, weasels, and even snakes. Wild animals know that they can score free meals hanging around shelters. Even the most frugal thru-hiker occasionally drops a grain of rice or two. But many critters aren't content with food that just happens to drop their way—as soon as the head-lamps go out and the snoring starts, they try to rummage through food bags.

You'll see nails protruding from the beams and rafters of shelters. These are for hanging your food. To stop mice from climbing down the drawstrings of food bags, you'll see an ingenious invention consisting of an empty can, a stick, and a piece of string hanging from the nail. Simply hang your stuff sacks from the stick at the end; the can makes it impossible for mice to crawl down to your food.

GEAR

Very few hikers end the Appalachian Trail carrying the exact same gear they started with. There are two reasons: first, the demands of the trail; and second, the change in climate. On a typical northbound thru-hike, temperatures can drop into the teens at night in Georgia, then rise to 100 degrees during the day on the rocky ridges of the Middle Atlantic States. So you'll need to start with warm clothes, shed them as summer catches you, and then retrieve some for the high mountains of New England. For example, I arranged to have a lighter sleeping bag sent to me in Virginia. When I received it, I sent the heavier bag home—with a note telling my mail-drop person to keep it "on hand" because I expected to need it again in northern New England.

Long-distance gear is described in Chapter 4. The following discussions cover issues particular to the AT.

Boots

The trend of thru-hiking in sneakers has met with limited success on the Appalachian Trail. Rocky trail, steep footway, and lots of mud make this trail tough on footwear (and feet). Only a minuscule number of hikers have hiked the entire AT wearing sneakers. Most prefer a lightweight fabric-and-leather boot with Gore-Tex, or sturdy all-leather boots with or without Gore-Tex linings.

Sleeping Bags

Most AT hikers prefer synthetic bags, because on the rainy AT, synthetic bags offer a measure of insulation, even when wet. The vast temperature differences mean that few hikers use only one bag for the entire hike. They may have a 20-degree bag for the southern Appalachians in March and April, and a 40-degree bag for summer. If you're a do-it-yourself type, you may want to experiment with making your own lightweight sleeping sack or quilt for the warmer months, when even a lightweight sleeping bag is too warm.

Raingear and Clothing

You'll need to change raingear and clothing as you go.

A northbounder in March may hike in shorts during the day, but will need warm clothes—perhaps long underwear, a fleece jacket, and a hat and gloves—for night. As the weeks wear on and the temperature climbs, hikers start to abandon layers. Some hikers send home raingear when temperatures rise into the 80s and 90s. Certainly, a full set of raingear—Gore-Tex jacket and pants—is overkill in the Middle Atlantic summer. But even in the summer months, rainstorms can be surprisingly chilly. Water wicks heat away from skin; you can quickly find yourself uncomfortably cold. If you're caught in a sustained cold rain without raingear, you'll have to find a shelter or put up your tent and sit it out. If you do get rid of your heavy-duty raingear in the warm months, you should take at least a lightweight, water-resistant jacket. Plan to retrieve your full raingear and some of your warm clothes in Vermont; you'll need them in northern New England.

Southbounders will do pretty much the same thing. Take warm clothes and raingear to start. Once you're past the White Mountains, you can get rid of the unnecessary layers; then add them back as temperatures drop in the fall.

Tents, Tarps, and Bivvies

The AT's 250-plus shelters range from primitive structures to elaborate rustic palaces complete with sleeping lofts, picnic tables, and in at least one case, a gazebo and porch swing. Most of them have nearby tentsites as well. Even if you plan to stay in shelters, you'll need some sort of backup for those nights when the shelters are full. This is especially true at the beginning of the hike before people have started to drop out—you may find yourself in the company of fifty others. Later, competition for shelter space is a little less fierce. But beware of holiday weekends, especially in national parks!

Some hikers prefer staying in a tent to staying in shelters. Tents offer more privacy, especially if you choose some of the AT's many campsites that are located away from the shelters. For solo hikers, a tarp, bivvy, or one-person tent makes sense because it minimizes weight. Small one-person tents with two poles provide enough room for you to change clothes, lean outside and cook, eat (albeit lying down and propped up on one elbow), and stash your gear. Their only disadvantage: they're not free-standing.

If you're starting early (mid-March or earlier), you may not be comfortable sleeping in a bivvy or under a tarp in a snowstorm. After the weather warms up, tarps—lightweight, roomy, and airy—are a great choice. However, like shelters, they don't protect you from bugs. Some hikers have rigged up bug screens made of mosquito netting.

Packs

Lately, equipment reviewers have been resurrecting the idea that external-frame packs are good for established trails, and for some reason, they always seem to mention the AT as an example. In actuality, most AT hikers prefer internal-frame packs because the load hugs the body more closely, making it easier to handle the trail's steep climbs and rock scrambles.

Stoves

Stove fuel is widely available on the Appalachian Trail. Many local businesses such as hardware stores and motels keep white gas on hand, which they sell to thru-hikers by the ounce. The thru-hikers' guides can tell you where you can usually find fuel.

Downed wood is also readily available (although not always at shelters and established campsites), so wood-burning stoves are also an option—and they weigh less than gas-burning stoves and fuel bottles.

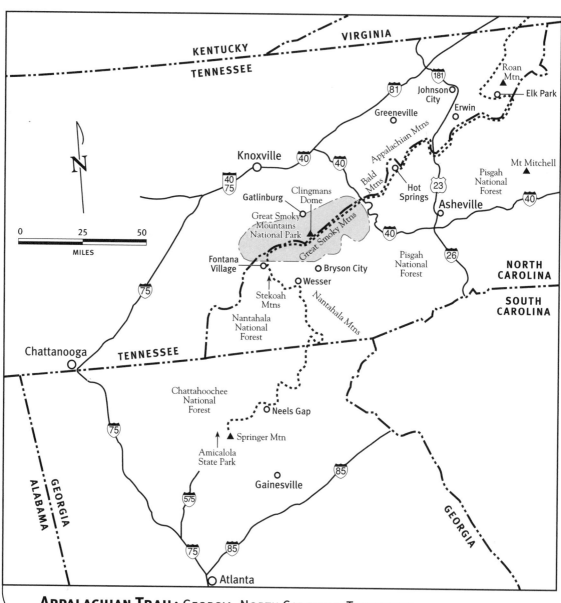

APPALACHIAN TRAIL: GEORGIA, NORTH CAROLINA, TENNESSEE

CHAPTER 6

Georgia, North Carolina, Tennessee

The traditional starting point of an AT thru-hike is actually 8 miles before the AT even begins, at Amicalola State Park, where an uphill blue-blazed approach trail takes you to the summit of Springer Mountain. There you'll see a plaque, a register, and the first of many thousand white blazes, 2 inches by 6 inches, which—if you keep following them—will take you to Maine. By AT standards, the approach trail is actually pretty tame, but if you're not used to lugging a pack up a mountain, it may not seem so easy. Hard to believe, but some prospective thru-hikers have actually given up the idea of an AT hike on the approach trail, before they even reached the summit and the first white blaze.

Forest Road 42, which crosses the AT 0.9 mile *north* of the Springer Mountain summit, is another popular drop-off point. Hikers who are dropped off there start their northbound AT hike by making a pilgrimage 0.9 mile *south* to the official start of the trail, where they can announce in the register their intention to walk to Maine.

Is it necessary to do that? Or just a meaningless gesture? In the months ahead, questions like these will occupy many hours of intense discussion in AT lean-tos.

THE TRAIL

Georgia's 75 miles of trail are rolling and curving, following switchbacks that were built by the Civilian Conservation Corps (CCC) back in the 1930s. The Nantahala Mountains are beautiful, but despite the switchbacks, these ups and downs are much steeper than anything you'll see on the PCT. Unless you're in tip-top shape, you'd be wise to plan low mileage for your first couple of weeks.

In North Carolina, the trail enters the Stekoah Mountains, which were once regarded as some of the AT's toughest miles. Today, the Stekoahs, too, have been largely tamed by switchbacks. Still, expect steep climbs and elevation gains of as much as 3000 feet.

In the Smokies, the AT runs along the border of North Carolina and Tennessee, and the hiker can, as Justice William O. Douglas gleefully remarked, walk with one foot in each state. The 70-mile traverse of the

MAP KEY

road

trail

state border

national park border

Indian reservation border

(40) interstate highway

(395) U.S. highway

(14) state route

O o city

▲ mountain

■ point of interest

lake

river

"Even though the South is not noted for severe winter weather, it receives a fair share of sleet and frozen rain. At elevations above 3000 feet, footing on steep climbs and descents can be a problem. I carry four-point cleats that strap onto my boots. They are light and easy to put on and take off. I have seen hikers use crampons, but they are expensive and heavy and not really necessary for this region. I use a good pair of trekking poles, too. I have not fallen once since using them and have fallen plenty of times without them."
—Douglas Greenfield

Smokies is one of the AT's highlights, although the overcrowded shelters leave something to be desired.

After the Smokies, the trail passes the town of Hot Springs, then climbs into the Tennessee Balds, where it steepens and the switchbacks disappear. But by this time, you'll be in shape to handle it. The Balds repay the hikers for their effort with vast expanses of big, rounded, treeless mountains that seem to occupy space on a western scale. By the time they cross the Virginia border, most hikers no longer think of themselves as prospective thru-hikers. With 400 miles under their boots, they are thru-hikers for real.

Seasons

The AT in the South can be hiked in any season of the year, although an occasional blizzard can force you to either hole up until the snow melts or hike out as fast as possible. Instep crampons (see Chapter 12) are a good idea in January and February, when the trail is frequently icy. In April and May the flower bloom starts, covering the hills with dogwood, azalea, and rhododendron. At the higher elevations, rhododendron is at peak in June and is especially beautiful in the area around Roan Mountain in Tennessee.

July and August are hot, sometimes with stultifying humidity even at the higher elevations. Bring plenty of water, and plan conservative mileage. September and October are comfortable, although some springs may be dry. Fall foliage starts in October and goes through Thanksgiving. December is cold and can be snowy, especially at the higher elevations. Most of the snow tends to fall after the New Year.

Strategies for Starting

By the time you start your hike, you're stuck with the results of your pre-hike decisions: to work out or not to work out; to pay attention to your pack weight or to carry the kitchen sink. But there are some things you can do to ease the shock of starting out.

Start Slow!

Limit your early mileage to 10 or fewer miles a day. This is a no-lose situation. If you find you can handle bigger mileage, there's nothing stopping you, and you'll have the satisfaction of being ahead of schedule. Starting slowly not only minimizes aches and pains but also helps prevent blisters, which often start forming at the end of long days early in the hike.

Opposite: Hiking through Laurel Gorge in Tennessee

The Rest Step

Mountaineers use the rest step to help them climb steep slopes. It works for backpackers, too. By momentarily taking pressure off the muscles and putting

it on the skeletal system, this technique gives you a small break with each step. As a result, you'll be able to keep going at a steady, if slow, pace.

As you take a step forward, simply pause with all the weight on your back leg and your knees locked. Then transfer weight to the forward leg, pick up your back foot and prepare to take the next step. As you take that step forward, pause with all the weight on the back leg.

The Shakedown

Look at the first 30–40 miles of trail as your shakedown cruise—a time to learn about the terrain, your body, and your equipment, and how they are working together.

Trail lore has it that you can walk along the AT in Georgia during April and pick up enough discarded gear to outfit a troop of Scouts. This isn't entirely true, since the quality and type of gear discarded is usually on the order of 5-pound cans of beans, bath towels big enough to wear, and economy-sized bottles of shampoo—stuff any self-respecting Scout troop would eschew.

If you think I'm exaggerating, consider this:

Every spring, the proprietors of Walasi-yi, a trailside store at Neels Gap located just 30 miles from the summit of Springer Mountain, stock up on boxes and tape and make nice with the UPS guy because they know they'll be shipping two tons of stuff (yes, tons) to hikers' homes. The postmaster at the Suches, Georgia, post office, 2 miles off the trail and only 20 miles into the hike, claims to have sent home a Russian army helmet and bows and arrows—along with the more usual hiker paraphernalia.

True enough, most people don't show up with a Russian army helmet. But it's the rare hiker who doesn't fine-tune something about his or her kit at Walasi-yi. No matter how much experience you have, it always seems that the beginning of the trail has a few surprises in store.

Psychological Factors

Once, many years ago, in a rush of misguided ambition coupled with parental expectations, I thought I would become a doctor. In college, I attended an orientation for pre-med students, in which a dour-looking man announced that only one out of every four of us would make it. (Obviously, in that case, I was in the majority!)

Odds are even worse for an AT thru-hike.

Who knows, that pessimistic professor may have been the AT hiker, who in a lean-to in Georgia, told an assembled group of hopeful thru-hikers that only one in ten of them would make it—and then proceeded to say which ones he thought those would be!

> "Most hikers in the South do not carry a sleeping bag rated for winter use. They carry a three-season bag, usually rated for 20 degrees. It may not snow a lot down here, but in the winter and early spring the temperatures can fall into the teens at night and well below zero with the wind chill. I have learned the hard way. Now I carry a 5- to 10-degree bag, and I use an air mattress."
> —Douglas Greenfield

Psychological factors drive a lot of hikers off the trail: boredom, not having a good time, getting tired of dealing with the same obstacles day after day, and lack of confidence. At some point, it's going to seem as though you've been walking forever—and you *still* have 2000 miles to go. It's easy for a new hiker to be intimidated by more experienced backpackers or by others who seem to have more confidence. Resist the temptation to obsess about more mileage, especially this early in the game. There are always more miles than you can do today. Remember that the trail is a gentle and patient teacher. Thousands of ordinary people have made it the whole way, including scores of beginners, many of whom had never spent a night in the woods before arriving at Springer Mountain. The trail will teach you what you need to learn.

The Great Smoky Mountains run along the Tennessee–North Carolina border, and offer views of forests that contain as many species of trees as all of western Europe.

Highlight Hike
GREAT SMOKY MOUNTAINS NATIONAL PARK

WHERE: Fontana Dam to Davenport Gap (Tennessee Route 32)
DISTANCE: 71 miles
DIFFICULTY: Moderate
BEST TIME TO GO: Spring and fall
GUIDE: *Appalachian Trail Guide: North Carolina/Tennessee*

Walk the ridge of the Great Smoky Mountains with one foot in Tennessee and the other in North Carolina. Beneath you are rows and rows of undulating mountains. Great Smoky Mountains National Park is rich not only in scenery, but also in biological diversity. It contains more than 300 species of trees—more than in all of western Europe. The high point of this hike, Clingmans Dome (6643 feet), is also the high point on the Appalachian Trail.

Highlight Hike
Tennessee/North Carolina Balds

No one knows why Tennessee's Balds are treeless, but they offer some of the AT's best views.

Where: Nolichucky River (near Erwin, Tennessee) to Elk Park (U.S. Route 19 E)
Distance: 46 miles
Difficulty: Challenging
Best time to go: Spring, summer, and fall
Guide: *Appalachian Trail Guide: North Carolina/Tennessee*

These bare humps aren't technically above treeline, but they have the feel of big western mountains with wide open views. Steep ups and downs make the going slow at times. In addition, the summits can be fogged in, making navigation difficult. In good weather, expect views of endless blue ridges. The rhododendron bloom in June is especially beautiful.

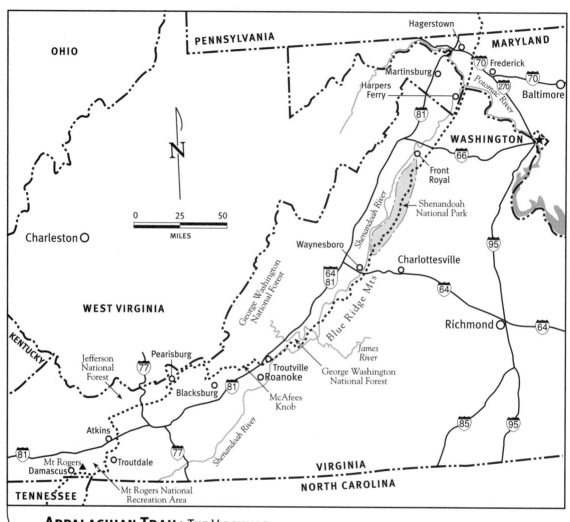

APPALACHIAN TRAIL: THE VIRGINIAS

CHAPTER 7

The Virginias

With 530 miles, Virginia has the most mileage of any Appalachian Trail state. It's also the easiest mileage, with gentle grades and generally good footway. Northbounders hike Virginia in the temperate, beautiful spring, through forests filled with dogwood, flame azaleas, and rhododendrons.

But as with everything else in long-distance hiking, there are those who disagree that Virginia is "easy." I remember meeting a couple of southbounders in a North Carolina shelter, just a couple of hundred miles from the end of their hike.

"You know, I kept waiting for the hike to get easy," one of them said. He was a man in his mid-20s, tall, lean, and fit. "I kept hearing about how easy Virginia was, but I have to say that there hasn't been a single day that was easy."

Nonetheless, by the time northbound hikers reach Virginia, they tend to ratchet up their mileage—either because after 400 miles they are fit or because the mileage is indeed easier. It's common for hikers to do 18- to 20-mile days through much of the state.

THE TRAIL

The trail enters Virginia near the town of Damascus (known, with good reason, as the friendliest town on the trail). From there, it climbs into the Mount Rogers National Recreation Area, which boasts Mount Rogers (the state's highest point), a network of trails, wild ponies, and spectacular open scenery.

Most hikers arrive in Virginia in early May, which is when the town of Damascus hosts its annual Appalachian Trail Days festival, an event that draws almost every hiker off the trail—and plenty of thru-hikers from previous years.

Do *not* get rid of your cold-weather clothing until *after* the Mount Rogers National Recreation Area. Mount Rogers is very exposed; it can be quite cold up there well into May. Even if the weather has thus far been warm, keep your warm clothes until your next resupply, usually in Atkins, a few days north.

Past Atkins, the trail follows long ridges, descends into valleys and farmland, then climbs again. This is the height of the wildflower bloom. If you have an eye for photography, be sure to bring a macro lens.

Virginia is more rolling and pretty than wildly dramatic, but it does have plenty of scenic highlights. In southern Virginia, the Mount Rogers National Recreation Area is a stand-out. In central Virginia, classic views include the Dragons Tooth, McAfees Knob, and Tinker Cliffs, all near Roanoke, near

> "Don't think that you're hiking to the trail's end (Big K, Canadian border, Mexican border, whatever); instead, think that you're hiking to the day's destination. That's a high-falutin' way of saying 'One Day at a Time,' but it sure helped me."
>
> —Charlie Wood

the site where Annie Dillard wrote her Pulitzer Prize–winning book, *Pilgrim at Tinker Creek*.

Continuing north, the trail roughly parallels the Blue Ridge Parkway and follows the Blue Ridge Mountains (a subrange of the Appalachians) across the James River and into a lovely and rather rugged, remote section of Virginia in the George Washington National Forest. Entering Shenandoah National Park, the AT parallels another scenic highway, Skyline Drive, whose construction bitterly divided Appalachian Trail advocates in the 1930s. The trail crosses the parkway countless times and passes close to picnic areas and the park's restaurants and snack bars. You'll see far too many cars and people in Shenandoah, but you won't have to carry much in the way of food.

North of Shenandoah, the trail hits a short section that surprises many hikers with its incessant nickel-and-dime ups and downs. You'll also see unusual wildlife—including zebras and antelopes. The National Zoo has a facility here, and the trail runs right alongside its fence. Finally, the AT descends to the Shenandoah River and crosses into historic Harpers Ferry, West Virginia. A short walk takes you up the hill to Appalachian Trail Conference Headquarters and then down to the Potomac River, crossed on a pedestrian bridge. Maryland is on the other side.

SEASONS

Virginia can be hiked any time of year. In January and February (and sometimes March), expect snow at the higher elevations. Thru-hikers arrive in peak hiking season—early to mid-May, when the forests are ablaze with spring flowers and the climate is relatively temperate. Nonetheless, weather at the higher elevations can be extremely variable, ranging from cold rainstorms in 40-degree temperatures to heat waves in the high 80s or low 90s.

In June, July, and August, temperatures can be uncomfortably hot, so carry extra water and keep the mileage down. Most southbounders arrive in Virginia in September and October, which are much cooler, although some of the springs on the ridges may be dry. Fall foliage starts in mid- to late October, depending on the elevation.

CHALLENGES OF THE TRAIL

Despite its reputed ease (or perhaps because of what happens when hikers realize it's not quite as easy as advertised), Virginia's AT does offer some challenges.

Virginia Blues

One challenge of this section of the trail is the so-called "Virginia Blues," when hikers realize that they've been hiking for what seems like forever—and still have 1500 (or more) miles to go. For true lovers of nature and hiking, that realization can lead to a feeling of joy. But for those undertaking the AT as a challenge (or worse, for bragging rights), the knowledge that you've only just scratched the surface can be disconcerting—especially if you've developed a gimpy knee and it's been raining for a week.

The legendary Grandma Gatewood, a three-time end-to-ender, said, "Hiking takes more head than heel." Virginia is where that theory gets put to the test.

By the time you reach Virginia, the grand challenge of the Appalachian Trail has been cut down to size. There's nothing in Virginia any harder than what you've already done in Georgia, North Carolina, and Tennessee. The romance of saying "I'm going to hike the AT" has given way to the reality of putting in the mileage. At this point, hikers realize that they *can* do it—that, if they've walked 500 miles, it is overwhelmingly likely that they can walk 1500 more. The question is: Now that they know what this thru-hiking business is all about, do they want to?

Nutritional Deprivation

After 500 or more miles on the trail, hikers who go for weeks on end eating prepackaged noodles-and-sauce for dinner and instant oatmeal for breakfast are like high-performance racing cars running on low-grade gasoline. Young, skinny men—the kind whose long legs lope along the trail and who seem built for major mileage—are most at risk for malnutrition. One friend of mine suffered from severe malnutrition when, as a recent college graduate, he hiked the AT sharing boxes of macaroni-and-cheese with his partner after hiking 20-mile days. His problem: He had no idea of how much a hiker needed to eat (see Chapter 2). Today, he hikes with protein powder, energy bars, and as many extra calories as he can carry. He also makes a point of eating not only copiously but well in town.

An oft-cited academic study by former thru-hiker Karen Lutz concluded that thru-hikers used as much as 6000 calories a day, but could not carry enough food to replace them. The effort of carrying more food uses more calories, leading to a vicious cycle. For most thru-hikers, one result is significant (and for some of us, welcome) weight loss. But if you start the trail in peak condition or are underweight, weight loss on the trail can be a problem.

Signs of nutritional deficiencies can include snapping at your partner, bad moods, and depression—all of which might be your body's way of telling you that you need a good meal. Listen to it! Eat well in towns. Try to eat lots of veggies and salads, because you're not getting enough fresh food on the trail. Listen to cravings: An appetite for ice cream might be telling you that you need more calcium.

Finally, take a daily multivitamin on the trail.

Friction with Hiking Partners

You're beginning to feel that you know what you're doing. Your hiking partner is starting to feel the same way. And now that the two of you have more confidence

> "One of the things that seems to bite all long-distance hikers is boredom, regardless of the scenery and adventure of the trail. Listening to books on tape really makes the day go fast. You get the best of both worlds: You are on the trail and are 'reading' some things you have always wanted to."
> —Steve "Switchback" Fuquay

An overcrowded shelter in Shenandoah National Park makes the argument for small groups and minimum-impact techniques.

and knowledge, you may be coming to very different conclusions about how you want to hike.

Hiking partnerships vary. Husbands and wives or romantic partners are committed to hiking together; it's rare for one partner to drop out and the other to continue. Good friends from home are also often motivated to stay together—especially if they share gear and food drops. Looser partnerships form on the trail. Some people end up sharing gear and hiking together for hundreds of miles. Other partnerships are completely informal, with both partners independent.

Partnership problems may be the result of physical inequality (one partner is stronger and faster than the other), temperament (one partner is planful, the other spontaneous), or habits (one partner is a get-up-and-go type, the other likes to stay in and sleep). The more equipment you share and the more committed you are to staying together, the more you have to agree on: when to take breaks, when to stop for the day, when to get up, how many miles to do, whether to hop off the trail for a treat, and whether to stay an extra night in town when it's rainy.

Physical disparity can affect the success of a partnership, especially if the strong partner is also the one who always wants to go farther. Spending six months with an exhausted, bitter romantic partner (or a frustrated one) is no way to thru-hike a long trail. Some romantic partners deal with the differences in physical strength by giving the stronger partner a little more weight to carry. Also, the AT is well marked, and it's difficult to get lost, so partners can split up for a while to walk at their own pace and get a little private time. If you do split up, be sure you have agreed when and where to meet. You should each have what you need for the day—food, insect repellent, sun lotion, some sort of trail description, and other items that you may be sharing.

Differences in habits and personality simply need to be negotiated—over and over and over again.

TRAIL DAYS

One of the highlights of a northbound AT thru-hike is the Trail Days festival in Damascus, Virginia. Festivals in Hot Springs, North Carolina, and Erwin, Tennessee, have sprung up in recent years, but none matches Trail Days (or, as the hikers call it, Trail Daze).

In 1987, Damascus began the tradition of hosting a celebration of the AT, scheduled to take place just as the average northbounder reached Damascus, usually in the second week of May. Hikers ahead of or behind the "average" schedule frequently hitchhike forward or back to take part in the fun. Also attending are hikers from previous years, gear manufacturers, and people from local communities. The hostel is jam-packed, with hundred of tents either on the lawn or in one of several designated camping areas in town. A thru-hiker parade, a talent show, lectures, slide shows, a square dance, and a town green filled with vendors selling food you won't find on the trail make this festival a rollicking good time.

APPALACHIAN TRAIL CONFERENCE HEADQUARTERS

The Appalachian Trail Conference (ATC) grew out of friendship and collaboration among various hiking clubs in the northeast and mid-Atlantic states. In its supervisory and management role for the AT, the conference works with the National Park Service on land acquisitions and trail corridor protection issues, advocating for trail-building programs in Washington, D.C., and in state capitals. It also orchestrates a vast volunteer trail maintenance effort, drawing on the membership of venerable clubs such as the Potomac AT Club, the New York–New Jersey Trail Conference, the Appalachian Mountain Club, the Green Mountain Club, and the Maine AT Club. The Appalachian Trail

"Before splitting up with your partner, carefully divide your gear. If one person carries the tent, the other should carry the groundcloth and some rope to make a shelter. If one carries the stove and pots, the other should carry food that doesn't need to be cooked. If one of you has the water filter, the other should have the backup iodine tablets. We have a backup plan if we get separated: We decide where we should meet or stop for the day. We don't go beyond that point until the other catches up."
—Gary Greaser and Sharon Burrer

Conference provides extensive information and sound hiking advice to the public as well as to its thousands of members.

Thru-hikers are welcome to visit the conference's friendly headquarters, just up the hill from Harpers Ferry National Historic Park, where the trail passes through town and over the Potomac River. You can have your picture taken with the ATC sign behind you, and you can sign the hikers' log. After you complete your thru-hike, the ATC invites you to "certify" your accomplishment by reporting the details of your adventure. The ATC's archive collects hundreds of these thru-hiking stories. An extensive AT bookstore at headquarters carries nearly every title a hiker could ever want to read about the trail, including all the maps and thru-hike planning guides. In the bookstore, a most amazing raised relief map about 15 feet long captures the entire Appalachian chain from Georgia to Maine in one fell swoop, tracing all of the trails ups and downs. A few moments spent looking over this map will give you a clear visual sense of how far you've come and how far you have yet to go.

Highlight Hike
MOUNT ROGERS NATIONAL RECREATION AREA

A wild pony in the Mount Rogers National Recreation Area

WHERE: Damascus to Troutdale (Virginia Route 16)
DISTANCE: 49 miles
DIFFICULTY: Easy
BEST TIME TO GO: Spring, summer, and fall
GUIDE: *Appalachian Trail Guide: Southwestern Virginia*

At 5729 feet, Mount Rogers is Virginia's high point. The summit is just ½ mile off the AT via a side trail. Much of the Mount Rogers National Recreation Area is wide open country, with big views and a large network of trails. Staying at the Thomas Knob shelter promises an evening with an eyeful of views. A special treat: Wild ponies may visit your campsite.

McAfees Knob in Virginia is one of the Appalachian Trail's famous beauty spots.

Highlight Hike
DRAGONS TOOTH, MCAFEES KNOB, AND TINKER MOUNTAIN

WHERE: Trout Creek (Virginia Route 620) to Cloverdale (near I-81)
DISTANCE: 32 miles
DIFFICULTY: Moderate
BEST TIME TO GO: Spring and fall
GUIDE: *Appalachian Trail Guide: Central Virginia*

This hike takes you past the Dragons Tooth and McAfees Knob, two of the best-known beauty spots on the Appalachian Trail, both of which offer glorious views, as well as on a ridge walk on Tinker Mountain. The landscape is full of gently rolling hills, but plan conservative mileage, because this section boasts some surprisingly steep ups and downs.

*Deer in Shenandoah
National Park, Virginia*

Highlight Hike
SHENANDOAH NATIONAL PARK

WHERE: Rockfish Gap to Front Royal
DISTANCE: 107 miles
DIFFICULTY: Easy
BEST TIME TO GO: Spring and fall
GUIDE: *Appalachian Trail Guide: Shenandoah National Park*

The AT in Shenandoah crosses Skyline Drive countless times, making it easy to arrange shuttles or plan a hike of almost any length. The trail varies, wandering from gentle woods to high rocky ridges, but for the most part the grade is gentle, making for easy walking and (if you like) high mileage. You won't have to carry much food on this hike, since roadside stores and restaurants abound.

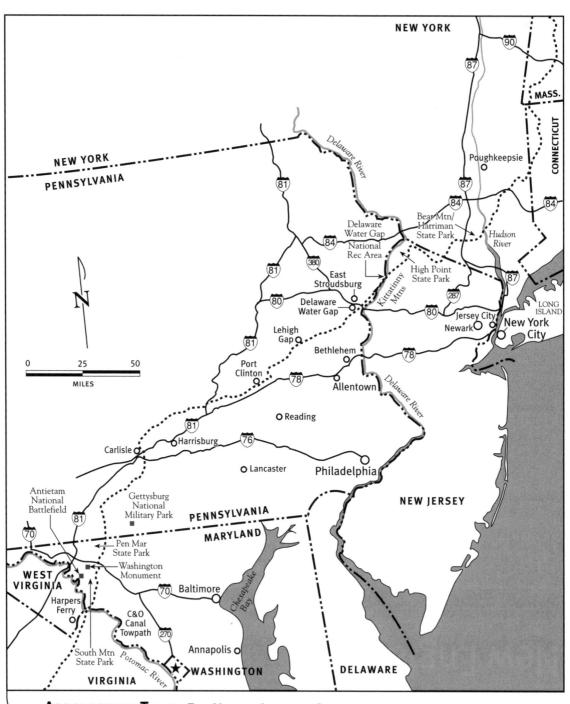

APPALACHIAN TRAIL: THE MIDDLE ATLANTIC STATES

CHAPTER 8

The Middle Atlantic States

In the Middle Atlantic States, the Appalachian Trail goes through the much more densely populated countryside of Maryland, Pennsylvania, New Jersey, and New York. Here the mountains are lower, the scenery less dramatic, and the road crossings more frequent.

Because of its proximity to major cities, this section of the Appalachian Trail gets a lot of day-hiking and weekend use. Thru-hikers sometimes think of it as the "boring" part, although it does have its charms. New Jersey's trail is lovely, although I prefer it during the off-season: I once hiked it in the dead of winter and saw not a single hiker for a week. New York's mountain laurel bloom in June is one of nature's grand and extravagant displays, hardly something you'd expect to take place within sight of the Empire State Building.

In such a heavily populated area, it's a miracle the Appalachian Trail Conference has found a thin corridor of wild lands, but it has. Many hikers report seeing bears in Pennsylvania and New Jersey, along with other wildlife including pileated woodpeckers, deer, and even the occasional eastern coyote. Unfortunately, each year development creeps closer and closer. Still, the Middle Atlantic AT boasts some stunning views, climbs that will surprise you, and more solitude than you would expect, all conveniently located within a short drive of the Northeast's major cities.

THE TRAIL

Leaving Harpers Ferry, West Virginia, the trail follows the C&O Canal Towpath along the Potomac River for a few miles before climbing to Weverton Cliffs and its famous view of Harpers Ferry. Next, the trail runs along South Mountain. You'll pass Antietam Creek, which feeds downhill to the famously bloody Civil War battlefield. You'll also pass some Civil War trenches, a memorial to Civil War journalists, and the nation's first Washington Monument.

Entering Pennsylvania, the trail soon crosses the Mason-Dixon Line and the official AT halfway marker (which is moved from year to year, as trail relocations change the exact halfway point). Pennsylvania is known to hikers as Rocksylvania, because of the glacial debris left behind at the end of the last Ice Age. Rocks the size of trucks form obstacle courses, while rocks the size of baseballs roll underfoot. There's a rumor that AT trail maintainers go out and

The mountain laurel bloom in the Middle Atlantic States is one of nature's extravagances. It takes place in June.

sharpen the rocks at night just in time for the current crop of thru-hikers. The bottom line: slow going, even in relatively flat terrain.

The trail crosses into New Jersey at the Delaware Water Gap, through an underpass beneath I-80. New Jersey is a lot prettier and wilder than you might expect, as you'll see in the next few miles. At Sunfish Pond, a glacial tarn, you might see one of the resident bears. In June, hikers are treated to profligate displays of mountain laurel along the ridges. The trail goes through High Point State Park, so named because it boasts New Jersey's 1803-foot high point.

New York State is pretty, too, with more rocky ridges and beautiful wildflowers, although there is almost always a sense of being close to a road or town. Harriman State Park is perhaps the most remote stretch in New York—it's here that the first miles specifically intended to be included in the AT were built. The elevations are modest, but don't be fooled: Short, stiff ups and downs of 400 and 500 feet quickly add up; it's not unusual for thru-hikers to gain more than 6000 feet of elevation in a single day's hike!

After descending from Bear Mountain, the trail goes through a zoo featuring local wildlife (if you haven't seen a bear yet, here's your chance), then crosses the Hudson River on the Bear Mountain Bridge, where hikers used to have to pay a toll. A traditional stopping point is the Graymoor Monastery, which puts hikers up for a small donation. A day later, hikers reach a shelter that occupies a suburban lot surrounded by homes! The trail then meanders through the Harlem Valley, weaving and dodging to avoid private property, before entering Connecticut.

SEASONS

The trail in the Middle Atlantic States can be hiked in all seasons, although in winter be prepared for snow, especially after January 1. Four-point instep crampons can help you handle iced-over rocks.

Fall and spring are especially pleasant times to hike. May and June are beautiful, and May has the added advantage of generally comfortable temperatures, usually in the 70s. The mountain laurel is at peak in June.

Summer is the most popular hiking season, although you should try to avoid heat waves, which are at their worst in July. In autumn, the foliage starts turning in early October and is usually at peak in late October. Some of the springs dry up in the autumn, especially on the ridges, so pay attention to your water supply.

Dealing with Heat and Humidity

Somewhere between Pennsylvania and New York, thru-hikers leave spring behind and enter summer for real. Heat spells drag on for days, and in the Northeast, heat comes with matching humidity.

Take advantage of the Northeast AT's proximity to towns and stores: You can hop off the trail every once in a while for a cold drink. Some hikers find that diluted electrolyte-replacement drinks help a lot, and they are widely available at convenience stores near the trail.

The trail is especially hot on exposed ridges, where the rocks soak up heat and reflect it back on the hiker. One particular danger spot is the northbound climb out of Lehigh Gap in Pennsylvania. This is an uncharacteristic stretch of trail that requires rock scrambling. Fumes from a nearby zinc smelter have deforested the whole mountain, so there isn't a stick of shade anywhere—and not much water. Take at least two or three quarts on a hot day.

> "It's easy to think that you should be doing big miles in Pennsylvania because the state is so flat, but then you come up against the rocks. Don't think about how you'd like the trail to be; just accept it for what it is."
>
> —Dan Smith

HIKING THE SUBURBS

Benton MacKaye's words about "smoky beehive cities" have resonance here. In spring, summer, and fall, the trails can be crowded; in winter, the curtain of foliage falls to reveal houses and towns. From several places, including High Point, New Jersey, and West Mountain, New York, you can even see the Twin Towers of New York City.

With some two-thirds of their mileage complete, foot-sore northbound thru-hikers may find little to engage their interest. Just when the trail should be getting easier and easier (after all, the elevations are low, the climbs short, the profile maps almost flat), summer temperatures start to bake the exposed ridges, and rocky terrain twists ankles and frustrates those with mileage on their minds.

A good way to cope is to focus on the treats that hiking so close to civilization offers. At many road crossings, you can go a short distance off-trail for sodas and snacks. Hiker appetites can be sated with New York deli sandwiches.

This is also a good place to invite family members to join you for a picnic or a day hike. Most thru-hikers find that it doesn't work well to have friends and family join them for multiple days of hiking, because non-thru-hikers can't keep up. But frequent road crossings make day hikes feasible—and there are even opportunities to take public transportation to several sections of the trail.

And here's an idea for an interesting day off: If you've never been to New York City, you can hop on a commuter train at the Appalachian Trail Station (yes, it's actually called that) near Patterson, New York, and be at 42nd Street in an hour and a half. (For the schedule, call Metro-North, 800-638-7646.)

Getting water from a well in New York

SAFETY

The AT is located in easy proximity to major urban centers. It's also located close to rural communities, some of them quite impoverished. Although hiking the trail is relatively safe, crime does occur, especially on parts of the trail that are within a short walk of roads. Although violent crime is rare, there have been nine murders on the Appalachian Trail. There have also been several rapes. It's never unwise to be cautious, especially when traveling alone.

In the Middle Atlantic States, the density of the population increases the likelihood of crime. Some hikers have reported unpleasant or frightening encounters with the kind of characters you'd prefer to see in a movie and not in real life. More commonly, there are incidences of theft.

The strategies discussed in Chapter 3 apply here. Keep an eye on your gear. Don't tell strangers where you plan to stay for the night. Camp in shelters with other hikers you know, or camp out of sight of the trail in your tent. Avoid shelters that are only a hop, skip, and a jump from roads. Pay attention to your belongings: Don't set up your tent and go for a stroll to a viewpoint; you might find (as my husband did, in Maryland) all your gear gone when you get back. If you and your hiking partner or friends are going into a restaurant or a business, ask if you can stash your packs inside. (Businesses near the trail are used to dealing with hikers. You won't be the first to ask to bring a backpack inside.) If you can't, leave someone outside to guard them, place them in clear view—or, if you have a choice, patronize another establishment. It only takes a few seconds for someone to toss a pack into the trunk of a car and take off. These suggestions are appropriate on all trails, but in more populated areas, more caution is advised.

Hunting Season

Hunting season is a consideration on many parts of the AT. In the Middle Atlantic States, this is mostly a fall and winter issue, so it pertains more to southbounders, section hikers, and day hikers than northbound thru-hikers. Although hunting is popular in most rural areas, in the Middle Atlantic States higher population coupled with less public land means more hunters in any given area. In Pennsylvania, the beginning of deer hunting season in late November is practically a state holiday.

If you hike during hunting season, wear hunter orange—as much orange as you can stand, from head to toe. Decorate your pack in hunter orange, too. (The ATC sells a reversible pack cover that is orange on one side.) If you have a dog, he should wear hunter orange as well. Be aware that there are several overlapping hunting seasons that start at different times—not just deer season, but deer by bow-and-arrow or powder, grouse, turkey, bear, and a slew of others. The ATC can give you detailed information about hunting season along the entire trail.

> "I discovered that I needed to make plans for meeting my honey rather than saying we'll figure it out when you're out there. If the date or place is set, then there is something special to look forward to, and some days that really makes a difference in your attitude."
> —K. A. "Goose" Cutshall

Previous page:
The upward thrust of the Appalachians plus glacial scouring left sharp-edged, oddly tilted rocks—sandstone, basalt, quartzite—along much of Pennsylvania's AT.

Highlight Hike
MARYLAND'S AT: SOUTH MOUNTAIN

WHERE: Harpers Ferry, West Virginia, to PenMar State Park on the Pennsylvania–Maryland border
DISTANCE: 40 miles
DIFFICULTY: Easy
BEST TIME TO GO: Any season; summer can be hot
GUIDE: *Appalachian Trail Guide: Maryland and Northern Virginia*

*Previous page:
View of the Potomac River
from Weverton Cliffs near
Harpers Ferry, headquarters of the ATC*

After exploring historic Harpers Ferry, the trail crosses the Potomac River and runs along the C&O Canal before climbing to Weverton Cliffs, with their spectacular views of the Potomac and Harpers Ferry. From here on, the trail is easy, running the ridge of South Mountain, past several Civil War sites and state parks.

Highlight Hike
NEW JERSEY'S AT: KITTATINNY RIDGE

WHERE: Delaware Water Gap to High Point State Park
DISTANCE: 44 miles
DIFFICULTY: Easy
BEST TIME TO GO: Can be hiked year-round
GUIDE: *Appalachian Trail Guide: New York–New Jersey*

*Rattlesnake Mountain in
New Jersey: The AT in the
Middle Atlantic States is an
all-season trail.*

From the dramatic cleft of the Delaware Water Gap, the AT climbs onto Kittatinny Ridge following sparkling Dunnfield Creek past Sunfish Pond, a glacial tarn. From here the trail largely follows rocky ridges, with views that sometimes extend clear to Manhattan. In June, the mountain laurel is spectacular.

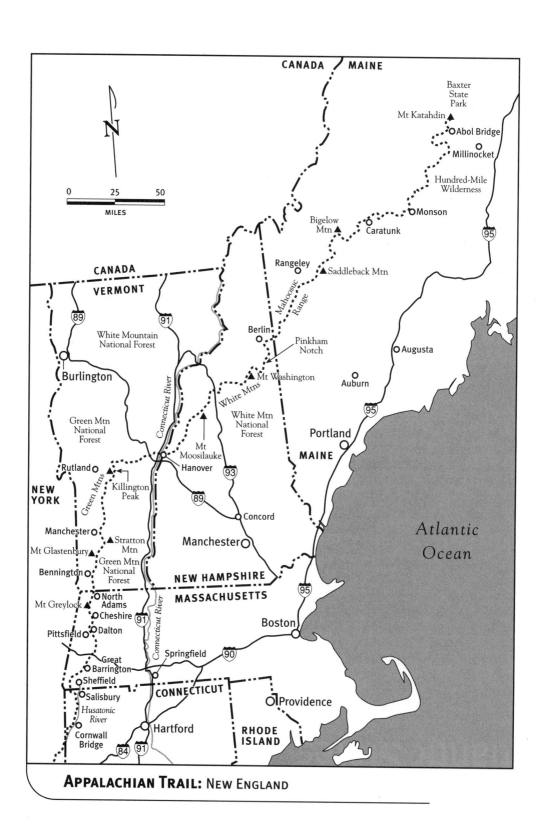

APPALACHIAN TRAIL: NEW ENGLAND

CHAPTER 9

New England

The AT in New England is really divided into two sections. At the Connecticut border, the trail enters southern New England, with short ups and downs interrupted by occasional visits to typical New England villages with trademark white-steepled churches. As the trail continues north, the mountains get progressively more impressive, reaching their highest point on 6288-foot Mount Washington in New Hampshire. In Maine, it's more mountains, and pristine wilderness ponds—and a grand finale atop 5267-foot Katahdin, meaning, in the language of the native Abenaki, "the greatest mountain."

THE TRAIL

Most thru-hikers notice immediately that the trail in Connecticut is much more rural than it has been for the last few hundred miles. Tracts of public land are larger, private property less obvious, roads fewer and farther between. Although Connecticut can't be called especially dramatic, it is extremely pretty, with a pleasant walk along the Housatonic River and a fine 16-mile ridgeline traverse just north of Salisbury, Connecticut.

In Massachusetts the trail continues the same pattern of modest ups and downs—with two notable exceptions, one south, one north. At the southern end the Mount Everett Range reaches 2602 feet (and grand views), providing a workout as the footpath rises steadily in deep forest from the Connecticut state line. The descent at Jug End into the Housatonic Valley is precipitous and fun. Great Barrington makes a good resupply or rest town, though the AT is a few miles from the village center. Up on the Berkshire massif, east of the Housatonic Valley, the trail meanders through rolling woodlands, with many miles in huge state parks, passing the tiny, pastoral village of Tyringham and wonderfully isolated Goose Pond. Black bear and much other wildlife are common here. There are no other towns until Dalton.

Some advice: Put your compass away (so that you won't know you're going in a circle!) and enjoy the walk; from here on, it only gets better.

In northern Massachusetts the AT traverses Mount Greylock (at 3491 feet, the state's highest point) in another massive state forest with dozens of feeder trails. Handsome Bascom Lodge provides shelter and hearty meals at the top, but not cheaply. After a steep descent to North Adams, the AT rises again, crosses into Vermont, and follows the Long Trail, America's first long-distance trail. Now the mountains—Glastonbury, Stratton, Killington—rise and the

Puncheons over boggy areas near Lonesome Lake Hut in New Hampshire's White Mountains

distances between roads stretch. If you've been traveling light, you should re-trieve at least one layer of clothing before Mount Greylock, as well as your better raingear, because these are real mountains and rainstorms on the high peaks can be cold.

North of Killington, the trail drops for the intermountain crossing between the Green Mountains of Vermont and the White Mountains of New Hampshire. This is another up-and-down stretch with lots of nickel-and-dime climbs and circuitous routing. Most hikers complain in the trail registers that it's a lot longer than advertised.

The trail crosses into New Hampshire at Hanover, home of the Dartmouth Outing Club, which maintains a stretch of the AT. Now warm layers are man-datory, since you'll shortly be climbing above the treeline into the White Mountains, as you tackle the mighty Presidential Range, which boasts some of the most treacherous weather in the world. People die in the Whites at an alarming frequency, and while many of the deaths are caused by falls or hypo-thermia during the winter months, an unsettling number of people have been killed by hypothermia and storms in the middle of August. You need raingear, at least one warm layer of insulating clothing, a hat, and gloves.

Oh, and another thing: The trail is about to turn rough. Through the Whites and for the first 90 miles of Maine, expect to scramble over, under, and between boulders and rocks, to pull yourself up steep rock faces with your hands, and to descend ever so carefully.

The route eases after Saddleback Mountain in Maine. The homestretch becomes a glorious grand finale, passing lakes and ponds abundant with wildlife, including moose and loons. The so-called "Hundred-Mile Wilderness," between Monson and Abol Bridge near the southern boundary of Baxter State Park, is the last challenge before massive Katahdin looms ahead. Although not especially difficult (compared, that is, to what you've already done), this is a long stretch without resupply, so you'll have to carry however much food it takes you to walk approximately 100 miles. Then it's Katahdin, triumph, and the top—and the end of a way of life as you contemplate what you've accomplished.

Ready to go home? Or to turn around and start walking back? It's been done . . . .

SEASONS

New England's AT can be divided into a southern and a northern section. In Connecticut and Massachusetts, the trail can be hiked at any time of year, although in winter, depending on the snowfall and accumulation, you'll need basic snow-camping and travel skills, including the ability to use crampons and snowshoes. Despite the modest elevations, this is real winter camping, with temperatures that can plummet below zero. In southern New England, spring, summer, and fall are all popular hiking seasons, although spring can be muddy and summer temperatures can be hot and humid. Fall is especially lovely, with comfortable temperatures and flaming foliage.

In northern New England (from Mount Greylock north), winter is off-limits to anyone without full-fledged winter mountaineering experience. In New Hampshire's White Mountains, people die almost every year from falls and hypothermia; Maine attracts fewer winter hikers, so there are fewer accidents reported, but the conditions are every bit as harsh, with temperatures far below zero and brutal winds.

Spring in northern New England is also a difficult season. Snow lingers, and some parts of the trail in Vermont may be closed to prevent erosion during the "mud" season. Much of northern New England is infested with blackflies until July. By far the best seasons to explore this beautiful terrain are summer and fall. Summer offers the most temperate weather—but also the biggest crowds. Fall offers a spectacular foliage display, but after mid-September, temperatures drop and at the higher elevations, snow is a real possibility.

THE HARD PART

To those who would argue that western trails are harder, I have one response: Come hike northern New England's Appalachian Trail.

From Mount Moosilauke at the southern end of New Hampshire's White Mountains to Saddleback Mountain in Maine, the AT becomes diabolical.

This area encompasses the White Mountains in New Hampshire and the Mahoosucs and Bigelows of Maine. Many hikers erroneously think that their work is done after they cross the White Mountains; in reality, you're only halfway through the rough stuff when you reach the Maine border. Notorious Mahoosuc Notch, a boulder-choked cleft between two mountains, and Mahoosuc Arm, a steep climb out of the notch, are only the best known of many difficult scrambles. It's not unheard of for hikers to break their legs or twist ankles and knees as they haul themselves over boulders, clinging to the roots or branches of any plant unfortunate enough to be growing near the trail. Prepare for low mileage. Many thru-hikers who have happily been whizzing by at 20 miles a day slow down to 10 miles a day in the Whites and Mahoosucs. Give yourself some extra time. Also budget some extra cash, because the cost of town stops goes up in this heavily touristed area.

A note for seniors: Many older thru-hikers have complained about this section of trail; some have suffered broken bones. This is a good place to hike with a partner, carry a cell phone, or at least check in with someone at home. You might want to sit out rainy days, because the rocks are not only steep, but slick.

Four strategies can help you through this section.

Lighten up. The lighter your pack, the better your balance. By this time, you have enough experience to know what gear you've been using and what you haven't. It's time to clean house. However, don't skimp on clothing; the above-treeline passages can be extremely dangerous in bad weather.

Pack your heavy gear lower than usual. Most pack manufacturers recommend that you pack lightweight items such as sleeping bags and clothes

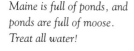

Maine is full of ponds, and ponds are full of moose. Treat all water!

at the bottom. The normal assumption is that the heavier items should be a little higher up for the pack to ride most comfortably. However, on rough terrain, the rules change. Keeping the heavy stuff down low puts your center of gravity low, too. In addition, many hikers find that internal-frame packs hug their bodies better and are more comfortable when rock scrambling.

Use trekking poles to help you keep your balance and take some weight off your knees. Poles are helpful when you have to take large steps down from big rocks. They can get in the way, though, when you have to scramble. Telescoping poles can be compressed and lashed to a pack, leaving your hands free.

Plan low mileage here. In the Mahoosucs, a 10-mile day is an achievement even for fit, young thru-hikers.

Southbounders will find northern New England especially challenging because unlike their northbound brethren, they are not yet in peak shape. Cut yourself some slack with the mileage—don't worry, you can pick up steam later.

THE WHITES

Exposed, Above-Treeline Travel

"STOP: THE AREA AHEAD HAS THE WORST WEATHER IN AMERICA!"

There is nothing subtle about the sign that greets you on the trails leading to treeline in the Whites.

The unique conditions here are caused by the collision of three weather systems that just happen to intersect atop the highest point for hundreds of miles. Northbound fronts coming up the Atlantic Coast, eastbound fronts racing across the Great Plains and the Midwest, and southbound Arctic fronts from Canada meet smack in the middle of the Presidential Range, the most rugged and highest mountain range in the Northeast.

As a result, weather in the Whites is vastly changeable. This is the arctic-alpine life zone, where the only life forms are lichens clinging to rocks. A perfect blue-sky day can change in the blink of an eye to a foggy mess where you'd be lucky to see your hiking partner unless you were close enough to hold hands. The AT in the Whites is marked by humungous cairns blazed not only with the AT's signature white blazes, but with yellow paint, to make them more visible in fog and storms. Think about that before you cavalierly decide to hike up there using only a garbage bag as raingear!

True, there are places to bail out or get help in the Whites. There is a system of backcountry huts and a summit house atop Mount Washington where you can buy food and drinks. There are also well-trained (and busy) search-and-rescue teams. But storms can be so severe that a disoriented hiker may be unable to cover the last ½ mile to safety. Rescue teams have been unable to respond to calls for help due to the weather. Hypothermia, discussed in Chapter 3, is a very real concern here, even in July and August.

AMC Huts

The White Mountains are one of the few places in America that have a European-style system of huts. Managed by the venerable Appalachian Mountain Club (AMC), one of the nation's oldest outdoor recreation organizations, the huts offer dormitory-style accommodations and hearty meals.

Among thru-hikers, the huts have a mixed reputation. It's not easy to walk by a hut (especially above treeline in foul weather) without wanting to stop in. While thru-hikers and anyone else are welcome to pay a visit, accommodations are reserved in advance—sometimes months in advance. Very few thru-hikers can plan their schedules so exactly. (But if you think you can, call 603-466-2727 to make reservations.)

The AMC does offer some thru-hikers the opportunity to work off a stay by donating labor. The jobs can be ridiculously easy—or a little unfair; it all depends on the hutmaster. Usually thru-hikers join the so-called "croos," helping to serve and wash up after meals and eating after the guests are done. Sometimes there isn't as much food left over as a hungry hiker would like. In past years, there have sometimes been conflicts between thru-hikers and croos (perhaps because each group vied for the admiration of the "normal" guests at the huts!). More recently, as thru-hikers have become croo members and croo members have undertaken thru-hikes, interactions have been more positive.

If you want to work, there are a few things you can do to improve your chances. First, realize that the croos only have room for one or two workers, maybe three or four, but not usually more than that. Get there early. Understand that even though you may prefer to do your work the day you arrive, AMC policy is that most jobs will be done in the morning before you leave. If you get along with the hut croo and do a good job, you can ask them to radio ahead and reserve you a working slot at the next hut.

Some hikers do manage to stay in the huts as paying guests. If you're the totally planful type who sets a schedule and follows it, you can make reservations in advance (several months in advance is not too early!). Or you can wait until you have a pretty good idea of when you'll arrive and call then. With a little bit of luck (people do cancel their reservations, and not all the huts are always booked) you might find a spot, especially if you can be flexible. You can also inquire about participating in the AMC's guest naturalist program. Guest naturalists are people with special expertise on outdoors-related subjects. If you are a good public speaker, you can volunteer to give a talk in exchange for room and board (but you still need a reservation). Only make these plans when you're sure you'll be able to stick to them!

Camping Regulations

Or you can skip the huts entirely. Forget about those homemade meals and the fact that the hut croo packed in a whole fresh turkey. You're supposed to be camping, remember?

> "In northern New England, prices are higher, the AMC huts are expensive, and there are lots of B&Bs that take in hikers. The terrain is tough and you'll want to treat yourself sometimes, so budget to spend a little more money here."
>
> —Dan Smith

But now the bad news: Camping in the White Mountain National Forest can be as frustrating as trying to stay in the huts. To prevent overuse, erosion, and impact on fragile alpine vegetation, camping is prohibited above treeline and elsewhere is limited to designated campsites and shelters for which you have to pay. Tentsites are on wooden platforms, on which it can be difficult to pitch a non-free-standing tent, not to mention a tarp.

If campsites are full when you arrive, you'll be sent to the next one—even if that means leaving the AT and losing hundreds of feet of elevation. Most thru-hikers, used to the almost unlimited freedom of the trail, chafe under the regulations.

Your best strategy for the Whites: Plan short days so that you can get to camp or the huts early. Remember that the regulations are an attempt to help preserve this vulnerable environment and that there are too many thru-hikers to be granting exceptions. Don't expect camping in the Whites to be as foot-loose and fancy-free as it is on the rest of the trail. Look at the upside: You're walking through the most spectacular country on the East Coast.

Descending Maine's Katahdin, the northern terminus of the Appalachian Trail

BAXTER STATE PARK

Katahdin, the AT's northern terminus, is located in northern Maine's Baxter State Park, which is, like the White Mountain National Forest, tightly regulated to protect its fragile environment. If you can plan in advance, you can reserve a lean-to at Katahdin Stream Campground, which is the closest campground to Katahdin. (Contact Baxter State Park Authority, 64 Balsam Drive, Millinocket, ME 04462; 207-723-5140.) However, camping spots at Katahdin Stream are often reserved months in advance and may be difficult to get. Otherwise, a lean-to at Daicey Pond is reserved for thru-hikers. Shelter space is free, first-come first-served, but if there are too many of you, you can camp around the shelter.

The climbing season on Katahdin is from sometime in May to mid-October, depending on the weather. Usually, rangers "close" Katahdin in mid-October due to danger from snow and ice. After that, you need special permission to climb.

Highlight Hike
BERKSHIRE RIDGELINE

WHERE: Salisbury, Connecticut, to Jug End, Massachusetts
DISTANCE: 17 miles
DIFFICULTY: Moderate
BEST TIME TO GO: Spring, fall, summer
GUIDE: *Appalachian Trail Guide: Massachusetts and Connecticut*

This lovely walk begins in the quaint village of Salisbury. After climbing to the ridge that runs north near the New York–Connecticut border, it passes several viewpoints that look out upon the Housatonic River Valley, the Berkshires, and the Taconics. Pretty Sages Ravine makes a perfect campsite, with numerous small waterfalls and pools that offer a refreshing dip at the end of the day.

Highlight Hike
NEW HAMPSHIRE'S WHITE MOUNTAINS

Approaching Lakes of the Clouds Hut in New Hampshire's White Mountains

WHERE: Franconia Notch to Pinkham Notch

DISTANCE: 53 miles

DIFFICULTY: Extremely challenging; plan no more than two-thirds of your normal daily mileage

BEST TIME TO GO: Summer and early fall

GUIDE: *Appalachian Trail Guide: New Hampshire and Vermont*

This famous above-treeline traverse takes in the Presidential Range, including Mount Washington, at 6288 feet the highest peak in the Northeast. The trail is difficult, with lots of rock scrambling that can reduce a hiker's pace to no more than 1 mile per hour. Take extra warm clothes and good raingear—the region boasts the "worst weather in America"! On a clear day, the 100-mile views are spectacular.

The Appalachian Trail's northern terminus is Katahdin, "the greatest mountain."

Highlight Hike
MAINE'S "HUNDRED-MILE WILDERNESS" AND KATAHDIN

WHERE: Monson, Maine, to Baxter Peak
DISTANCE: 118 miles
DIFFICULTY: Challenging
BEST TIME TO GO: August and September
GUIDE: *Appalachian Trail Guide: Maine* (Map 2, section 3)

This north-country stretch is the most remote part of the Appalachian Trail. Dotted with ponds and lakes, the land is prime territory for moose and loons. Unfortunately, the name "wilderness" is a misnomer. Between Monson and Abol Bridge, some sections of the trail do go through protected areas, but in several stretches you'll see rather too much evidence of logging. Nonetheless, the combination of mountains, lakes, and wildlife makes this an AT highlight. In this 118-mile section, the only on-trail opportunity to resupply is at the small, poorly stocked (and expensive) store at Abol Bridge, just south of Mount Katahdin. Most hikers, therefore, carry enough food for the entire hike. Thru-hikers can do this section in 6 or 7 days, but unless you're in a rush (and as fit as a thru-hiker) you'll want to take more time, even though that means your pack will be heavy with food.

PART III

Pacific Crest Trail

A smooth stretch of the PCT leads through the northern Cascades.

CHAPTER 10

A Trail of Extremes

The Pacific Crest Trail could hardly be more different from its eastern cousin. While the Appalachian Trail largely wends its way through temperate forest, the PCT is a trail of extremes: the scorching desert valleys of southern California's sere and severe drylands, the sky-spearing snow-covered pinnacles of the Sierra Nevada, the giant volcanoes of the Cascades, and the thousand-year-old trees of the old-growth forests of the Pacific Northwest. It is a trail of awe-inspiring nonstop views.

Ranging from 140 feet above sea level at the Columbia River Gorge to 13,180 feet at Forester Pass, the PCT has the greatest elevation range of any of the three trails. It crosses six out of North America's seven ecozones (all except the subtropical). Hikers walk through high and low desert, montane forest, old-growth forest, and arctic-alpine high country.

CHARACTER OF THE TRAIL

Although many hikers who attempt a thru-hike of the PCT are AT veterans, it's not necessary to have AT experience to successfully hike the PCT. In fact, in many ways the trails are so different that hikers expecting to revisit their Appalachian Trail experience are often disappointed. While some AT trail traditions have migrated to the PCT (for example, trail angels, trail names, and registers), there are fewer people, fewer trail towns, fewer festivals—and fewer of the diversions that both distract and delight hikers on the AT.

CHALLENGES OF THE TRAIL

You might hear as you plan your hike that the PCT is easier than the AT. Any such generalizations are as full of holes as a thru-hiker's old socks. All three of the Triple Crown trails are difficult in their own different ways.

Yes, the PCT does have a much better footway than the AT, and the tread is indeed easier to walk on. AT veterans are sometimes shocked to realize that on the PCT, they can meander along looking at views instead of obstacles underfoot. You can make better time and cover more miles per day on the PCT—by that measure, almost all of the PCT, when hiked in the optimum hiking season, is indeed easier than almost all of the AT. But that does not mean that a PCT *thru-hike* is easy.

For the long-distance hiker, the PCT poses several challenges:

Its length. At 2658 miles, the PCT is about 500 miles longer than the AT.

The hiking season is shorter. To complete the PCT in the snow-free season requires a five-month pace. Maybe, if you're lucky, the season will last five-and-a-half months. Figure on 20 miles a day if you take 1 day off a week to rest and resupply. Sometimes, as in the High Sierra, your mileage will be lower. Other times, as in the desert, it might be higher because of water scarcity. In Oregon, many hikers cover 25 miles a day or more. Most AT vets find that their PCT mileage is about one-third higher than their AT mileage.

The extreme environments. Searing heat in the desert, blazing sun, long distances between water sources, snow in the Sierra, streams swollen with runoff, and always the prospect of not making it to Canada before winter comes to the North Cascades, are all challenges the PCT hiker faces.

Difficulties at the very beginning. The environment conspires to make starting the PCT trail more difficult than starting the AT. On the AT, you can hike short days to break in. On the PCT, the availability of water often requires that you be able to hike 20 or more miles—or else carry many pounds of extra water to see you through a night in a dry camp.

Bigger wildernesses. The wildernesses are bigger, and the distances between roads are longer, so the average PCT hiker carries more food.

A less-developed hiker and trail community. If you're an AT veteran, don't expect as many services geared to hikers. The AT community is close-knit and intense. Hikers traveling together at roughly the same rate often encounter each other and form deep friendships that last far beyond the trail. While there are certainly other hikers on the PCT, and plenty of trail angels, the fact is that hiking the PCT is not anywhere near the social experience that the AT is. Without shelters to clump people together, it is easy to find yourself camping alone night after night.

As PCT hikers approach the High Sierra, they get glimpses of the snow they'll have to contend with.

Long-Distance Considerations

Which Way?

As with the AT, northbound is the preferred direction of travel on the PCT. Most hikers start from the Mexican border in late April. In recent years, for example, there has been a low-key kickoff party at Lake Moreno County Park, 20 trail miles north of the Mexican border, during the last few days of April. A start date in late April in an average year means that hikers should be clear of snow in the higher mountains of southern California. They can then cover the 700 miles to Kennedy Meadows (where there is usually a gathering of thru-hikers) in six to seven weeks and start through the Sierra in mid-June, which will put them in a good position to make it to Canada before winter.

Unlike the AT, seasonal conditions can vary so much that the typical starting date becomes impractical. In a low-snow year, the higher elevations of the Laguna and San Jacinto Mountains may be clear a few weeks earlier than usual, and an earlier start date would be possible, especially if snow in the Sierra is also at average or lower levels. The opposite can also happen, with snow in southern California's mountains lingering well into June. Before starting out, check current conditions with the Pacific Crest Trail Association (PCTA); see Appendix 2.

Southbounders start in mid- to late June and almost always wallow in snow from the Canadian border through the Glacier Peaks Wilderness. Once out of snow, southbounders are in serious bug season for a few weeks, usually until somewhere in Oregon. Then, there's an easy run through northern California. You should plan to be through the Sierra by the end of September. Fall in southern California is more comfortable than late spring, but most of the natural water sources will be dry.

Resupplies

There are fewer resupplies on the PCT than on the AT, and some of them are located much farther from the trail, which requires hitchhiking. Even so, with few exceptions, most hikers don't carry more than 5 to 6 days' worth of food at a time. The biggest resupply problems are the High Sierra (200 miles between road crossings, with several opportunities to take side trails out for resupply) and southern Washington (147 miles; most hikers do this section in about 7 or 8 days).

Permits and Regulations

Backcountry permits are required in all national parks and in many wilderness areas. If you are doing a short section hike, you'll have to check with the individual management agency regarding regulations. Fire permits are also required in some areas. The PCTA offers members free thru-permits for hikes of more than 500 miles. Contact the PCTA, giving them your approximate start and finish dates and places; they will send you a permit.

In general, camping is permitted anywhere along the PCT, as long as applicable local regulations, including minimum-impact guidelines, are followed. For example, you should camp no less than 200 feet away from water, and if you camp in a site that has not been used before, make sure that when you leave, it is as pristine as when you found it. In places that attract a lot of hiker traffic, such as the High Sierra, some campsites will be very oft-used and obvious. Camping in less-obvious sites is sometimes referred to as

"I copy guidebook pages onto lighter pages which can be trimmed. I use four different-colored highlighters to mark proper names mentioned in the text, water sources, good camping spots, and intersecting trails or roads. This way, at any given moment—when tired or in a storm—I don't have to grope my way through a page of 'equal-looking' text, as I wonder how far to the next water or campsite."

—Bob Ellinwood

stealth camping, a slight misnomer, because it implies something possibly illegal. In fact, a "stealth" site is nothing more than a site that is off the beaten path. There are only a handful of shelters, most of them run-down, on the entire PCT.

Finding Your Way

The PCT is not as frequently marked as the AT, but it's usually marked well enough that few hikers get lost. There is no consistent pattern of blazes. The PCT may be marked with "candle-in-the-woods" ax blazes (one long blaze for the candlestick, topped with one short, round blaze for the flame), metal chevrons, wooden markers, and trail signs. The maps and directions in the guidebooks are adequate. For thru-hikers, the only problems are likely to be in the High Sierra and the North Cascades, where snow can obscure the trail. In such situations, you'll need to be able to use a map and a compass.

The PCT is not as frequently marked as the AT, but "candles in the woods" blazes like this one help hikers stay on the trail.

GEAR

In recent years, the Pacific Crest Trail has been a laboratory for new ultralight techniques, and indeed, new thinking about backpacking equipment, thanks partly to the influence of ultralight guru Ray Jardine and partly to the fact that the climate on many parts of the PCT during the main thru-hiking season is warm, dry, and generally forgiving of hubris and mistakes.

Ultralight is more than a trend here; it's an obsession. At annual trail events, hikers show off new inventions in gear and compete to see whose homemade stove will boil water the fastest. It's all good fun in the sunshine of southern California, where the possibility of hypothermia seems a million miles away (although, in actuality, thru-hikers can climb to hypothermic conditions a mere 40 miles from the Mexican border). Hike parts of the PCT in the wrong season, and your homemade poncho-tent is really going to have its work cut out for it.

Basic ultralight backpacking is covered in Chapter 4; the following comments address specific gear issues on the PCT.

Footwear

The PCT is where the trend of hiking in running shoes or other lightweight footwear began. The key issues in deciding what kind of footwear works for you will be your own sense of how much support you personally think you need, your intended mileage, your pack weight, and the climate and snow (see Chapter 4).

The debate over boots versus sneakers will continue to generate heated discussion for years to come. The following considerations might help you make your choice for the PCT.

If you're hiking in a high-snow year, boots will help you stay warm and kick steps, and they have more traction than sneakers, which is important on slippery ice. Heavyweight boots are not necessary. Lightweight fabric-and-leather models are adequate.

If the trail is dry and you're hiking with a light pack, consider running shoes or trail shoes. Many PCT hikers wear sneakers; some even wear sport sandals, sometimes in conjunction with Gore-Tex socks.

You may want to organize your resupplies or floater box so that it's easy to switch back and forth. For instance, you might use sneakers in southern California (assuming that the trail is clear), then switch to boots in the High Sierra, where you will spend many miles on snowpack. In California and Oregon in an average year, you might switch back to shoes in mid-July. Then in Washington, your decision would depend on when you get there and what you're comfortable with. In the rain and snow of late September, boots may be a better choice.

All that said, some people have gone the whole way in sneakers, others in boots.

Tents

On the PCT, you need (or will occasionally wish you had) shelter from rain, cold, sunlight, and bugs. The best bug shelter isn't necessarily the best rain shelter. You may want to switch from one to the other at different points in the hike.

Tarps are the lightest-weight choice, and are especially appropriate for southern California, where it's almost guaranteed not to rain, but where you might appreciate shelter from the sun in the middle of the day.

The start of bug season depends on the snowpack and the rate of snow-melt. In an average year, you'll hit it somewhere in the High Sierra and/or in Yosemite National Park, and you'll definitely be happier in a tent or in a tarp outfitted with mosquito netting. By the time you get to northern California, the snow and most of the bugs should be gone. In Oregon and Washington, your decisions will depend on when you get there. Just after the snowmelt, both states swarm with mosquitoes; you'll need some sort of bug protection to preserve your sanity. If you arrive later in the season, a simple tarp might suffice.

Some hikers go the whole way using tarps, but most of them have at least a few uncomfortable nights.

Sleeping Bags

Whatever sleeping bag you choose, it should be able to keep you warm (perhaps in conjunction with a tent or extra clothes) in temperatures below freezing, even in southern California. Most hikers take one 20-degree bag for the whole trip. Because most of the PCT is in a relatively dry climate (in the thru-hiking season), down bags are a good choice, since they are warmer for their weight and more compressible than synthetics. If you try your hand at homemade sleeping sacks, keep the temperature rating in mind.

"You don't need a tent in southern California: no bugs and very little inclement weather in the first 700 miles. It's a good idea to have one from there on."

—David Cossa

Stoves

White gas is not as available on the PCT as it is on the AT, but enough hiker-savvy businesses and trail angels have sprung up along the way that it's generally possible to fill up a fuel bottle. If you have a multifuel stove, you can always use unleaded gas. Some hikers use the propane-butane stoves and mail themselves the canisters. If you do this, you *must* label them properly and ship them via ground transportation only. Homade alcohol-fueled hobo stoves made from tuna cans or soda cans are a current PCT trend. They are an especially good solution for patient cooks who favor the just-add-water school of cuisine. The Zzip wood-burning stove also works well, but you won't be able to camp spontaneously above treeline.

> "I used a wood-burning stove on the PCT and loved it. Only 1 pound, and I could cook for 45 minutes and not worry about fuel. I used one AA battery every 4 days."
> —David Cossa

Packs

Many PCT hikers start the trail psyched about their super-lightweight packs—only to find that those packs can't comfortably handle the water loads they have to carry. I've seen a number of people start the PCT with lightweight packs, only to abandon them after the first long water carry and send home for their heavier, and more comfortable, old packs. Remember: Even if you have cut your base pack weight way down, you still have to carry water and food. Most hikers find that once their total pack weight exceeds 25 pounds, they need a decent suspension system.

One strategy you might consider: Start with a pack that can handle heavier loads, and then, once you get past the High Sierra and you don't have to carry so much clothing, food, or water, switch to a bare-bones, stripped-down, lightweight model.

Umbrellas

I admit that I am sometimes a reluctant convert to new equipment. Usually, the best way to sell me on a new piece of gear is to hike with me. If I find myself getting jealous because you have two shock-absorbing, spring-loaded, collapsible walking sticks and I have an old broom handle, I'll be a convert. That happened with trekking poles (see below), but it didn't happen with umbrellas. I hiked with two umbrella-carrying guys for all of southern California, and my observation was that umbrellas didn't provide much protection from the heat while walking. Much of the heat that attacks hikers in desert conditions radiates from the ground, which has been baking for hours. Putting momentary shade over it doesn't reduce the temperature that much. Instead, I carried lightweight, light-colored pants and a long-sleeved shirt to keep the sun off my skin, and also a sun-reflecting, wide-brimmed hat that shaded my face. My friends used their umbrellas. All of us were satisfied with our choices.

Trekking Poles

Most of the grade along the PCT is gentle enough that it doesn't cause the knee-wrenching injuries that are so common on the AT. However, if you have

weak or aging knees, or if you (or your pack) are overweight, trekking poles can absorb a lot of stress. They are extremely useful in the High Sierra and the North Cascades for stream crossings. Note, too, that some of the new light-weight tarp-tents use trekking poles as part of their support system; you can also use trekking poles to rig a standard tarp.

Ice Axes and Instep Crampons
This is the only unequivocal statement in this book: Northbound PCT thru-hikers should always have ice axes in the High Sierra in June—regardless of what the grapevine says, what the snow survey says, what the guy in the next campsite who seems to know everything says. An ice ax could save your life.

Instep crampons are not required. However, they make traveling over snowfields easier and a little safer. For a few ounces, you're buying yourself some security that you might appreciate.

Raingear
In southern California (in spring and fall), northern California (in July), and Oregon (in July and August), a lightweight, mostly waterproof rain jacket is adequate. In the High Sierra and in Washington, you should have a good rain jacket and either nylon wind pants or full-fledged rain pants, depending on your degree of caution.

Many of my decisions are based on my own experience, although I'm not averse to learning from others. In the case of the Sierra, I learned from my own experience—the first time I hiked the Sierra, I didn't take rain pants. A mid-summer squall and downpour taught me to take them on subsequent visits.

Previous page:
Overflowing streams filled with snowmelt are one of the challenges of a PCT thru-hike.

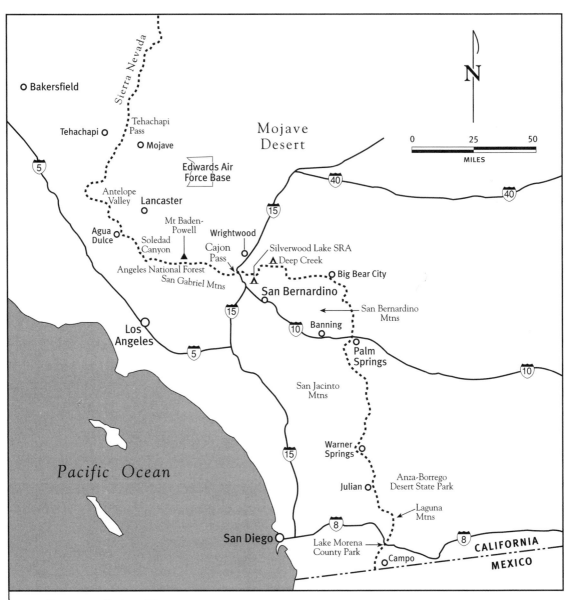

PACIFIC CREST TRAIL: SOUTHERN CALIFORNIA

CHAPTER 11

Southern California

Hikers in southern California invariably talk about hiking through the desert. Technically, that's not exactly true. While the trail does cross some of southern California's desert valleys, for the most part it stays high and dry on chaparral-covered slopes.

But from a hiker's point of view, one thing is true of almost all of southern California: For 700 miles, there is too much sun and too little water.

THE TRAIL

The trail leaves the Mexican border near the tiny town of Campo, which boasts a railroad museum, a store, and an INS station. In May you can expect temperatures in the 90s. But almost immediately the trail shows its chameleon character. In a mere 40 miles, it climbs from chaparral to the Jeffrey pine–shaded Laguna Mountains where temperatures in May are often below freezing. You may be surprised at how glad you are to shiver and see some trees!

Next the trail descends along the border of the fierce Anza-Borrego Desert. After some mild ups and downs, it climbs for real into the San Jacinto Mountains where many PCTers encounter their first snow. This roller-coaster pattern continues; no sooner has the trail reached the high country than it starts back down on trail switchbacked so relentlessly that you sometimes feel that you're losing no more than a few inches per mile. Some 25 miles later, you're back in the low Sonoran Desert as you cross the creosote-dotted valley of San Gorgonio Pass.

Then it's back up—7400 feet back up, to be precise—to the San Bernardino Mountains. The trail passes near Big Bear (a popular recreation area and thru-hiker resupply), then descends along Deep Creek to the Mojave River Dam. Now exposed and dry, the trail passes Silverwood Lake State Park, climbs through more chaparral, and descends to Cajon Pass. The next 25 relentlessly uphill miles are among the PCT's more difficult, as the trail climbs the waterless north face of the San Gabriel range. (Take plenty of water.)

Once in the San Gabriels, the trail stays largely above 7000 feet, occasionally rising to 8000 or even, atop Mount Baden-Powell, 9000 feet. Temperatures are cooler, the trail is shaded, and water is spaced at more reasonable intervals (although it's never abundant enough to let hikers be casual about where their next drink is coming from).

After descending to Soledad Canyon, the trail goes through the hiker-friendly town of Agua Dulce, zigs and zags over the Pelonas Mountains, then

Near Mount Laguna, elevations rise and delicate wildflowers bloom—but at these higher elevations, temperatures can drop below freezing.

descends to cross the Antelope Valley of the Mojave Desert. Second only to the Sierra in snow-melt, this is the most feared section of the PCT. But most thru-hikers find that by the time they get there, they are acclimated, fit, and used to dealing with the challenge of too much heat and not enough water. The trail climbs yet once more, following a far-from-ideal route that was developed as a compromise between the Forest Service and the owners of the mammoth Tejon Ranch. At Tehachapi Pass, the trail officially enters the Sierra Nevada, although the climate and terrain for the next 150 miles is a transition zone and not yet truly montane in character.

Seasons

This may be one of the few sections of trail on all of the Triple Crown trails that doesn't have an optimum season. That's because of the wide variance in elevations (1200–9200 feet)—wider than on any other section of any other trail. When it's comfortable in the desert valleys, it's snowbound up high. When it's passable in the high country, it's broiling down below. And in autumn—when it's at least a little cooler, and there isn't any snow—there isn't any water either!

The higher elevations of the Laguna, San Jacinto, San Bernardino, and San Gabriel Mountains may have significant accumulations of snow in the winter months. The snowpack generally lasts through April or May and, in heavy snow years, can pose a hazard well into June or even early July.

Springs and ephemeral water sources start to dry up in April or May (later in a high-snow year).

In the desert valleys, February and March can be lovely because of the wildflower bloom. The lower sections of the trail can be hiked in winter.

Gear

Gear considerations for the PCT as a whole are discussed in Chapter 10. In addition, in southern California consider the following:

Shelter. Most PCT hikers carry a tarp in southern California. You need shelter from the sun more than shelter from the rain. To cast enough shade to be helpful, the tarp must be dark colored—forest green or navy blue; not bright yellow. A space blanket placed on the tarp with the reflective side facing up can deflect more of the sun's rays.

Water carriers. You need at least a 6-liter capacity for carrying water.

Trekking poles are handy for staking tarps and fending off rattlers.

Raingear. Don't bother with rain pants. Ultralight wind pants, however, could be a good thing to have in a late-spring storm at the higher elevations. A light rain jacket can be part of your layering system up high.

Packs. Packs for the PCT are discussed in Chapter 10. Whatever your school of thought, your pack must be comfortable with base weight plus food plus water.

Footwear. See the questionnaire in Chapter 4 to decide whether to wear sneakers or boots. Boots should be well broken in and a little on the roomy side, because your feet will swell in the heat. You needn't bother with Gore-Tex–lined boots in southern California. If you use sneakers, have them sized so that there's room for wool socks and poly liners (*not* cotton socks). If your feet expand, you can take off the wool socks. Inserts can provide extra heel and arch support.

STARTING OUT

It's a mantra among hikers that "the only way to get ready to hike a long trail is to hike a long trail." That works—to some extent—on the AT, where shelters are only a few miles apart from each other and water is plentiful. On the AT, if you like, you can hike 5 miles a day until you break in.

But on the PCT, water sources don't allow the luxury of a leisurely break-in. On the very first day, the distance between the Mexican border and the first reliable water source at Lake Moreno County Park is 20 miles. If you're not fit enough to do a 20-mile day, you have to carry enough water to walk the distance *and* camp overnight. This early in the hike, your body isn't used to the heat, the exertion; to climbing, sweating, regulating its temperature. You probably need more water than you think you do.

PCT hikers, even hikers who trod the AT relatively blister-free, seem to have more foot problems than hikers on other trails. Even hikers in running shoes get blisters if they don't stop and treat hot spots. The worst pair of feet I ever saw belonged to a sneaker-wearing, light-backpack-carrying, very fit hiker who did 20 miles by 1 P.M. the first day out—and suffered for the next three weeks as his multiple blisters slowly healed.

Blisters are discussed in Chapter 3. Here it's worth noting that the ground temperatures in southern California frequently reach inferno levels—150 degrees or even more, which makes feet especially vulnerable. Be vigilant. Make sure your boots or shoes are big enough. Stop and treat any hot spots before they become blisters. If you are doing big miles, take breaks during the day. Perhaps the biggest mistake hikers make in the first few days is to be too cavalier, too tough, and too ambitious. It's very difficult to strike a balance, even if you are fit: Do you do the big miles between water sources? Or do you carry more water, dry-camp (see "Dryland Hiking Strategies" later in this chapter), and take longer—which puts more weight on your back and feet and also contributes to blisters? There's no right answer, but if you do opt for the

> "For a change of pace, eat your main meal at lunch. Without having the pressure of having to cook in the evening, you might do more mileage in the comfortable evening hours, and you can camp anywhere—you don't need to carry or find enough water to cook dinner."
>
> —Dan Smith

big-mileage days, take lots of breaks and try to sit out the heat of midday. It stays light until 9 o'clock. You have plenty of time to cover the distance.

WATER STRATEGIES

Water and heat shape the beginning of a northbound PCT thru-hike. The sooner you adopt a "desert" mindset, the sooner you will acclimate to this new environment.

Think water! You should always know where the next reliable water source is, and you should never walk past a water source without tanking up. Don't wait until you are thirsty to drink—by the time your brain is receiving thirst signals, your body is already a quart low. Some hikers swear by hydration systems that let them drink continuously as they walk.

How much water do you need? As a rule of thumb (after all, you have to have some basis for your first couple of days of decision-making), figure that between cooking and walking, you're going to need a minimum of 8 liters of water a day. (You'll use much more if it is readily available.) Eight liters sounds like a lot, but before you try to skimp by on less, consider that many thru-hikers on the PCT end up severely dehydrated and some of them quit the trail because of the thirsty misery caused by running out of water in the first few days. (Some even quit at Lake Moreno, only 20 miles into the trip.)

The "8 liters of water" figure is based on recommendations from Grand Canyon rangers and nurses, who spend an inordinate amount of time tending to and sometimes rescuing people who don't listen to them. Another way of calculating the amount of water you need is 1 liter per hour of heavy exercise in hot weather. Figuring a pace of 2½ to 3 miles per hour, that works out to 6–8 liters to go 20 miles. The U.S. military, which trains soldiers in Southwestern deserts, recommends similar amounts and stresses that newbies, overweight people, and people who have had prior problems with dehydration are most at risk. You may indeed find that over time you need less water, especially as you become both more fit and better acclimated to the heat and aridity. But starting out, you should be conservative. If you have to dry-camp, you'll need a couple of liters more for cooking and to sip during the night.

Learn about your body. All of the above notwithstanding, don't listen to others to try to learn how much water you need! I have seen some hikers get by on a quart of water while their partners needed a gallon. I have seen some of the strongest hikers in the world knocked flat by dehydration so severe that they could barely walk 30 feet to shade and shelter. How do you know whether you need to carry a little or a lot? This is something you really can't learn from someone else (or a book). The numbers above are only a starting point; from there on, you need to learn from your own experience. A warning: Don't try to extrapolate from your experience on the Appalachian Trail. Hiking in arid lands is an entirely different situation. Be conservative until you know how you adapt to dry heat.

Water Availability

In May and early June, reasonably reliable water sources will usually be found on or near (within ½ mile of) the PCT every 8–12 miles. There are many stretches where water is found every 12–20 miles. Only in a handful of cases will you have to walk 20–30 miles (rarely more) between *reliable* water sources. Unfortunately, one of those long waterless days is the very first, unless you have information that Hauser Creek is running. And there are two other long waterless stretches within the first week. Take heart: If you make it to Warner Springs with your feet intact, you're well on your way to successfully hiking southern California.

Southbounders should note that very few of southern California's surface water sources run during the fall.

Finding Water

Many hikers, especially those from the better-watered East Coast, think of natural water sources as streams and springs that run year-round. On the southern California PCT, most of the natural water sources are ephemeral, and many of them start to dry out during the thru-hiking season. Exactly when they dry is a reflection of how heavy a snowpack there was. The more snow, the longer the water lasts. In addition to natural sources (such as streams and springs, which may be permanent or ephemeral), you will find temporary sources such as caches provided by people in the hiking community and tanks for livestock, as well as campground spigots, stores, and private homes.

If you come to a water source that appears dry, don't just give up! Streams don't dry out all at once. First they slow down, then they dry in patches, and then they leave puddles and pools, usually in shady places. A stream that is dry in one place may be running only a few yards away. (This is notably true of Hauser Creek, the important but unreliable water source 16 miles from the Mexican border. Hauser Creek starts to dry up in late April or early May. If you don't see water, go downstream about 20 or 30 yards; you may find a lingering pool.) Experienced desert hikers look under shade-giving rocks, near moisture-loving willows and cottonwoods, and in deep depressions.

In recent years, former hikers and trail angels have tried to help out hikers in the early miles of southern California by providing emergency caches in some of the longer waterless sections. Unfortunately, some hikers have taken to relying on these water sources, only to find when they get there that the party of hikers just ahead has taken all the remaining water. Caches should be regarded as supplemental and emergency sources—not as a substitute for

To find water in arid environments, look for ravines surrounded with lush vegetation.

"My wife and I always walk from south to north on long-distance trails to avoid UV rays. This means that about 70 percent of the time the sun is shining on our backs instead of in our faces. We always cover ourselves with loose-fitting clothing (big hats, long-sleeved shirts with collars up, long nylon pants). We also wear lightweight gloves to protect the backs of our hands, which get more sun than any other part of your body, and are usually the first place that becomes sun-damaged. Most younger hikers probably think that we're crazy to dress like that, especially when it's really hot. But surprisingly, we don't really suffer that much from the heat. When the sun is hot we use our umbrellas."

—Roger Stephens

carrying the water you need to safely complete a section of trail. Please leave some for the hiker behind you—and carry out empty jugs.

The following resources provide information on water:

PCT help-line toll free number (1-888-PCTRAIL). The PCT's trail reports number is oriented to thru-hikers. Here's how it works: You call the number, and a recording gives you trail conditions as reported within the last week. If you have anything to report, you can leave a message, and your information will be included in the report. The PCT's trail reports can only be as accurate as the information given by the hikers. Also, there could be as much as a week's lag time between when someone left a message saying that there was water in a certain spring and when you get to the spring—during which time the spring could have dried up. When you are giving info, try to be as specific as possible (the spring was gushing, trickling, almost dry, choked with dust) and mention the date you were there.

PCT guidebooks are accurate about water sources and their reliability. But conditions change from year to year, so it's useful to develop some experience in interpreting and supplementing the information they contain. Your first strategy is to *extrapolate* based on information you've gathered so far. Has it been a dry year or a wet year? Was the snowpack high, normal, or low? How have the springs and streams thus far been running? If, for instance, you had to ford a gushing Hauser Creek in early May, you can reasonably extrapolate that the springs and streams are running better than usual, because Hauser Creek is usually dry by early May.

DRYLAND HIKING STRATEGIES

Have you ever noticed how still the desert seems in the middle of the day? Then there's the ditty about mad dogs and Englishmen—the moral being, Stay out of the noonday sun! If you can possibly arrange your day so as to spend lunchtime in the shade, do so. Or put up a tarp and create your own shade.

Get up early so you can be walking at first light, about 5 A.M. Let's use as an example an extreme scenario, the 24-mile stretch in the San Felipe Hills between Mount Laguna and Warner Springs; assume 100-degree temperatures and totally exposed conditions. You could hike from 5:30 A.M. to 10 A.M. and from 3 P.M. to 8 P.M., a total of 9½ hours hiking time. At 2½ mph, you would cover the whole 24 miles without even moving during the heat of the day! This not only conserves water—it saves your feet from the most blistering heat.

Don't insist on camping near water. Where and when you camp and eat will depend on a lot of things including the mileage you can do, the heat, and how water sources are spaced. If you get out of the "I must camp near water" mind-set, you'll be able to eat your main meal in the afternoon by a water source, drink as much as you can during the time you're resting, then load up with water and hike when it's cool. You'll also reduce your pack weight because you won't be carrying your dinner and the water needed to cook it during the last miles of the day.

Drink smart: Give up caffeine (a diuretic—something you definitely don't need). Try using electrolyte-replacement drinks to replenish sodium and potassium lost to sweating. These drinks are available in powdered form; they're effective in diluted quantities, so use them at half strength to ration them. You'll also find them in some of the campground stores near the trail.

Be respectful of the desert, and recognize your vulnerability as a human in an environment that isn't exactly friendly. I know several people who thought they really might die in southern California. It wasn't the terrain that did it. It was their lack of respect for it. They just didn't understand how vulnerable a human body can be.

OTHER CHALLENGES IN SOUTHERN CALIFORNIA

Just to make things interesting, here are a few other challenges you might face:

Bugs. In the chaparral zone, flies can be merciless, but they disappear at night. They tend to be found in localized areas. They may torment you in one place and be gone a few miles later. Carry DEET.

Rashes. Heat rashes can be a real problem here. Biking shorts help prevent them; hydrocortisone helps treat them.

Poison oak. According to some botanists, poison oak is the most common shrub in the chaparral zone. Most thru-hikers start before it has unfurled its telltale leaves in clusters of three. Look for thin, graceful stalks that arch out, then up, like deer antlers (see Chapter 3).

Rattlesnakes. You can expect to see rattlesnakes throughout most of this section's 700 miles, although they tend to stay out of the high country (here about 8000 feet). For more on rattlesnakes, see Chapter 3.

UNDOCUMENTED IMMIGRANTS AND HIKER SAFETY

They have very different motivations, but most undocumented immigrants are trying to do exactly what you are: get through the drylands. Without adequate clothing or any information about water sources, some of them die, either of hypothermia or of dehydration (something to consider when you're planning how much water to take on a long, dry stretch). There have been a few instances of theft of hiker property, food, and water. There have also been a few instances of thru-hikers walking companionably along with would-be immigrants. The Mexicans tend to travel in groups, and they do use the PCT. Check with local rangers and INS officers (at Campo) about current "hot" areas. Avoid camping at Hauser Creek. After Mount Laguna, most of the immigrants have dispersed via roads and highways and are no longer seen on the trail.

"Hiking in hot weather, we get a very early start. If there is a long, hot climb ahead, we often make camp about noon and start the climb at 3–4 P.M."

—Roger Stephens

"Pesky, annoying gnats love to follow PCT hikers through parts of southern California in hot weather. They are usually found around the live oak trees that are abundant along the trail at lower elevations. The more you sweat, they more they attack. DEET doesn't seem to slow them down at all. But for some reason, the gnats only seem to attack while you are moving. As soon as you stop for a break, they leave you alone. Also, use your umbrella. As soon as you pop it open, 95 percent of the gnats will disappear."

—Roger Stephens

San Jacinto Mountains

Highlight Hike
SAN JACINTO MOUNTAINS

WHERE: Pines to Palms Highway 74 to San Gorgonio Pass (near I-10)
DISTANCE: 58 miles
DIFFICULTY: Extremely challenging
BEST TIME TO GO: Late spring and fall
GUIDE: *Pacific Crest Trail: California*

This rugged and difficult hike gives you a sampling of southern California's environment, from the blazing, low Sonoran Desert to shady and sometimes snowy montane forests. The San Jacinto escarpment, created by the San Andreas fault, is a stark and dramatic formation that looms more than a vertical mile over the San Gorgonio valley floor. The difference in elevation between the high point (9030) and the low point (1195) is a mind-boggling 7800 feet. Carry lots of water, and bring good maps in case you have to bail due to water shortages at the lower elevations—or too much snow up high!

Highlight Hike

SAN GABRIEL MOUNTAINS, ANGELES NATIONAL FOREST

WHERE: California Highway 2 near Wrightwood to Highway 2 near Pasadena Camp

DISTANCE: 34 miles

DIFFICULTY: Easy

BEST TIME TO GO: Late spring

GUIDE: *Pacific Crest Trail: California*

The PCT follows the Angeles Crest through the San Gabriel Mountains, running near and occasionally crossing the Angeles Crest Highway, which makes it possible to plan hikes of varying lengths. Wide open views abound. The PCT reaches its highest point (9245 feet) in southern California near the summit of Mount Baden-Powell; an additional 150 feet takes you to the summit, where you'll see phenomenally twisted limber pines that may be as much as 2000 years old. Be aware that in a high-snow year, the upper elevations may be snow-covered into June.

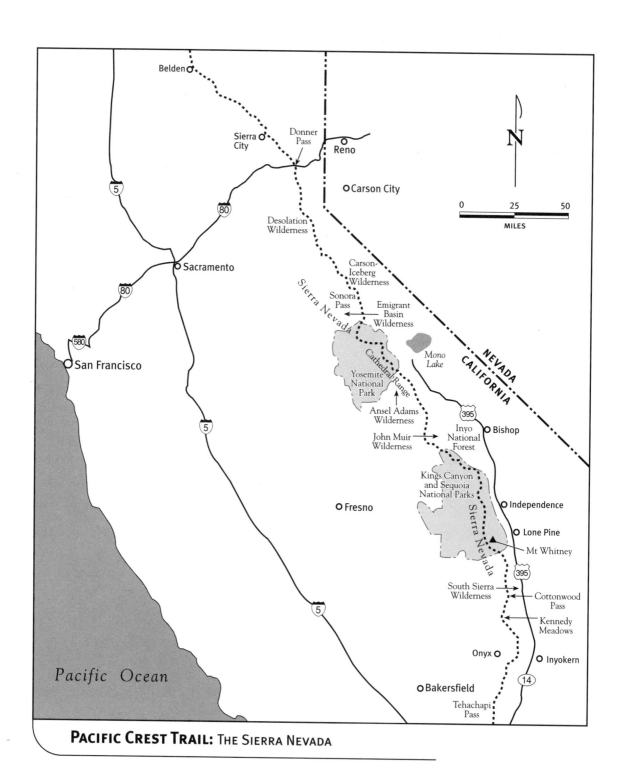

PACIFIC CREST TRAIL: THE SIERRA NEVADA

CHAPTER 12

The Sierra Nevada

Although the Sierra Nevada technically starts at Tehachapi Pass, located between Mojave and Tehachapi, the terrain between Tehachapi Pass and Kennedy Meadows is more transitional than alpine, with the familiar chaparral, the blazing sunshine, and the occasional companionship of rattlesnakes, jackrabbits, and a plethora of horned lizards. Most hikers consider this section a continuation of southern California. Certainly the true Sierra Nevada *experience* begins at Kennedy Meadows, a Forest Service campground that is the last resupply point before a 200-mile roadless stretch encompassing the High Sierra, one of the crown jewels of the PCT.

The Sierra Nevada is a land of superlatives. This 400-mile-long mountain range (800 miles by trail) contains the longest wilderness, highest mountain, and deepest canyon in the contiguous forty-eight states. For long-distance hikers, it is a mammoth challenge. Numbers tell the story:

- 200 miles between road crossings
- Elevations between 8000 and 13,200 feet
- Nine passes with elevations between 11,000 and 13,000 feet
- As much as 10 feet of accumulated hard-packed snow blocking the route

For novice PCT hikers, the High Sierra's icy passes and snowmelt-swollen streams are fearsome obstacles. But it is because of such challenges that the PCT is such a mammoth achievement—in the words of the PCTA, the "Everest of backpacking." After a traverse of the High Sierra during snowmelt, you may well feel, as have many hikers before you, that you have had the adventure of a lifetime.

Some of the fast-packing strategies covered in Chapters 4 ("Ultralight Backpacking") and 13 ("Fast-packing with Ultralight Gear") can actually be implemented in the northern Sierra as soon as you leave the snow for gentler terrain. In an average year, the trail is snow-free after Sonora Pass. After Sonora Pass, the trail should be both easier and less obstructed; you can then pick up the pace.

THE TRAIL

From Kennedy Meadows, the PCT continues north on an uphill trend through chaparral. The only hint of what is to come is the occasional view of a snow-capped peak ahead. Watch your water for the first 2 or 3 days, because water can be scarce. (This is especially true later in the season.)

Sometimes a "bridge" is nothing more than a rolling, treacherous log placed, in this case, above water eyeball deep at Rae Lakes in the High Sierra. In midsummer, after the snowmelt, this crossing may be only ankle deep.

All that changes once you reach Cottonwood Pass, 40 miles from Kennedy Meadows. Now surrounded by glacial cirques, granite pinnacles, massive moraines, and rushing streams, everything is different. Water surrounds you in the form of snow up high, in roaring rivers down low.

Only 20 miles after Cottonwood Pass, you have the opportunity to climb Mount Whitney via a side trail. In an average year, the climb to the highest point in the forty-eight contiguous states is not as difficult as you might think, even in early season, and can be done by "average" thru-hikers. Near Mount Whitney, the PCT joins the John Muir Trail; the two are nearly contiguous for 200 miles.

After Mount Whitney, the trail approaches the high passes, each presenting its own challenge. The scenery is outstanding; there may not be a single place on the trail where if your camera shutter went off accidentally, you wouldn't get a good picture! The trail's pattern here is to gently approach a high pass for several miles, then steeply climb it. The descent down the other side is steep at first, then gentle; after hitting the bottom of the next valley, and perhaps meandering a while, the trail starts back up to the next pass. Plan conservative mileage; with the snow and the elevation changes, most thru-hikers do only 15–18 miles a day. The first on-trail resupply is at Reds Meadow, near Devils Postpile National Monument, although most hikers choose to leave the trail and resupply in between, usually at Vermilion Valley.

The John Muir Trail leaves the PCT for good on the approach to Tuolumne Meadows, the major trailhead for the Yosemite high country. North of Tuolumne Meadows, the PCT enters a very difficult section of Yosemite National Park. Passes here are wooded and lower than in the higher mountains to the south, but the trail goes steeply across the lay of the land and can be slick just after the snowmelt. North of Sonora Pass, conditions become markedly easier. There may still be occasional lingering snow, but from here on, it's time to start making big miles.

The trail passes near Lake Tahoe, the Desolation Wilderness, and historic Donner Pass. Multiple use is evident in some places, and after the spectacular isolated beauty of the High Sierra, the views seem a little subdued. But for the first time in the hike, thru-hikers have an easy trail, enough water, and gentle weather all at the same time.

Geographers disagree on what marks the exact northern end of the High Sierra. Somewhere near the small town of Belden on the North Fork of the Feather River, thru-hikers enter the volcanic Cascades.

> "You can make well-educated early Sierra snow condition predictions based upon the snow survey info on the web (check out *www.PCTA.org*). You don't have to rely on sporadic, hyped-up reports. This information can save you from having to wait in Kennedy Meadows for the snow to melt or from starting too late and suffering heat, sparse water, and the hurried pace to beat the snow in the North Cascades."
> —Greg "Strider" Hummel

SEASONS

Weather isn't usually a major problem in the Sierra's summer dry season. Parts of the eastern High Sierra actually look like an alpine desert. But, as with any mountain range, summer storms can surpass you, and if you do get caught in cold alpine rain or snow above treeline, you need to be able to shelter yourself. Remember: The average elevation is 10,000 feet.

In an average snow year, the trail becomes reasonably passable in mid-June for hikers starting from Kennedy Meadows. "Reasonably passable" means that you can slog through with ice axes; it doesn't mean the trail is clear.

From mid-July through mid-September, the Sierra is usually reliably snow-free in an average year. After mid-September early winter storms start to dump new snow at the higher elevations. By early October, this new snow may start to stick.

KENNEDY MEADOWS GATHERING

In the second week of June, thru-hikers start congregating at the Forest Service campground in Kennedy Meadows. Conventional wisdom has it that the High Sierra becomes passable to hikers with ice axes (and the ability to use them) somewhere between June 10 and 15. Conveniently, if you start your hike at the Mexican border at the end of April (when, in an average year, most of the snow is gone from the Lagunas and San Jacintos) and if you maintain a steady pace, you will indeed arrive at Kennedy Meadows in mid-June.

A snowmelt Sierran crossing is a lifetime hiking highlight and a true adventure. But there is some danger. Fording a raging river requires a cool head and a confident sense of balance. So does crossing the steep slopes of the high passes. A solo traverse of the High Sierra during the snowmelt is not advised. (The unofficial gathering at Kennedy Meadows is a good time to hook up with a hiking partner if you don't have one.) In 1999, a thru-hiker fell to his death in a storm in the Sierra. He was not carrying an ice ax—and he was traveling alone, having let some faster companions go on without him. Such tragedies are, fortunately, rare. Groups traveling together can take turns kicking steps and can provide moral support. They also tend to make better decisions than hikers traveling alone, and of course, can help each other in an emergency.

However, too many hikers talking, guessing, and fretting about what lies ahead can have a negative effect. I've seen people needlessly scared out of the Sierra on the basis of unfounded rumor. I've heard the words "The highest snow year on record . . . " at least five times in the last 10 years. Although the High

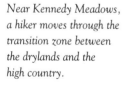

Near Kennedy Meadows, a hiker moves through the transition zone between the drylands and the high country.

Sierra was, in each year, widely declared "impassable," the fact is that each year, somebody—usually at least a moderately experienced hiker, but not necessarily a "super-hiker"—managed to get through. It's worth hiking the 40 miles to Cottonwood Pass to check things out for yourself. You can easily bail out there if there's a problem.

Crossing the Passes

During the main hiking season (mid-July through mid-September), crossing the high passes is only a matter of being able to walk uphill. Note, though, that if you're section hiking, you'll want to schedule in some slow days to start. Altitude sickness can be a problem if you're not acclimated.

But the High Sierra late-spring snowpack presents one of the most notable, important, challenging, fearsome, adventurous, and spectacular parts of a PCT thru-hike. Each pass has its own character and challenges, so it's useful to look at them one at a time. The comments below refer to the passes in mid-June in an average snow year.

Cottonwood Pass (11,160 feet) is somewhat indicative of snow levels ahead. The PCT doesn't actually go over Cottonwood Pass, but it does ascend to it. Instead of crossing the pass, the trail swings around the shoulder of the mountain. This is the true entry to the High Sierra. From here until Yosemite, you'll rarely be at elevations below 8000 feet, and you'll constantly be surrounded by mountains. If Cottonwood Pass is relatively snow-free, you are probably traveling in an "average" snow year. "Average" means that you can expect to be wading in plenty of snow, but nothing that a fit and competent outdoors-person with an ice ax and a positive attitude can't handle. If you're trudging in knee-deep (or more) snow at Cottonwood, you could be in for trouble ahead, including many miles of on-snow travel. You can bail out at Cottonwood by taking the Trail Pass Trail.

Forester Pass (13,180 feet; the PCT's high point) is the first pass that you actually climb up and over. You reach it about a day's walk from Crabtree or Whitney Meadows (the base camps for climbing Mount Whitney). From a distance, Forester Pass looks like nothing more than a tiny notch in a towering wall. During midsummer, it presents no major problems; you simply ascend via a switchbacked path blasted into the rock. During snowmelt, that path may be snow-covered. Coming from the south, some hikers erroneously assume that Forester Pass is the more prominent pass to the right, near Junction Peak. This pass is reputedly used in winter, but Forester Pass is the smaller notch to its left—the one above a prominent and long-lasting cornice, which you'll have to cross. Coming down the north side of Forester Pass, traverse the slope to your left at first, before starting downhill. Once you get out a little ways on the slope, you'll see the route clearly. Beware: This can be an avalanche-prone slope; cross it one at a time.

> "Try to hike on snow when it's solid in the early-morning hours to avoid post-holing. Stay away from rocks and the trunks of trees, as they lend themselves to sunken or cavernous areas hidden by rotten snow."
> —David Patterson

Muir Hut atop Muir Pass offers emergency shelter.

Glenn Pass (11,978 feet) is a challenge, with a long and steep climb that is frequently covered with snow. Routefinding requires piecing together those patches of trail you can see—and being competent with your map and compass. If the descent is covered with snow, stay high and to the right for about 100 yards, and then start down. This is a good place for a glissade (see "High Sierra Skills," later in this chapter), if you have an ice ax.

Pinchot Pass (12,130 feet) is one of the easier passes—unless you misidentify it. Coming up the long valley, you'll see a prominent pass straight ahead of you. It seems logical to assume that this is Pinchot Pass; in fact, Pinchot Pass is the next pass over to the left.

Mather Pass (12,100 feet) is considered by many hikers to be the most difficult because it has a frightening cornice that lingers late into the season. The trail up Mather Pass is widely switchbacked, but if it's under snow, ignore the traces of trail, stay left of the tarn, and simply go straight up the left side of the pass. You'll have to climb over the cornice at the top; there's no way around it. The descent is fairly straightforward, although long, down the so-called Golden Staircase with its interminable tight switchbacks.

Muir Pass (11,955 feet) is different than the others. All the other passes have long, gentle ascents, and then a quick, steep climb over the pass itself. Muir Pass just has a long ascent, much of it above 10,000 feet and covered in snow. Even in a moderate snow year, you can expect to hike in snow for up to 10 miles. Routefinding is fairly straightforward, but the afternoon slog down from the pass can be exhausting if you end up postholing up to your hips. Console yourself that the hard work is done: The three passes that remain are much easier.

Selden Pass (10,900 feet) is one of the lower and more gentle passes and generally presents no problem.

Silver Pass (10,900 feet) is a straightforward climb; not so the descent. Don't simply hop over the pass and glissade down the other side. (If it looks like a shortcut, it's not.) Instead, follow the trail up and over to the right before starting downhill. You'll save time. Really.

Donohue Pass (11,056 feet) usually has more snow than Selden and Silver, but it's a gentle climb and in an average year, enough trail will be visible to keep you on the right track. If the entire area is under snow, you'll need to refer to your map.

SNOWED IN

In a high-snow year, hikers might consider "flip-flopping," which means doing a hike that is continuous in time but not direction. The problem on the PCT is that if the Sierra is snowed in, all of California is likely to be snowed in. The mountains of northern California may be lower, but the latitude is higher, so you're likely to find snow there, too. It is also possible that the Cascades will be snowed in. Sometimes flipping works—for instance, if the Sierra has had a high-snow year and the Cascades have had a dry winter. But often, the only thing to do is wait a while until the snow melts.

One possible alternate route is the Theodore Solomons Trail through the High Sierra, which follows lower terrain. Some hikers have also hiked on back roads through the Owens Valley. However, the High Sierra is a highlight of the PCT thru-hike, both for its scenery and for its adventure. It would be well worthwhile to douse your impatience and wait for the snow to melt.

GEAR FOR THE HIGH SIERRA

Footwear. Early-season thru-hikers should wear boots, not sneakers. If you haven't been using them, you'll want to switch. Lightweight boots are fine.

Ice ax. Not to sound like a broken record, but—you need an ice ax, period, to cross the snowpack. You should know how to use it. If you don't, beg a lesson from another hiker at Kennedy Meadows, then practice on the first snowfield you find.

Instep crampons. Instep crampons are small, lightweight, four-point crampons that attach to the instep of your boot. (They are not the same as the full-fledged ten-to-twelve-point crampon used by mountaineers.) Not many hikers carry them, and they are not necessary. But for the price of a few ounces, you get an awful lot of help. Contrary to commonly held belief, you *can* walk on dirt with them, so it's not necessary to take them on and off for short distances between snowfields. You must, however, take them off before attempting a glissade.

Tents. Bug season starts here. You will want a tent.

Clothing and raingear. You'll need an extra layer of clothing and decent raingear.

Snowshoes. Do not take snowshoes, even in a heavy-snow year. Snowshoes are virtually useless on consolidated late-spring-Sierra hard-packed snow. On traverses and sun cups, you risk twisting an ankle.

Rope. In an average year, rope is not necessary; and, let's face it, most backpackers don't know how to belay each other. Rope can actually cause people to drown during stream crossings because it can hold them underwater if they lose their balance and fall.

Gaiters are good for snow, stream crossings, and mud.

HIGH SIERRA SKILLS

Funny thing about warnings about skills and preparedness: Every year, a few hikers with few skills, inadequate gear, and cavalier attitudes skip happily through the High Sierra and report to their fellows that all this talk of ice axes and mountaineering skills is unnecessary.

It's true that nature is a gentle teacher. Most hikers, even the unskilled and ill-equipped, survive their encounter with the snowmelt Sierra, perhaps with some hair-raising tales, but none the worse for wear.

But it is also true that hikers—including at least one PCT thru-hiker—have died from falls in the springtime Sierra snows. In a high-snow year, potential avalanche slopes, tricky cornices, and heavy runoff present yet more obstacles. A little respect for the elements can go a long way in keeping you safe as you traverse this beautiful but potentially treacherous section. At the very least, those hikers who have taken the time to read about, learn, and practice basic mountaineering skills approach the Sierra with more confidence and less fear. The following pointers are the bare-bones basics; they are not intended to supplant in-field training and experience.

Ice Ax Use

Here's the basic how-to: Hold the ice ax in your uphill hand with the adze (the blunt part of the head of the ax) facing forward. If you fall, turn toward the ax, bring it up so that the head is near your shoulder, and dig the pick into the slope. There are also techniques for falling head-first, backwards, or head-first *and* backwards, but backpackers usually don't take such dramatic tumbling

> "It's important to live in the moment. I do my best to plan ahead, but don't waste time or energy on fear. It's an unnecessary distraction to worry about the snowpack 300 miles ahead. Conditions there will change on the way. It may be 'unbearable' thinking of hiking thousands of miles in cold rain or with bad blisters or mosquitoes. But the only hiking I have to do is right NOW. Tomorrow will take care of itself."
>
> —Brian Robinson

falls. Still, being able to use an ice ax properly is an invaluable outdoor skill; a few lessons are well worth your time.

Glissading

Glissading is a fancy way to say sliding downhill on your posterior. Hold your ice ax in two hands to one side of your body, with the pick facing the slope, ready to dig in if you start careening out of control and need to self-arrest. If you're hiking in shorts, you'll need to put on long pants before attempting a glissade, or your legs will be severely cut by the ice. Warning: Gore-Tex or coated nylon pants will speed your rate of descent. If that's what you're wearing, prepare for a fast ride—and have that ice ax ready.

FINDING YOUR WAY

Once under several feet of snow, it makes no difference that the PCT is well marked, well mapped, and well graded. The maps in the PCT guidebooks are generally adequate, but if you know you're headed into snowier-than-average conditions, good topos are even better.

Pay attention to major landmarks and features. If you're not used to high mountains, take time to look at the maps and the landscape and see how they correlate. Usually the trend through the High Sierra is to walk up a valley, climb a pass, then walk back down the next valley, cross a river, and so on. The number of differently shaped and sized lakes and tarns makes navigating fairly easy. From the top of a pass, for example, you can simply look down, see a tarn the trail goes near, identify it on the map, then look for the next tarn, identify that, and so on. Major creeks and streams are other obvious landmarks, as are designated campsites with bear boxes.

You'll be able to see plenty of evidence of the trail. Look for little bits and pieces of trail on dry ground between snowy patches. Look for cairns and rockwork, too. As you approach the pass, identify it by using your map; thru-hikers *have* climbed to the wrong pass.

RIVER FORDS

If you've been to the Sierra in August, you may have seen pretty little streams trickling down mountainsides. In June, these streams may be torrents. Some hikers find river fords the most dangerous and frightening aspect of the PCT.

The guidebook notes which streams are likely to be problematic during peak melt-off. Your first strategy for "problem" creeks is to try to camp near them and cross first thing in the morning. The snowfields up high generally refreeze at night, slowing the flow of water. Morning crossings are thus easier—if frigidly cold!

Realize that different people will freak out over different obstacles. A surefooted hiker may walk over a slippery log bridge, but tremble at a thigh-deep white-water crossing. Don't be afraid to turn back if you start across and find yourself in deeper or faster water than expected. Sometimes you'll be better off choosing a route different from the trail. Go upstream or downstream to find a crossing you're comfortable tackling.

A few other river fording tips and techniques:

- Wide means shallow. When the water is a deep, beautiful dark green, it's likely to be shoulder high.
- Although you can cross on snow bridges or logjams, both can be dangerous. Snow bridges can break under your weight. Logjams are unstable, and your weight and movement could shift the logs enough to break the jam and send them—and you—hurtling downstream.
- Look downstream for snags that you might be washed into if you fall.
- Two hiking sticks really help; ice axes are too short. (This begs the question: Do you really have to take both? Most hikers don't. I did, and was glad of it.)
- Don't go barefoot. Feet can get stuck in between rocks, especially in white water. Sport sandals are good. If you have only one pair of footwear, remove insoles and socks before crossing; then cross in your boots. With dry socks and insoles, your feet will feel drier even if the boots *are* wet.
- Try to avoid getting feet and footwear wet as you're climbing to a pass. You'll be in snow for several hours, and the result can be a painful chill, or possibly even frostbite.
- Face upstream, into the force of the water, and aim diagonally upstream. It's easier to keep control and balance when facing into the current.
- Undo your pack straps before the crossing so that if you have to get out of the pack quickly, you can.
- Use waterproof stuff sacks for your sleeping bag. But don't worry too much if you get a dunking; there's lots of sun to dry things out.
- Protect your camera in a plastic bag.

BLACK BEARS

High Sierra black bears are different from the other black bears you'll see almost anywhere along the PCT (with the exception of southern California's desert valleys). High Sierra bears have PhDs in getting food. They are physicists. They understand ropes and gravity, cause and effect, and they have more persistence than even the most dauntless thru-hiker. Since they are not hunted in national parks, they have no fear of humans; quite the opposite, they regard us as walking delicatessens. Having learned that hikers carry delicious food, they have followed us to elevations far higher than their normal habitats (below 8000 feet). In the high country, natural bear food is scarce, so bears gravitate to hikers. Each year, hikers lose food to hungry, persistent, clever bruins.

The traditional technique of hanging food from a tree limb doesn't work here. Even counterbalancing (hanging the food with two bags, each as a

counterweight, and pushing them up as high as they will go with a walking stick) doesn't work; mama bears send cubs out onto the branches to tear at the ropes or jump onto the food sacks.

Fortunately, during the thru-hiking season, bears are only just getting themselves up and about after their winter's nap. Many of them are still in the low country; most thru-hikers get through the Sierra without having their food molested. Later in the season, it's a different story.

Many, but not all, well-used campsites in the Sierra have bear-proof food storage lockers. (A list of current locations is available from the various national parks and from the PCTA.) These metal trunks are chained to trees and boulders and provide secure storage (although I do have one photograph of a bear cub standing atop a food storage locker).

Bears aren't always big—but they always want your food! Use storage lockers, if they are provided.

The Park Service additionally recommends (and in some places may require) using bearproof storage containers, which are rentable at the national parks. Traditionally, these weigh about 2–3 pounds and carry about 5–6 days' worth of food—not enough for a High Sierra traverse. More recently, newer, supposedly bear-proof storage stuff sacks have been introduced on the market.

Do not sleep with your food—not only is it illegal, but you may awaken one night (as a friend of mine did) to find a bear's jaw clamped around your ankle! If you can't make it to a campsite with a food storage locker and you are not carrying a bear-proof storage container, the best thing to do is cook in a campsite, then walk on. Camp in a spot that hasn't been used as a campsite and hang your food. Bears tend to scavenge in the same well-used sites; in a "stealth" camping spot, you may escape their attention. Go 100–200 yards from water, camp out of sight of the trail, and make sure no trace remains of your visit when you leave in the morning. Yosemite National Park literature recommends that if confronted by a bear, you stay together with any hiking partners, make noise, bang pots, and throw stones.

HIGH SIERRA RESUPPLY

It's not just the ice and snow and the treacherous streams that make the Sierra traverse so challenging. It's also the distance between opportunities to resupply. From Kennedy Meadows, it is 200 miles to the next on-trail resupply at Reds Meadow. In between, none of the options are exactly convenient. Here's a rundown.

No Resupplies

It *is* possible to hike 200 miles without a resupply. But forget about the 20-plus-mile days you were doing in southern California. Most hikers can't do more than 15–18 miles a day in the Sierra during snowmelt; some do significantly less. So figure 15–18 miles a day. Add a day to climb Mount Whitney. The result: You'll need to carry enough food for 12–14 days to get from Kennedy Meadows to Reds Meadow.

One Resupply

The most convenient resupply to the trail is at Vermilion Valley Resort on Thomas E. Edison Lake. This is also a hiker-friendly stop, with plenty of food, a thru-hikers' tent, and pies and ice cream galore. Resupplying at Vermilion Valley requires taking a 2-mile side trail to a boat ramp where a ferry (one runs in the morning, another in the afternoon; check the times with the proprietors when you make arrangements to send your food) takes you the remaining 4 miles to the lodge. But although Vermilion Valley is convenient to the trail, it's a full 174.3 miles from Kennedy Meadows, which means that the average thru-hiker who climbs Mount Whitney is going to take about 10–11 days to get there. Console yourself with the thought that you only have to carry

11 days' worth of food for the first day of the hike; after that you'll be eating through the weight on your back. Note: Like many backcountry businesses, the lodge charges a fee for collecting and holding packages.

One or Two Resupplies

If you can't stand the idea of carrying 10 days' worth of food, you might consider a second stop at Independence. The Kearsarge Pass side trail is located almost halfway through the Sierra, 87.5 miles from Kennedy Meadows. Add on 9 more miles (each way) on the side trail, a high pass to cross (11,600 feet), and a 15-mile (each way) hitchhike. Not exactly convenient, but if you can't or won't carry 10 days' worth of food, it may be your best option.

Other Resupplies

There are many other routes in and out of the Sierra, and some hikers use them to resupply.

Muir Ranch. Located 153 miles from Kennedy Meadows, Muir Ranch is only about 20 miles from Vermilion Valley, so thru-hikers don't stop at both. Muir Ranch's license allows it to serve or sell food only to ranch guests, which makes it a less than satisfactory rest stop—especially considering that you've hauled yourself over some of the biggest mountains in California to get there. But the ranch will pack in and hold resupply boxes for hikers (for a fee).

Trail Pass Trail. Although this is an easy resupply, it's only 42 miles from Kennedy Meadows. The Trail Pass Trail goes 2.1 miles to the Horseshoe Meadow Road, from which you hitchhike 23 miles to Lone Pine. Given that you only save carrying 2 days' worth of food (4 pounds), you may decide this resupply really isn't worth the bother.

Whitney Portal. This resupply route, which is 61.1 miles from Kennedy Meadows, is probably the most nonsensical of all—even if you plan to climb Mount Whitney. You'd have to climb almost to the summit of Mount Whitney, then plummet down to the Whitney Portal trailhead (a total of 15.5 miles from Whitney Meadows), then hitch 13 miles to and from Lone Pine. Coming back, you'd have to reclimb Whitney, then rehike the 15.5 miles with a full pack. Even if you are climbing Whitney just for the fun of it, this resupply doesn't make sense because of the extra mileage and the additional 5000-foot elevation loss and gain with a full pack. I've actually seen thru-hikers who, when they finally realized what they'd gotten themselves into, hitchhiked back to the Cottonwood Pass trailhead, hiked up to Cottonwood Pass, then rehiked the 16.7 miles back to Whitney Creek. Walking in circles is not a good way to get to Canada.

Banner Peak is one of the PCT's most photographed sights.

Highlight Hike
JOHN MUIR TRAIL

WHERE: Top of Mount Whitney to Yosemite Valley
DISTANCE: 212 miles
DIFFICULTY: Extremely challenging
BEST TIME TO GO: Mid-July through September
GUIDE: *Pacific Crest Trail: California*

This classic hike is contiguous with the PCT for most of its length. It crosses eight of the PCT's nine high passes—and starts atop the highest peak in the forty-eight contiguous states. Challenges include altitude, snowfields, stream fords, and resupply; the area is so remote that you'll see only one road crossing on the JMT. Reserve your permit early, and bring lots of film.

Highlight Hike
DESOLATION AND GRANITE CHIEF WILDERNESSES

WHERE: Echo Lake Resort to Old Highway 40 near Donner Pass
DISTANCE: 61 miles
DIFFICULTY: Easy
BEST TIME TO GO: Summer and early fall
GUIDE: *Pacific Crest Trail: California*

Both easier and more accessible than the John Muir Trail High Sierra, this hike through the lake-dotted Desolation Wilderness and the high and open Granite Chief Wilderness gives hikers interested in a shorter trip a taste of the glories of the High Sierra to the south. The elevations are lower, the trails more gentle, and there are no high passes clogged with snow.

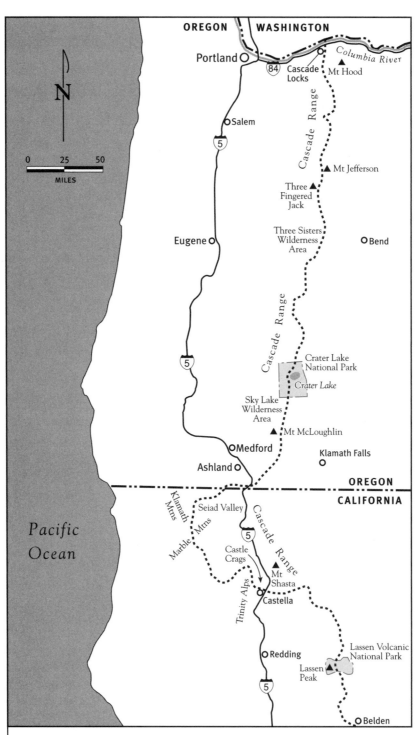

PACIFIC CREST TRAIL: SOUTHERN CASCADES

CHAPTER 13

Southern Cascades:
Northern California and Oregon

The PCT enters the Cascade Range north of Belden, California, close to the trail's halfway point. Having come 1300 miles, most hikers are somewhat taken aback to consider that for every mile they've walked thus far, there is one more mile yet ahead.

But the trail now is much easier, and it's the middle of summer. With easy footway, gentle (although sometimes hot) weather, and a broken-in body, this is an ideal time to experiment with ultralight fast-packing techniques. Indeed, this is the place to up your mileage and make up for any lost time. Both northbound and southbound thru-hikers are now in good shape for big miles.

THE TRAIL

A few days north of Belden, northbounders glimpse Lassen Peak, the first of the chain of mighty volcanoes that lead, like beacons, all the way to Canada. For many of the PCT's remaining miles, at least one of these great mountains will be visible.

But at first, the trail is less than breathtaking. With the exception of Lassen Volcanic National Park, much of the terrain from Belden to Castella (230 miles) is not the most scenic part of the trail and much of it is under multiple-use management. You'll go through lots of logged sections and a few areas that look more like tree farms than forests. On the other hand, in Lassen Park you'll see some interesting thermal and volcanic features reminiscent of Yellowstone's bubbling basins.

After Lassen, Mount Shasta comes into view. At Castella, the PCT starts making a wide arc to the west into the scenic Klamath Mountains, through the Castle Crags, Trinity Alps, Marble Mountains, and Russian Wildernesses. Finally, just north of tiny Seiad Valley, the trail crosses, after 1697.4 long miles, into Oregon.

After a resupply in Ashland (one of only two towns anywhere near Oregon's PCT) hikers head east, back to the main chain of the Cascades. Oregon's first 65 miles are dull and dry, but the rest of the trip through Oregon is quick and beautiful. Although much of Oregon's PCT stays below treeline, it passes numerous lovely lakes with pleasant camping, and there is plenty of dramatic scenery, including Mounts Thielsen and McLoughlin, Crater Lake,

> "I can't recommend enough taking a few extra pounds of down-home, cholesterol-laden, gut-busting, stop-you-in-your-tracks comfort food—there will be days when you really deserve the reward. After a while, you won't even feel the weight on your back."
> —Ben Shiffrin

155

The Eagle Creek Trail is a lovely alternate route as hikers descend to the Columbia River Gorge.

the Three Sisters, Three Fingered Jack, Mount Jefferson, and Mount Hood before descending, finally, to the Columbia River Gorge at Cascade Locks on the Washington–Oregon border.

SEASONS

The seasonal pattern here is similar to that in the Sierra; the more northerly latitude makes up for the lower elevations, and snow in the mountains can linger well into June. In high-snow years when the Sierra is blocked, some thru-hikers try to skip up to the southern Cascades, only to find that the trail is not passable here, either.

Note that although Oregon is usually an easy romp for both northbound and southbound thru-hikers, in a high-snow year the higher elevations around the Three Sisters, Mount Jefferson, and Mount Hood can be snow-covered into August.

Fast-packing with Ultralight Gear

Assuming an "average" year, the southern Cascades are an excellent place to dump some weight and gain some mileage. The trail is relatively obstacle free, and the gains and losses of elevation are much gentler than anywhere else (although there are a few multi-thousand-foot climbs—nobody said the trail was flat!). By this point, you're super-fit and you have a fair idea of how you like to hike. You know what you like and don't like about your gear. You know the range of weather conditions and how your body reacts. Granted, you've probably modified your gear several times before. But this is a good time to clean house.

Shelter. Once you're through the worst of the bug season, you can go back to a tarp.

Stoves. There's plenty of fuel for wood-burning stoves. Gentle conditions make this a good place to experiment with that homemade hobo stove you've been dying to try. For traditionalists, Coleman fuel and canisters are available at most of the backcountry lodges.

Raingear. You're in the heart of the dry season, but occasional downpours do occur. You need some sort of rain jacket, although you could probably get

A tent is useful during bug season in northern California and Oregon.

away with a poncho on this stretch. (Have a piece of cord to hold it in place if it's really windy, and be willing to stop and make camp if you become chilled.) For pants, choose according to your preference: Some hikers just walk in shorts, others in polys, others in lightweight nylon water-resistant pants (which are also good against bugs). Heavy-duty rain pants probably aren't necessary.

Trekking poles. The trail is so flat that ski poles are unnecessary (except if you're like me and never hike without them). Adjustable ski poles work well with a tarp.

Packs. If you shrink the bulk of what you're carrying, you could lose several more ounces by sending home top compartments and extra pouches.

Shoes. If you can't hike in sneakers here, then you're not made for hiking in sneakers anywhere!

Crossing the California–Oregon border is one of a thru-hiker's milestones.

Halfway Blues

Many hikers report a little bit of depression at reaching the halfway point, when they realize that 1300 down means 1300 still to go. Arriving at the Oregon border, with 1000 miles still ahead, is only a little less daunting. It's also true that some parts of northern California and Oregon have less dramatic scenery and that multiple-use activities like logging and grazing detract from the hiking experience.

Realize that from here on, it only gets better, especially once you hit Castella and head into the Klamath Mountains, which is mostly in wilderness. Oregon's flat, easy trail gives you the sense that you are making real progress. You can visually record your progress as you pass from one volcano to the next.

A couple of other strategies to spice things up:

- Schedule a couple of breaks in "good" towns, like Ashland, Oregon, where the Shakespeare festival will be in full force.
- Take breaks or at least get a meal in some of the Oregon lodges (where most hikers resupply).
- Climb (if you are so inclined) one or more of the big peaks along the way.

Alternate Routes and Resupplies

In Oregon, most hikers rarely go into actual towns, with the exception of Ashland (at the southern end of the state) and Cascade Locks (on the northern border with Washington). In between, the PCT is just too remote, so most hikers resupply in private lodges, whose owners generously hold packages.

Not all of the lodges are convenient to the PCT. However, extant fragments of the older Oregon Skyline Trail (OST), a precursor of the PCT, offer access to some of them. The Oregon Skyline Trail is marked on the guidebook maps; additionally, Forest Service maps show large networks of trails. After you pick out which lodges you'll use for resupply, you can decide whether to detour to them via the OST.

There are two alternate routes you should know about. In Crater Lake, the trail splits into a hiker route (which follows the spectacular crater rim) and a less scenic equestrian route (the old PCT, which avoids the lake). Also, from either Indian Springs Campsite or Wahtum Lake in far northern Oregon, alternate routes lead to the Eagle Creek Trail, one of Oregon's most popular paths. This trail was not included in the PCT because of high usage and because it is not accessible to horses. Most hikers take it, regardless. It goes through a beautiful gorge and even passes behind a waterfall. If you plan to camp on the Eagle Creek Trail, camp in the upper part of it; the lower gorge closer to the parking lot can be very crowded.

Note: If you do use lodges for resupply, check the latest edition of the *PCT Thru-hiker's Town Guide* or call the lodges for instructions. Some of them require that you use a private delivery service such as UPS. Some lodges charge to hold a package; remember, they are doing you a favor.

"In California it's easier to think of going from range to range rather than state to state like most people do on the Appalachian Trail. Besides, California is two-thirds of the PCT. If you break it up into sections, it's a lot easier to swallow the pieces than the whole."
—David Patterson

"I dealt with the monotony of northern California in two ways: (1) plain old focus, focus, focus and chanting, "This too shall pass"; (2) the knowledge that I leased my house out for six months, so I really had no place else to go."
—David Cossa

Castle Crags in northern California is the beginning of the Klamath Mountains segment, which takes hikers through four wilderness areas—a welcome antidote after the logged lands to the south.

Highlight Hike
KLAMATH MOUNTAINS

WHERE: Castella near I-5 to Seiad Valley (Highway 96)
DISTANCE: 157 miles
DIFFICULTY: Moderate
BEST TIME TO GO: Summer and fall
GUIDE: *Pacific Crest Trail: California*

This long, remote hike goes through the Castle Crags, Trinity Alps, Marble Mountains, and Russian Wildernesses and features a variety of terrain—from the stark and dramatic Castle Crags, to high open ridges, to lakes and streams. But in some sections, water can be scarce. Several logging and paved roads enable you to fashion shorter hikes or arrange car shuttles.

Highlight Hike
THREE SISTERS WILDERNESS

WHERE: Road 600 near Irish Lake to Santiam Highway (U.S. Route 20)
DISTANCE: 72 miles
DIFFICULTY: Easy
BEST TIME TO GO: August
GUIDE: *Pacific Crest Trail: Oregon and Washington*

The Three Sisters are the only major volcanoes in the Cascades found in a cluster. Surrounding them are thousands of acres of volcanic rubble. The combination of glaciated peaks, stark black lava fields, cinder cones, pumice and obsidian, and pretty little lakes makes for one of the PCT's most dramatic and memorable landscapes.

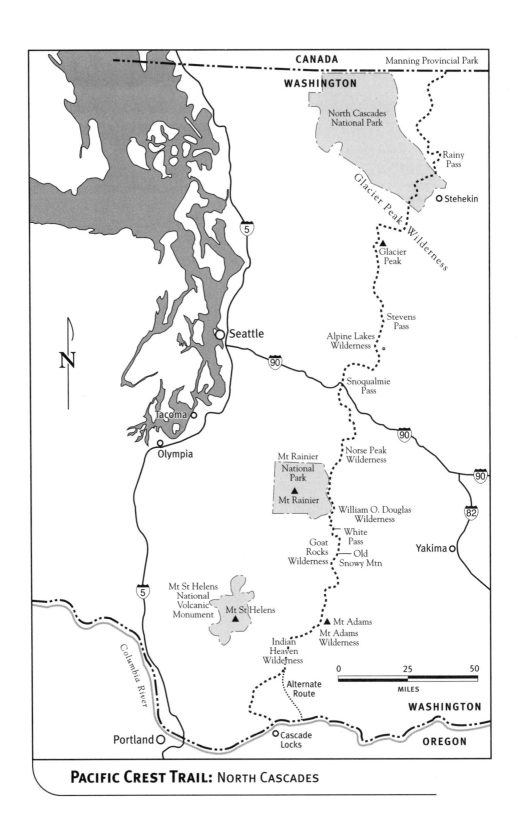

CHAPTER 14

Northern Cascades:
Washington

I have had one of the worst hiking experiences of my life in Washington—and also one of the best. I have had 24 (out of 30) days of soggy, dreary, misty, cold, incessant, spirit-drenching rain and I have had a month of clear blue skies, warm sunshine, and superb views of some of the PCT's—indeed, America's—finest scenery.

It's all about timing and luck.

Most thru-hikers enter Washington in late August; a few straggle up in early September. While August is Washington's dry season, September is the bridge season. It can be wonderful, with sunny days, buckets of huckleberries, and comfortable temperatures. Or so I am told. When I was there in September, it was cold, clammy, rainy, cloudy, drizzly, misty, and even snowy. The earlier you arrive, the better your chances of good weather. It's worth the effort. With the exception of one 40-mile stretch through logging country, most of Washington's scenery is among the best on the entire PCT.

THE TRAIL

The trail enters Washington on the Bridge of the Gods, named after an Indian myth about Mount Hood and Mount Adams throwing fire at each other (a common theme in Native American myths of the region). The first 36 miles are rather ordinary as the trail weaves and dodges to avoid private property, climbs some 3000 feet, then promptly descends almost all the way back down. Thru-hikers in a rush sometimes take what they somewhat disingenuously call an "alternate" route, which is not a hiking route; it's a road walk up Highway 14 and Wind River Road to the Panther Creek Campground. This alternate route makes sense in bad weather or if you're pressed for time. Warning: From Cascade Locks north to Crest Campground in the Indian Heaven Wilderness, water sources are scant, so watch your canteens.

From Panther Creek Campground, the route and scenery improve as the trail wends around ridges that give views back to Oregon's Mount Hood and forward to Mount Adams, Mount Rainier, and decapitated Mount St. Helens. Next up is the Indian Heaven Wilderness, a volcanic area with huge lava beds. Locals nickname it the Mosquito Heaven Wilderness; if you're hiking here in early to mid-July, consider yourself warned.

Don't be deceived by the easy-looking trail; the Glacier Peak Wilderness is one of the PCT's most rugged sections.

"We erect our tent on a very slight gentle slope, with our heads facing uphill. It seems to eliminate some of the heavy, flat feeling when sleeping. Plus it rains a lot in Washington. This way the rain rolls downhill and away from the tent, and we don't get the puddling around the edges of the tent. Remember to keep the groundcloth tucked under the tent so that as the water comes off the sides, it doesn't puddle underneath."
—Gary Greaser and Sharon Burrer

Then the trail climbs into the Mount Adams Wilderness, where it circles the west side of the mountain at an elevation of about 6000 feet. Mount Adams towers above, and Mount St. Helens rises 40 miles to the west. After Mount Adams, the trail climbs again into the Goat Rocks Wilderness, which many hikers rank among the PCT's scenic highlights (if, that is, they are there on a good day). Wild and lovely, exposed and rugged, the above-treeline traverse of the Goat Rocks is reminiscent of the High Sierra. There's even a glacier to cross: the upper slopes of the Packwood Glacier. Ice axes are recommended in early season; they are not necessary later in the year. If you don't like the look of the glacier, there's an alternate route, which leads up and over the slopes of

Old Snowy Mountain. This alternate trail is worth taking in its own right; from the shoulder of Old Snowy, a quick 300-foot scramble takes you to the 7930-foot summit. The view is well worth the climb.

The trail then descends into a high basin, climbs again, and traverses two open bowls where you might see mountain goats, then descends to White Pass, 147 miles (assuming you took the official trail) from Cascade Locks. White Pass consists of a campground, a convenience store, and a motel; basic it may be, but it is the only resupply in southern Washington.

For the next 50 miles, the PCT is characterized by gentle climbs along long ridges, as it crosses the William O. Douglas Wilderness, briefly touches Rainier National Park, then climbs into the Norse Peak Wilderness. Just past the wilderness boundary, you'll see one of the PCT's few shelters, Urich Cabin, a well-maintained, fully enclosed cabin with a pot-bellied stove and sleeping loft.

After that, the logging debacle begins. For the next 40 or so miles, you'll see up-close-and-personal what clear-cuts do to a forest as you walk through miles of them. At Snoqualmie Pass, the trail heads into the jagged and forbidding North Cascades, first through the popular Alpine Lakes Wilderness, and then into the wild and craggy Glacier Peak Wilderness, a vertical landscape that features glaciated peaks, precipitous and tightly serrated mountains, waterfalls, and the looming mass of Glacier Peak. After resupplying in the town of Stehekin, hikers are on the homestretch north to Rainy Pass, a high-country traverse, and the final descent to Canada.

Approaching Mount Rainier

“How quickly gear dries out is very important. Boots stay dry a little longer than running shoes, but running shoes dry out faster. A tarp is easier and faster to dry out than a tent. How much water a garment absorbs affects its weight. Many waterproof/breathable garments have water-absorbing layers. Truly waterproof material doesn't soak up any water, even when it's wet on both sides. Since it's less wet to start with, it also dries more quickly. Close-fitting damp clothing worn to bed will usually be dry by morning. You can't always stay dry, but properly designed clothing can keep you warm anyway. Don't be afraid to get it wet if you need to wear it to stay warm.”

—Brian Robinson

SEASONS

August is the best month for hiking in Washington. But most southbounders arrive in late June (bugs and snow). Most northbound thru-hikers arrive in late August and September (rain and possible snow). The hiking window in Washington is fairly short; the farther north or higher up, the shorter the snow-free season. July can be full of mosquitoes, so if you're hiking in early summer, you might want a tent, not a tarp.

Most rangers and experienced PCT hikers recommend that thru-hikers hiking during the season's "bookends" not attempt to use ultralight strategies. After seeing extremely experienced and well-equipped thru-hikers forced to bail out to a town after days of downpours and soaking-wet gear, I concur. You can encounter severe hypothermic conditions that last for several days—or much more. Much of Washington is not only rugged, but extremely remote. It's not always easy to walk out to the nearest road if you get into conditions your gear can't handle.

Northbound Strategies

Try to be north of the Columbia River by September 1, if possible. If you get to Cascade Locks after the 1st, try to limit your rest days. Thru-hikers can easily do 20 miles a day through just about all of Washington. October 1st should be your target finishing date. No, it doesn't promptly start snowing on the 2nd—but it could, and often does.

Southbound Strategies

Lingering snow and late-spring storms can make June in the Cascades extremely dangerous, even in an "average" year. *Most* southbound thru-hikers have tales of having to navigate for many miles over trailless snow. Fire Creek Pass, in the Glacier Peaks Wilderness, is often snow-choked in early season, forcing hikers to take long detours. During late June and early July in one recent average snow year, register entries in Skykomish, just south of the Glacier Peaks Wilderness, included comments such as "It's beginning to look a lot like Christmas," and "Now I know how to use my ice ax."

FINDING YOUR WAY

Routefinding in Washington can be a little tricky if the trail is snow covered, especially if you are in thick fog or white-out conditions.

While in normal (sunny) conditions you can navigate from large landmark to large landmark, in bad visibility you'll need to work on a smaller scale, paying close attention to your direction of travel and to smaller landmarks that you pass. Often you'll be able to "feel" your way, occasionally confirming that you are on the trail because of breaks in vegetation, cairns, or blazes on trees. If you are hiking southbound in June or intend to push on no matter what the weather in October, you might want to take the USGS 1:24,000 maps,

166   Pacific Crest Trail

Rain in the North Cascades can last for days—or weeks.

which show more detail. Mark the PCT route on them with highlighter before you leave.

To keep in aural contact with your partner when scouting routes in a whiteout or in fog, use a police whistle. Develop a system of codes: Three blasts, remember, is commonly used to indicate "I'm in trouble."

GEAR

Tents. If you use a tarp, be sure it's big enough to come down close to the ground. Your groundcloth should be large enough to keep you and your gear out of the mud. If you use a small tent, consider also taking a small tarp for cooking. Conditions drove us to this solution in the wet September of 1997. Some of our fellow hikers reveled in their larger tents, which allowed them to sit up and eat. In July, Washington has fierce mosquitoes; a tent can save your sanity.

"When using a tarp in bug season, sew some very lightweight mosquito netting into the shape of an oversized pillowcase. It should be long enough to fit from head to hips, and wide enough to give your arms freedom of movement. Add elastic completely around the open end so that it gently hugs your torso. At night, pull the netting over your head and down beyond your waist, or pull it completely around your sleeping bag. Sometimes I wear my cap so the bill keeps the netting off my face."

—Roger Carpenter

"During really bad rains, don't even try to stay dry. I wear what I call 'sacrifice clothing' (quick-drying Supplex nylon) that I allow to get drenched. After making camp, I switch to dry clothing and, if it has finally stopped raining or let up to a drizzle, build a campfire under a sheltered tree and dry out everything that has become wet."

—David Cossa

Goat Rocks Wilderness

Stoves. This is no place to be messing around with stoves that take half an hour to boil a pot of water. Wood-burning stoves may not be the best choice; while they can burn wet wood, you'll definitely need to fuss with them more than hikers with standard canister or white-gas burning stoves.

Full raingear. This is the time to break out the good stuff. In addition to a jacket and pants, pack gaiters and maybe a rain hat in your Labor Day resupply box.

Extra warm clothes. Throw in an extra layer—not only is it getting colder, but in a long series of rainy days, you may not be able to keep everything dry. Extra socks are similarly a good idea. This may also be a good time to try out Gore-Tex socks.

Waterproof stuff sacks. An obvious item.

BEARS

Black bears are common in the North Cascades, and in well-used campsites you should hang your food to prevent them from helping themselves to a meal. The North Cascades are also considered a grizzly bear recovery area, although the grizzly population in the area is miniscule. There have been only a small number of verified grizzly bear sightings in the North Cascades, and it is extremely unlikely that you will encounter one. But their presence is yet one more reason to make sure that your food is carefully stored and hung out of reach.

Highlight Hike
MOUNT ADAMS AND GOAT ROCKS WILDERNESSES

The trek around Washington's Mount Adams gives good views of the summit, as well as Mount St. Helens to the west.

WHERE: Panther Creek Campground to White Pass (U.S. Highway 12)
DISTANCE: 112 miles
DIFFICULTY: Moderate
BEST TIME TO GO: Mid-July through September
GUIDE: *Pacific Crest Trail: Oregon and Washington*

The trail goes through the Indian Heaven Wilderness, then circles around the shoulder of Mount Adams with excellent views of both Mount Adams and nearby Mount St. Helens. The small Goat Rocks Wilderness is one of the PCT's highlights, with a stark traverse above treeline complete with a glacier to cross, open cirques, and the possibility of seeing mountain goats.

The Alpine Lakes
Wilderness in Washington

Highlight Hike
ALPINE LAKES WILDERNESS

WHERE: Snoqualmie Pass to Stevens Pass
DISTANCE: 78 miles
DIFFICULTY: Moderate
BEST TIME TO GO: Summer
GUIDE: *PCT: Oregon and Washington*

This is a classic alpine hike. A stiff climb from Snoqualmie Pass brings you to the high country. From then on the trail undulates across these tightly serrated peaks. The elevation gains and losses are large, so plan conservative mileage and plan to spend at least a week (unless you're a thru-hiker, in which case you'll probably cover the distance in 4 or 5 days).

PART IV

Continental Divide Trail

The CDT in New Mexico goes cross-country through miles of sagebrush.

CHAPTER 15

The Wild Child of the Triple Crown

In some ways, the PCT and the CDT are very similar. They both run through Southwestern deserts; they both climb to alpine passes. They both pass through legendary landscapes of the American West. And they both force hikers into encounters with unpredictable weather, thunderstorms, snowmelt, stream fords, bears, and long stretches with no convenient way to resupply.

But there is a big difference. Younger, wilder, less complete, and almost unknown, the CDT is the wild child of the Triple Crown family. It is as different from the PCT as the PCT is different from the AT.

The CDT is the brainchild and lifelong passion of Jim Wolf, who has worked for more than 30 years to establish the trail as a wilderness path through some of the country's most stunning scenery. Designated as a National Scenic Trail by Congress in 1978, the CDT has suffered from being conceived in an era of environmental conflict and special-interest politics. Multiple use is the management mandate of much of the region—with land-use conflicts a common result. Water allocations, grazing, mining, hunting, fishing, water sports, motorized use, ski area development, and local politics (in one case involving disputes over a centuries-old Spanish land grant) are just some of the issues that affect the Continental Divide Trail.

Note that because there is no complete official trail, all mileages given in this and the following three chapters are approximate.

CHARACTER OF THE TRAIL

The CDT invites the hiker into the real West—both the untamed wildernesses set aside for nonmotorized recreation and the multiple-use lands. On no other long-distance trail will you spend as much time above treeline. On no other long-distance trail are you as likely to be invited into the homes of rural people—ranchers, Native Americans, loggers. It's a unique opportunity to see both the land and its people.

But the major difference between the CDT and its grown-up siblings is the fact that the CDT is not yet fully established, marked, and mapped—which has a profound effect on the hiker's experience. About 70 percent of the CDT exists in some form or another—back roads, cairned cross-country, actual footpaths—but that doesn't mean that it's marked or noted correctly on maps.

History is a constant companion on the CDT. These Anasazi ruins are above Inscription Rock at El Morro National Monument.

One thing is for sure: You won't get into conversations about what "everybody" said or what "everybody" is doing, because you're not likely to meet a lot of other thru-hikers. Also, any other hikers you meet will, like you, be concentrating on routefinding.

Some social habits from the AT have migrated west. AT traditions like registers, trail angels, and trail names are becoming part of the PCT hiking experience. Not so on the CDT. A register left in a post office can go for years without an entry from another hiker. It is possible to thru-hike the entire trail and never see another thru-hiker. The result: This is an individualistic wilderness experience where hikers make their own decisions. It is a supreme adventure.

CHALLENGES OF THE TRAIL

The first major challenge of the CDT is its length. The actual Continental Divide from Mexico to Canada is 3100 miles; depending on your route, a thru-hike of the CDT might be a little less, but in any event, it is significantly longer than the Pacific Crest Trail. Thru-hiking it means covering those miles in the same short snow-free season.

But that's not all. Not only is the CDT longer than the PCT, it's also higher. Thru-hikers can encounter snow conditions in many of Colorado's 800 miles, in Wyoming's Wind River Range, and in northern Montana. The *average* elevation of the trail in Colorado is above 11,000 feet. Consider that the PCT only goes above 13,000 feet once, for the quick hop over Forester Pass. On the CDT, I once climbed five 13,000-foot peaks in a single memorable day.

The lack of a clearly defined trail poses difficulties. Even where cut foot-trail exists, it may not be marked and easily recognizable as part of the CDT. There is more roadwalking than on any of the other trails—also more bushwhacking and more cross-country travel. All hikers need to be competent with map and compass, and it doesn't hurt to have a GPS.

LONG-DISTANCE CONSIDERATIONS

Which Way?

Unlike the AT and the PCT, there's no consensus on which direction to travel. Some years, a majority of hikers go southbound; other years, the flow, such as it is, is northbound. Starting dates and direction are influenced by snowfall in the northern Rockies (a lower-than-average snow accumulation being more conducive to a southbound start) and in Colorado (a lower-than-average snow accumulation being conducive to a northbound start).

A word of warning: If you have your heart set on a one-direction, single-season thru-hike that follows the official route as much as possible, you'd be better off choosing another trail. Very few people are able to hike the CDT in one season while sticking closely to the "official" route, not taking shortcuts, and not changing directions somewhere along the way. The weather usually doesn't permit it. If you can't average 20 miles a day (even above 11,000 feet in snow in Colorado), chances are you're not going to be able to finish in one season without making some adjustments in route or direction of travel.

Conditions being favorable, a northbound start is easier in terms of footway, breaking in, and blisters because the trail in New Mexico often follows gentle dry roads, not steep wet trails. If you start in late April or early May, you should arrive in Colorado in the second or third week of June, depending on your route in New Mexico. (Straight-line road warriors will get there faster.) In an average snow year, arriving in Colorado in mid-June means encountering quite a few snowfields, some of which will be big enough and steep enough to force you to find a way around them. In a high-snow year,

"Above all, flexibility is important. Go with the wind, and let the trail direct your course. The CDT is a gem: the glorious areas are farther apart than on other trails, but well worth the effort because they're really magical places unlike anywhere on Earth."
— David Patterson

you may have to wait until July to get through the Colorado high country.

After Colorado, northbounders face hiking Wyoming's hot and dry Great Divide Basin in August, and then have to race winter to get to the Canadian border before snow does.

A southbound start forces hikers to immediately cope with snowmelt in Glacier National Park and the Bob Marshall Wilderness, where snowfields, steep slopes, and raging streams present dangerous and frightening obstacles, and where routefinding will be a real test of your skills. Once past the Montana snowmelt, hikers have fairly clear sailing through the rest of Montana, Idaho, and Wyoming, although they will arrive in the Great Divide Basin in the heat of midsummer. Like northbounders, southbounders have to race winter. In this case, it's southern Colorado and the south San Juan Mountains, which start to get snowy in October. Once you reach New Mexico, you should be able to finish. Most southbounders sticking to the actual route of the Colorado CDT end up having to cope with early-winter storms, especially in the San Juans. Some use snowshoes.

As on the PCT, flip-flopping can help you extend the hiking season, although it takes time and sometimes money. Each year's conditions, your starting date, direction of travel, and mileage are variables you'll have to consider.

Resupplies

The CDT is more remote than the PCT. To go to a town can require hitchhiking 20 miles or more. The length between resupplies is a little longer than it is on the PCT. Nonetheless, hikers rarely carry more than 8 days' worth of food. Many of the resupply stations are small and remote. Often you won't be able to buy any food, so most CDT thru-hikers use mail drops (see Appendix 3).

Permits and Regulations

Camping is permitted all along the Continental Divide Trail. In general, you can put up your tent wherever you like (of course, taking care to follow minimum-impact principles and any local regulations). Permits are required in Yellowstone and Glacier National Parks. They are also required if you intend to camp in Rocky Mountain National Park (unlikely, since the trail only briefly touches the park). In Yellowstone, rangers will issue permits over the phone to thru-hikers arriving on foot. Glacier's permit system does not make special allowances for thru-hikers, and getting a permit to cross the park can be more difficult (and certainly more frustrating) than the hike itself. Some wilderness areas also require permits. In addition, you will need permission if you intend to cross Indian reservations or private land; this is mostly an issue in New Mexico, where the route is not yet fully designated, and in Montana, where the trail crosses a small section of the Blackfeet Indian Reservation. Neither the CDTA nor the CDTS currently provides thru-hiker permits.

"You have to use a lot of maps on the CDT. We numbered them consecutively and marked the route on them with highlighter."
—Dan Smith

A rare trail sign on the CDT

Finding Your Way

Unlike the AT and the PCT, the CDT actually has two trail organizations. The Continental Divide Trail Society (CDTS) is headed by trail veteran and visionary Jim Wolf, whose work on the CDT has spanned three decades and was largely responsible for the inclusion of the CDT in the national trails system. The Continental Divide Trail Alliance (CDTA) is a newer, nonprofit group, founded in 1995. The CDTA has an agreement with the National Forest Service to be the primary nonprofit partner in managing the trail. It works with corporate sponsors and clubs to help build and maintain the trail. Each of the organizations sells CDT-related materials.

There are two sets of guidebooks for the CDT (see Appendix 1). The CDTS guidebooks, by Jim Wolf, are models of clarity in guidebook writing. Along with periodically published supplements, they include both the officially designated route along with Wolf's recommendations for alternate routes that may be more remote or scenically pleasing. "Map-Paks" are available for five of the six volumes in the series. The series of guidebooks, published by Westcliffe Publishers, is sanctioned by the CDTA and describes the official route.

Even with these resources, routefinding is the major challenge on the CDT, especially in New Mexico and southern Wyoming. Almost every CDT thru-hiker has had the experience of seeing a plate-sized CDT sign at a trailhead—and not a single indication of which way to go 10 feet beyond the sign. If you see the CDT marked on a map, don't make the mistake of thinking that it will be clearly marked on the ground (or even, sometimes, exist!). The trail is most complete in Colorado and Montana, although in parts of southern and central Montana there is still plenty of work to be done. In northern Wyoming (the Wind River Range and Yellowstone National Park), it's easy to piece a route together. New Mexico and southern Wyoming will challenge your navigation skills—and also your ability to pick out a pleasant backcountry route that stays off roads and avoids private land.

Chapters 16, 17, 18, and 19 offer specific leads on route-planning resources and routefinding.

GEAR

Because conditions along the CDT are similar to those found along the PCT, many of the same gear considerations apply (see Chapters 4 and 10). There are a few differences in climate and terrain, however, which will affect some of your gear choices.

- New Mexico is generally not as hot as the lower elevations of southern California.
- Colorado is much wetter than the Sierra Nevada, with daily thunderstorms, usually but not always in the afternoons. Hikers in Colorado also stay much higher for longer periods on exposed ridges.

- There is a fierce hot and dry section in southern Wyoming which both northbounders and southbounders hit during midsummer.
- There is more cross-country travel and more roadwalking, particularly in New Mexico.

Aspens changing color and gathering clouds warn of changing weather. Through Montana, northbound hikers are in a race with winter.

Boots

Very lightweight boots are perfectly good for the trail's dry stretches. Some hikers use sneakers, but find that sagebrush seeds, prickles, snow, and other detritus from cross-country travel are constantly sneaking inside. Gaiters can keep this junk out. If you're planning a route that requires a lot of roadwalking in New Mexico, you might consider sneakers, because they have more padding under the foot to absorb the impact of walking on hard roads. On the other hand, in Colorado, waterproof boots help keep feet dry even after miles on snow. Also, much of the trail above treeline isn't actually a cut trail; it simply follows cairns through rocks, hummocky grass, and tundra, so the added ankle support of boots is a benefit.

Tents

In New Mexico in the spring, a tent is hardly worth its weight; you'll be sleeping under a billion stars most nights. A tarp is perfectly adequate and offers the advantage of being able to provide midday shade. But in late summer, during New Mexico's monsoon season, and for much of the rest of the trail, mountain weather can be fierce. On the CDT, most hikers prefer a sturdy, wind-worthy tent that can handle an above-treeline storm.

Sleeping Bags

A 20-degree bag should be fine for most of the CDT. If you use a down one, keep it in a waterproof stuff sack, and be especially careful if you use a tarp.

Stoves

As on any trail, your stove decision is related to how you like to cook. Stove fuel is readily available in towns catering to outdoors-people (especially in Colorado), but it can be hard to find in some of the smaller towns, especially in New Mexico. If you use a wood-burning stove, you won't be able to cook in some above-treeline campsites. If you use a butane-propane stove, you can mail yourself the canisters if you send them by ground.

Ice Axes

Northbounders need ice axes in Colorado. Send them to your resupply in Chama, and have them when you climb out of Cumbres Pass. Southbounders need them at the start and can usually send them home from Lincoln.

Snowshoes

You won't find snowshoes particularly helpful in dealing with the late-spring snowpack (either in Colorado or Montana). The problem is that late-spring snow is consolidated, so snowshoes don't "float." Also, much of the trail runs along the sides of steeply slanted slopes. Because the snow is hard, the snowshoes can't cut into it, but instead torque in the direction of the hill, which is ineffective, uncomfortable, and potentially dangerous—if you slip and fall, you could break an ankle.

However, if you are skilled in winter travel, snowshoes could get you through early-winter storms in Colorado or Montana. Be sure to take enough food if you expect to be traveling on snowshoes; it's going to affect your mileage.

Instep Crampons

Instep crampons (see Chapter 12) aren't necessary, but they do provide a little extra traction and security that might enable you to cross certain slopes rather than bushwhacking around them (which can add miles and take hours).

"You need a water filter. The CDT has the worst water of any trail I've hiked. Shepherds graze their flocks along creeks and streams, and the sheep devastate the surrounding areas. It's so bad I could smell urine from over a mile away approaching a water source. Essentially, few if any (except maybe in parts of New Mexico) riparian areas are protected from livestock."

—David Patterson

Trekking Poles

As on other trails, this is a question of personal preference. On the New Mexico CDT, they are useful as snake detectors. They also help you keep your balance while crossing streams and going cross-country.

Water Filter

Water quality on much of the CDT is the worst on any of the national scenic trails. Grazing is one problem; so are old mines and beavers. High-country wildernesses tend to have good water, but multiple-use lands down below are suspect. In addition to a water filter, send yourself replacement canisters every month or so in your mail drops. You should use a prefilter to remove pond scum, dead animal parts, cow pies, and other biological delights from what may be the only water source for miles around. Also bring iodine pills to use in emergencies.

Raingear

For most of the trail, you'll need good-quality raingear. The only exceptions are New Mexico in the spring and southern Wyoming in midsummer, where you can get away with lightweight inexpensive jackets or ponchos.

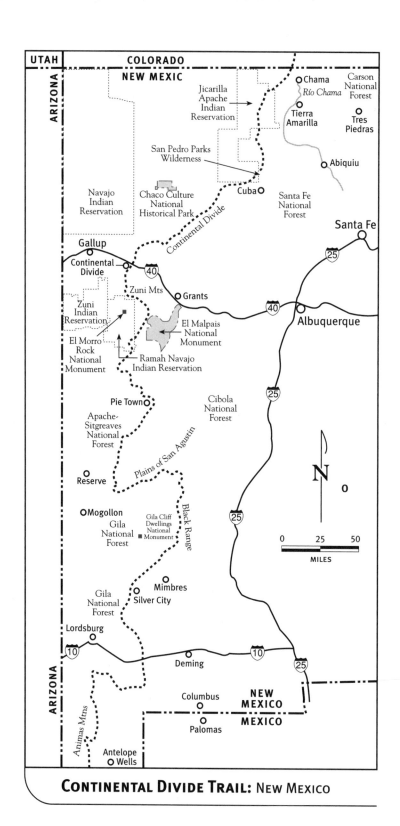

CONTINENTAL DIVIDE TRAIL: NEW MEXICO

CHAPTER 16

New Mexico

You'll encounter the first of the New Mexico CDT's many challenges the minute you sit down to plot out your route.

Route? What route?

Several factors have delayed establishing a continuous route through New Mexico. First is the always prickly issue of private land. Second, much of the land along the Continental Divide is leased for grazing or logging, and potential conflicts of interest are regarded warily by land managers and lease-holders. Third, the Continental Divide in New Mexico passes through Navajo and Apache lands. Fourth, in northern New Mexico, a bitter land ownership dispute between the local Hispanic community and the Forest Service is holding the CDT hostage to local politics. And fifth, water shortages are a real concern.

As a result, some of the proposed segments have had 40-mile stretches with no reliable source of water, making the "official" route untenable. The New Mexico trail also suffers from the lack of a strong local constituency. New Mexico has only one urban center, Albuquerque. Many outdoors-people eschew the piñon-juniper drylands in favor of New Mexico's beautiful northern mountains. So the local volunteer base is as underpopulated as the state.

THE TRAIL

The Continental Divide crosses the Mexican–American border in the middle of dusty nowhere, and immediately the hiker is faced with a choice: Where to start?

The nearest official border crossing (and hence, road) is about 14 miles from the Divide, at Antelope Wells in the boot-heel of New Mexico. Trail managers have chosen a route near the Antelope Wells border crossing as the beginning of the official CDT, but the "route" is unfinished.

Farther away (more than 60 air-miles east of the Divide) is the better-traveled and more accessible border crossing between Palomas, Chihuahua, and Columbus, New Mexico (site of Pancho Villa's 1916 raid into the United States). An alternate route from here veers on dirt roads to the Three Sisters Mountains, then circles around (or, if you prefer, you can climb through) the Florida Mountains before reaching the town of Deming.

Hikers are split about evenly on which route to take. The Antelope Wells route is closer to the Divide, longer, and, at this time, involves more high-grade road walking. The Columbus route is farther from the Divide, shorter, and more scenic. Neither of the routes follows the exact Divide, which is privately owned.

View from Chaco Mesa in central New Mexico shows typical New Mexican terrain: wide mesas, piñon-juniper vegetation, big skies, and empty space.

North of Deming and west of Silver City, the trail climbs into the Gila National Forest, where there is again a choice. The official CDT follows the Continental Divide in a wide arc around the Black Range (where some trail is cut and marked). However, a wonderfully scenic alternate route follows the Middle Fork of the Gila River up to the Gila Cliff Dwellings, where Mogollon people lived in pueblos 800 years ago.

North of the Gila, the route becomes somewhat problematic. Many hikers cross the Plains of San Augustin and head into Pie Town, then head toward the slopes of Mount Taylor. Others stay to the west of the Divide and resupply in the small town of Reserve.

The official route is slated to go through Pie Town, but there is currently a debate about the trail between the Gila National Forest and the town of Cuba. Water shortages and private lands are the two main hindrances. In this section, the official route of the trail, which may end up being some distance east of the actual Divide, crosses miles of sparsely populated drylands and the Malpais Lava flow, stops in the town of Grants (on Interstate 40), climbs Mount Taylor, and then descends to the town of Cuba. Another possible route goes from Reserve, through Quemado, into the Ramah Navajo Indian Reservation, through El Morro Rock National Monument, and along the actual

Divide to the hamlet of Continental Divide on Interstate 40. From there, it continues north through Navajo lands, over Chaco Mesa, and to Cuba.

From Cuba, the route crosses the San Pedro Parks Wilderness, then descends to the wild and scenic Río Chama and the town of Abiquiu. Land rights arguments in this corner of northern New Mexico have again delayed selection of an official route. However, there is an excellent backcountry route through the Carson National Forest, described in Wolf's guide. Continuing north, you'll see white spots in the distant sky—not clouds, but the south faces of the high peaks of Colorado. How snowy the peaks are, how difficult the traverses of the colder north sides—all that remains to be seen.

Seasons

Most northbound thru-hikers start in April or May (any earlier, and you'll arrive in Colorado before the snow has melted). Temperatures can be hot (90s), and some of the springs will be dry. There also may be fire danger. In late March and early April, strong winds create dust devils that race across the mesas, making hiking difficult.

Late July and August is the so-called monsoon season, with occasionally ferocious storms. Hikers should avoid camping in dry gullies, which may be subject to flash floods.

Southbound thru-hikers arrive in autumn, a comfortable time to be hiking in most of New Mexico. Winter is also quite pleasant in the non-mountainous parts of New Mexico's CDT.

Planning a Route

Planning a route through New Mexico is likely to take more time than any other prehike task—including planning your route for the rest of the trail. First you'll need to gather the following resources:

The DeLorme *New Mexico Atlas and Gazetteer* shows the route of the Continental Divide itself through the entire state. It does not, however, show the actual route of the CDT, which does not always exactly follow the Divide. The atlas's 1:250,000-scale maps are not sufficiently detailed for hiking, but they do include many trails and jeep roads and rudimentary topographic information, which is helpful for comparing food drops and major chunks of the route.

Forest Service maps of the Gila, Cibola, Santa Fe, Apache, and Carson National Forests. Be aware that many roads and trails in national forests are not shown on National Forest maps. Ask for the most current map available, as these are updated frequently.

Bureau of Land Management (BLM) maps. Which maps you need will depend on the route that you choose. For the official route, the maps are: Alamo Hueco, Animas, Lordsburg, Silver City, Quemado, Fence Lake, Chaco

> "Even on a well-marked trail, I keep track of where I am on the map. The few minutes spent are good insurance against getting lost or walking by the last water for many miles."
> —Brian Robinson

Mesa, and Abiquiu. For real bushwhacking, though, the scale is uncomfortably small. Ask for the most current edition.

USGS 1:24,000-scale topographic maps. Because the route in New Mexico keeps changing, the list of maps needed to hike it changes, too. You can get the most current list of maps for the official route from the Continental Divide Trail Alliance. Buying seventy-five topo maps is expensive and carrying ten or so at a time is heavy, so most hikers don't do it. However, having them enables you to plot a true backcountry route, avoid roads, find much more water, and turn the New Mexico segment of your CDT hike into a real pleasure.

Guidebooks. The *Northern New Mexico Guidebook*, published by the Continental Divide Trail Society, includes Jim Wolf's recommendations for a route through northern New Mexico. Bob Julyan's *The New Mexico CDT Guidebook* (Westcliffe Publishers) describes the official route, only some of which is actually on the ground. The booklet *Alternate Routes to the CDT*, by David Patterson, is a handy little reference that outlines the official route and a few alternates. It does not, however, include all the possible alternates, and the routing information is sketchy. The CDTA's *Long Distance Planning Guide* is a handy compilation of contact people, agency information, a list of topo maps, and a list of resupplies. (See Appendix 1.)

The CDTS newsletter. Back issues of *Dividends* contain far more detail than other sources about different routes, but you'll have to wade through lots of discussion about trail management issues and routing debates to find the information you're looking for.

The next step is to choose your intended route and mark it on your maps. The CDTA can tell you where actual trail has been constructed, where it has been designated, and where it is still in flux. Using this information and the two New Mexico guidebooks, highlight the completed sections on your maps. In a different color, highlight your resupplies and the trails and roads that could be used to connect the completed sections. For suggestions, consult the CDTS and CDTA guidebooks, the *Alternate Routes* booklet, and back issues of *Dividends*. At this stage, it's best to work with Forest Service and BLM maps; the atlas is too general, and working with seventy-five topos would be too overwhelming. Once you've chosen a route, you can decide which topos you need. (The USGS has an index map that will help you locate what you're looking for; also the CDTA offers a list of topos needed for the official route.) Marking the route is tedious, especially if you are using USGS maps, but you'll be grateful you did it once you are in the field, because you'll be able to see your route at a glance. You'll also become somewhat familiar with where it is you plan to walk.

Once you have your route planned, number the maps. Our system was to identify the maps by food drop, then by number. (For the stretch between Cuba and Ghost Ranch, for example, the maps would be coded C-GR, then numbered in order.)

> "If a trail peters out in a meadow, I always look in the corners of the meadow for a continuation. Trails are often built on old animal paths. Animals spread out in a meadow to graze, and for some reason recongregate at the corners for the journey to the next meadow. So, if you're completely off trail, pretend you're a big, fat, lazy elk. Then pause to think, 'Where would I go to get up or down this hill with the least amount of effort?' Also, watch for their droppings. They're always a good sign that you're taking the path of least resistance. But keep your objective in mind, too."
>
> —David Cossa

FINDING YOUR WAY

No question, thru-hiking any major trail is a wilderness achievement that entitles you to regale your friends with stories about near encounters with bears, lightning, and the local trail lunatic. But the truth is, the CDT is the only one of the Triple Crown trails that requires you to be competent with map and compass.

If you don't already have navigation skills, the first thing you need to do—long before heading out—is get to an outfitter and buy a compass and a map of a local area. Then go on a hike and start matching the landforms (mountains, cliffs, depressions, ridges, valleys, flat spaces, etc.) to the map. Practice will make you proficient—which will increase your confidence when you find yourself in the middle of dusty nowhere.

Learning to navigate in parts of New Mexico is quite easy because the land is wide open, with lots of prominent landmarks. At the beginning, you'll be on easily identifiable back roads. This is a good time to practice navigating by landforms. For example, match the mountain in front of you to the map. How do you know it is that precise mountain? (Maybe it has a funny-shaped outcropping that shows up as a mass of black contour lines.) The crux of staying found is to keep paying attention to where you are so that you will recognize immediately when the map and the ground start to diverge. If you need to confirm your position, look for three points of congruence (for example, you're southeast of this mountain, you just crossed an east–west electric line, and you are walking past a dried up stream that runs north–south).

GPS is strongly recommended for the CDT. It is not a substitute for map and compass, but it can answer in a snap that panic-stricken: "Does anybody know where we are?"

ROADWALKING

Many CDT hikers, thoroughly frustrated and confused by the lack of route information, succumb to the temptation to take the quickest and easiest way, which almost always ends up putting a footsore hiker on a hard-surfaced highway. This is not the ideal way to see New Mexico on foot. But with a little planning, you can minimize the amount of walking you have to do on roads (though, unfortunately, you can't eliminate it altogether). When you do find yourself on roads, remember the following:

Yield to traffic. Forget anything you might have learned in driver's ed about pedestrians having the right of way—when a logging truck barrels through, it's you who needs to get out of the way.

Flag vehicles for water. Most hikers give New Mexicans the award for being the friendliest people on the CDT. Many drivers will stop to see whether you need help (why else would you be on foot?). This is one way to get water, although obviously not reliable.

Watch for blisters. Hard, hot paved roads and, even worse, high-grade

> "When I lose the trail/route, I just say to myself, 'I'm not lost, just temporarily inconvenienced!' In most cases, the route is not that far away."
> —Roger Carpenter

> "Walking on pavement day after day destroys the spirit of a person. Roads are dangerous and motorists unpredictable. Additionally, injuries such as tendinitis are prevalent from the repetitive and constant pounding. If a roadwalk is unavoidable, seldom-used dirt roads are preferable to paved highways. That said, there are numerous alternative routes that preclude extensive paved road walks."
> —David Patterson

Much of New Mexico's CDT follows back roads like these, which make for fast, easy hiking.

gravel roads are extremely hard on feet, especially when combined with the high mileage many hikers do on roadwalks. Inserts (if your shoes are big enough) can provide some cushioning. Sneakers aren't a bad idea if you're planning a lot of roadwalking. Watch for hot spots; on a road, they can turn into blisters seconds after you notice them.

WATER STRATEGIES

The same desert-like conditions that exist on southern California's PCT exist in New Mexico. Water sources can be 20 miles apart—sometimes more. But because of the New Mexico CDT's higher elevations, the heat is less extreme. While the PCT dips as low as 1200 feet in California, the CDT stays above 4000 feet, and its average elevation is between 6000 and 7000 feet, keeping it for the most part in the piñon-juniper zone. Nonetheless, temperatures in May and June often rise into the 90s. As on the PCT, there are different kinds of water sources:

Surface water. If you've never spent much time in the arid Southwest, you may be surprised at first to cross a bridge over a dusty ditch—and see a sign saying Río something-or-other. There's a reason why almost all of the surface water on the map is marked in broken blue lines: In New Mexico, there isn't much that is certain about water, except that there isn't enough. Both northbounders and southbounders arrive in New Mexico when some surface water may be available. The winter snowpack in the mountains replenishes the aquifer and springs. The so-called monsoon takes place in the late summer and early fall; southbounders might find a little bit of surface water (as well as rain).

Stock impoundments. Frequently supersaturated with mud and cattle feces, water in stock impoundments only looks blue from a distance. Up close, it is an unappetizing brown sludge. These tanks are usually marked on maps in broken blue (indicating that they are seasonal). Very few of them have water out of season, and the water is generally so thick and sludgy that it can't be filtered. If you need to try filtering it, let it settle first, strain it through a bandanna, then run it through your prefilter.

Windmills. Windmills pump water from deep beneath the earth. Generally, the water gushing from the ground through the pipes is safe to drink. But water that's been sitting for a while may be less appetizing—be sure you peer inside the tank before you drink; it's not uncommon to see a dead bird floating inside. Watch for honeybees, which are attracted by the water. In fact, beekeepers sometimes put out boxes for bees near windmills in New Mexico. You'll see windmills from quite a distance. Be aware that sometimes the blades are turned off so that they don't spin (which means, of course, that no water is being pumped, although there may be water in the tanks). It's also possible that the windmill may be broken or that the water is stored in a closed tank with no faucet—and no way to get a drink. Recent signs of cattle (no need to be more graphic than that) indicate that working windmills are nearby. Windmills are the most reliable of all of New Mexico's water sources.

PRIVATE PROPERTY

Private property issues are always controversial when a trail is being routed through land that is at least partly in private hands or leased for private use, such as ranching or logging. In New Mexico, these issues are exacerbated by antigovernment sentiment. Locals rightly point out that much of the state is in federal hands; they want control of the land that is locally owned. But while many New Mexicans are suspicious about yet another government project, they are also helpful to hikers—as long as the hikers are respectful of their property.

The local BLM office or Forest Service can tell you about the ownership of in-holdings or other private parcels that may be near your planned route. You need permission to cross private land and Indian reservations. On private land, refrain from making fires, practice no-trace camping, and leave gates as you found them.

> "Today it's nearly impossible to get truly lost. However, getting off the trail is commonplace on the CDT. Stay calm, remain patient, and try to retrace your steps until you find your bearings. If that doesn't work, try to locate a feature—a stream, a ridge, a peak, or a manmade structure—that will enable you to determine your whereabouts."
>
> —David Patterson

At the Gila Cliff Dwellings, hikers can see how the indigenous Mogollon people lived.

Highlight Hike
GILA NATIONAL FOREST

WHERE: Intersection of Highways 15 and 35 to Road 159 near Mogollon
DISTANCE: 50 miles (approximate)
DIFFICULTY: Moderate
BEST TIME TO GO: Spring and fall
GUIDE: Guidebook not available. Contact the Gila National Forest for a map of the Gila Wilderness.

This alternate route to the official CDT goes through the Gila National Forest, including a large section of the Gila Wilderness and the Gila Cliff Dwellings National Monument. It's well worth the detour. From the intersection of Highways 15 and 35 near Lake Roberts, take Trail 247 down to the Gila River. Upstream, at the Gila Cliff Dwellings National Monument, you can explore the long-abandoned homes of the indigenous Mogollon people. Continue up the West Fork (in the process, you'll ford the Gila River about 100 times!), and leave the river to climb Mogollon and Whitewater Baldies.

Highlight Hike
CUBA TO ABIQUIU

The wild and scenic Río Chama in northern New Mexico is one of only two major rivers hikers encounter in the entire state.

WHERE: The San Pedro Parks Wilderness and the Río Chama
DISTANCE: 64 miles (approximate)
DIFFICULTY: Difficult
BEST TIME TO GO: Spring and fall
GUIDES: Wolf, *Vol. VI: Northern New Mexico;* or Julyan, *The New Mexico CDT Guidebook.*

This short stretch passes through the surprisingly green San Pedro Parks Wilderness, then climbs to Mariana Mesa. A word of warning: The route down from the mesa is steep and can be difficult to follow. Once on the north side of the mesa, the trail follows the wild and scenic Río Chama to the red-rock cliffs of Abiquiu's Ghost Ranch, where Georgia O'Keeffe painted.

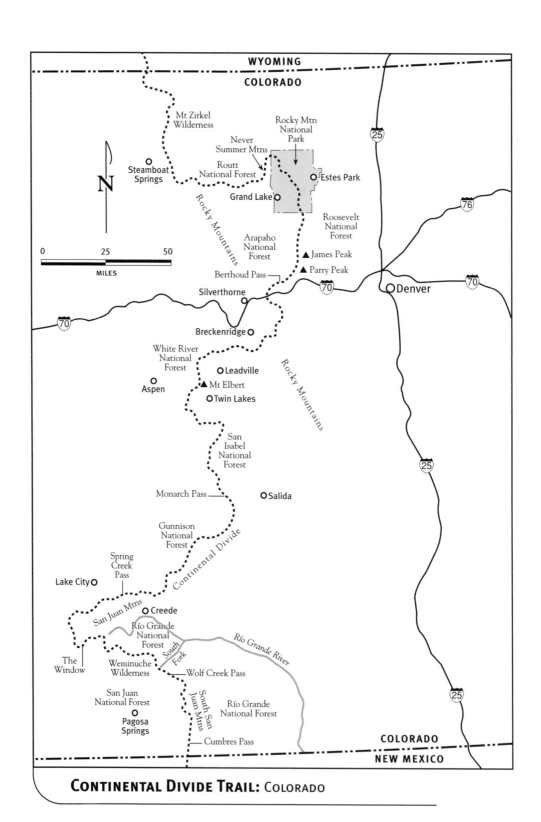

CONTINENTAL DIVIDE TRAIL: Colorado

CHAPTER 17

Colorado

Unlike the PCT, which jumps over the High Sierra's passes like a horse running a steeplechase, the Colorado Continental Divide goes up—and stays there. The trail's elevation averages more than 11,000 feet for most of the state. This makes Colorado's CDT the highest sustained stretch on any of the national scenic trails. In southern Colorado, sleeping at elevations of less than 10,000 feet usually means that you're sleeping in a bed in a town!

Much of the trail in Colorado is designated and is in good shape. There is very little roadwalking and an abundance of scenic high country. In one sense, Colorado trail managers had an easy job. Much of the Divide lies in designated wildernesses, many of which already had large trail systems. In many cases, the CDT was able to follow trails that already existed. However, trails may not be clearly marked as being part of the CDT.

Some of the official trail (described in the Westcliffe guidebooks) is lower and safer than alternate routes higher on the Divide (recommended by the CDTS guidebooks). For example, while there is a wild, high, and spectacular route along the actual Divide following the Front Range, the official route leaves the Divide in places to avoid some especially tricky climbs through exposed terrain.

In general, hikers can follow or devise a satisfying and remote single-track route through Colorado that is largely off-limits to motorized vehicles. But be aware that Colorado is one of the nation's key playgrounds. Mountain bikers, all-terrain/off-road vehicle users, and snowmobilers want access, too, and in many non-wilderness areas, they are permitted.

As everywhere on the CDT, Colorado's trail junctions aren't necessarily marked with a CDT logo, and in early season some of the trail will be snow-covered. Most hikers find that guidebooks and Forest Service maps are sufficient for routefinding, especially in wilderness areas where the trails tend to be in good shape. If you expect to hike in snow, however, you may find it worthwhile to have the USGS topos. Note that many of the USGS topos predate the trail, so you'll have to mark your intended route on the maps yourself (see Chapter 15).

THE TRAIL

The trail in Colorado starts at Cumbres Pass and immediately climbs into the South San Juan Mountains. The trail then enters the Weminuche Wilderness,

The south face of the South San Juan Mountains in late June of an average snow year

where it takes a long, meandering 270-degree arc around the headwaters of the Río Grande, joining the Colorado Trail as it swings back to the east. This detour is well worth the time, for it boasts some of the CDT's most dramatic scenery. The trail then follows the well-marked Colorado Trail until near Monarch Pass, where hikers have the choice of either continuing on the Colorado Trail or following the official Continental Divide Trail farther to the west. The Colorado Trail is tempting because it is well marked, but in this section, it can be a little frustrating as it gains and loses elevation (sometimes 3000 feet at a time) without the dramatic views you've come to expect. It also spends more time than you might like on multiple-use lands. The Colorado Trail and the CDT rejoin at Twin Lakes, pass Mount Elbert (Colorado's highest peak), and remain contiguous until the Copper Mountain ski area on Interstate 70.

The next section follows the Gore and Front Ranges between Silver-thorne and Grand Lake, where the Continental Divide rises above 13,000 feet. Again, there are several route choices in this area. The official CDT at first stays atop the Divide, then takes a longer, more circuitous, and up-and-down route to avoid some dangerous trail conditions between Parry and James Peaks. The more scenic route described in the CDTS guidebooks is difficult, requiring a gain of nearly 6000 feet of elevation and five ascents of peaks of more than 13,000 feet in a single hiking day. Other problems are finding sufficient water (there isn't much) and the perilous footway, which includes lots of ankle-twisting tundra and rock, along with a ridiculous scramble between Parry and James Peaks that makes even experienced hikers gasp. This route can be dangerous in bad weather. But if the weather is good, go for it!

The CDT then touches the corner of Rocky Mountain National Park and heads west. A longer alternative around the Never Summer Mountains is recommended by CDTS director Jim Wolf.

Now in northern Colorado, you'll find the climate drier and the mountains more open, with wide parks between them. A notable climb of Parkview Mountain will have you gasping for air. At 12,300 feet, it's not the highest peak on the CDT, but it is one of the most demanding. Colorado's scenic tour concludes with a crossing of the Mount Zirkel Wilderness, followed by a descent to the Wyoming border.

SEASONS

The CDT averages more than 11,000 feet in elevation and thus has a short snow-free season. Peak season is mid-July through mid-September in most of the state. Mosquitoes can be bad just after the snowmelt. It is possible to hike into October, although early-winter storms are likely and temperatures are cold.

SCHEDULING FOR SNOW

The Colorado snowpack is unpredictable. In some years, the high country is easily hikable in mid-June; in other years, snowfields last well into July.

In the elusive "average" snow year, an arrival at Cumbres Pass, on the New Mexico–Colorado border, between June 15 and June 20 should set you up for a fairly straightforward, if still challenging, passage. In a high-snow year, the trail could very well be completely impassable for several weeks more.

Note that the difficulties of a high-snow year in Colorado are much more serious than those of a high-snow year in California. In the High Sierra, you only rise above 11,000 feet when you are climbing one of the nine high passes. In Colorado, 11,000 feet is merely an *average* elevation.

By the time you get to Wolf Creek Pass, you'll have a good idea of snow conditions. But even if the snow cover is light, keep your ice ax until Spring

"After experiencing countless slide shows by hikers who couldn't remember just where this gorgeous view was or just where this campsite was, I vowed to treat my audiences (and myself) better. I put a tiny piece of masking tape on the top of every completed film canister and number each roll. I also keep a small 'photo log' notebook. Finally, I always use prepaid mailers so film can be processed from the trail, without my having to bother with time delays or potential heat threats to unprocessed film. On the mailer, I note the number of the film canister so I can match the processed slides to my photo log months later."

—Bob Ellinwood

Creek Pass, because snow lingers late in the Weminuche Wilderness.

If you've arrived too early in Colorado, you may find conditions impassable. In this case you have three choices: flip-flop (perhaps going up to Wyoming and starting southbound through the Great Divide Basin), wait it out, or take a shortcut. Generally, however, if you've made it through the South San Juans, you can make it through the exorbitantly scenic Weminuche Wilderness.

Faced with the snowpack, some northbounders take what is called the Creede cut-off, meaning that instead of following the Divide around the headwaters of the Río Grande, they cut straight across, saving high-country mileage. The cutoff takes a straight-line lower route from just north of Wolf Creek Pass to Spring Creek Pass. This is certainly one way to keep going forward, but the section you skip, including the incomparable Weminuche Wilderness, is one of the trail's finest. Other hikers, arriving too early, have simply taken a low route across most of Colorado. That is certainly an option—but it is not the Divide.

Southbounders need to make tracks through Colorado. Above 11,000 feet, snow can fall any time of year. (It's not for nothing that one of the ranges along the Divide is called the Never Summer Mountains.) Hiking Colorado in September is a cold prospect—you'll need a warm sleeping bag and extra clothes. In October the Colorado high country can turn seriously snowy; and weather and wind might force you off the ridges and peaks.

Equipment and Snow Safety

Northbounders should be competent with an ice ax. Instep crampons aren't a bad idea, either. Southbound hikers may need snowshoes if they arrive in southern Colorado when winter does. Snowshoes will help you get through soft, deep accumulations. Be warned that your mileage is likely to plummet, even though you'll be in excellent shape at this point in your hike. Snowshoes mileage is slow mileage, and in addition, you'll have to take extra time to navigate because the trail will be buried. Use snowshoes with two hiking sticks or ski poles with baskets.

Both northbounders and southbounders should take adequate maps so as to be able to navigate in snow. Forest Service maps show alternate trails and roads—which can be very useful if the CDT is impassable and you have to bail out.

THUNDERSTORMS

Colorado's thunderstorms are legendary, and when (not if) you're ever caught in one above treeline, you'll know why. Typically, thunderstorms come in the afternoons, so the standard advice is to plan your days so that you are below treeline by one or two o'clock. But the route doesn't always oblige; not only that, but the thunderstorms sometimes roll in well before noon. Chances are that at least once on the Colorado CDT, you're going to be stuck on a high ridge when clouds the color of bruises race across the sky. To minimize the risk, remember the following strategies:

If you can plan to be off the high peaks by early afternoon, do so. For example, if walking 3 miles farther one evening puts you right at the foot of the next day's big climb, it's worth doing those extra miles so that you can be up and over as early as possible.

Go downhill. You may not be able to reach shelter; you may not be able to get down to treeline, but you can get off the high point of a ridge.

Take an alternate route. Do not continue climbing into a thunderstorm. Wait until it passes, or take a lower alternative.

Reduce exposure. If the storm gods are indeed hurling their thunderbolts directly at you, get rid of any metal implements (ice ax, trekking poles). Stand on your sleeping pad. Crouch down, but do not put your hands on the ground. Putting your hands on the ground would, if you were hit by lightning, encourage the shock to go through your central and vital organs, perhaps from your feet through your trunk and out one or both arms. Stay away from shallow caves, protruding rocks, the base of cliffs, and the only cluster of trees in an open field, all of which attract lightning.

First aid for lightning strikes. If someone in your group is hit by lightning and appears dead, administer CPR. Once conscious, the victim should be treated for shock and should get medical help as soon as possible.

ALTITUDE SICKNESS

As on the PCT, thru-hikers are not likely to be troubled by altitude sickness in Colorado, because by the time they get there, they have slowly acclimated. Nonetheless, the increased altitude does have an effect, and you might find yourself being more winded than usual, getting tired more easily, and generally wondering why it's taking so long to get anywhere. It's more of a problem on the Colorado CDT than on the Sierra PCT because the average elevation is much higher for much longer. Your body is working a lot harder, so give it a break! Rest every once in a while, and drink frequently even if you don't think you are thirsty (see Chapter 3).

COLORADO RESCUE INSURANCE

Talk about a good deal! The state of Colorado offers a "Colorado Hiking Certificate" which helps defray the cost of search-and-rescue in the state. The cost: a mere dollar. Contact the Colorado Division of Wildlife, 6060 Broadway, Denver, CO 80216; 303-297-1192. Certificates are also available at Colorado outfitters.

"The best way to cope with lightning is to climb high early in the day and try to get somewhere low and away from any exposed ridges in the afternoon hours. There isn't a formula, because some mountains create their own weather patterns."
—David Patterson

The "Window," a 150-foot cleft in the Divide, is a notable landmark in the Weminuche Wilderness.

Highlight Hike
WEMINUCHE WILDERNESS AND SAN JUAN MOUNTAINS

WHERE: Wolf Creek Pass (U.S. Route 160) to Spring Creek Pass (Colorado Highway 149)
DISTANCE: 134 miles
DIFFICULTY: Challenging
BEST TIME TO GO: Summer
GUIDES: Wolf, Vol. V: *Southern Colorado;* or Jones, *The Colorado CDT Guidebook*

High and wild, this section of the CDT swings around the headwaters of the Río Grande, passing the famous landmarks of the Río Grande Pyramid and the "Window," a 150-foot-tall cleft in the Divide. This is a true high-country route; beware of electrical storms, late-season snow, and fierce mosquitoes.

Highlight Hike
FRONT RANGE AND GORE RANGE

Sparkling lakes and tarns nestle among the peaks in Colorado's Front Range.

WHERE: Silverthorne to Grand Lake
DISTANCE: 110 miles
DIFFICULTY: Extremely challenging
BEST TIME TO GO: Summer
GUIDE: Wolf, Vol. IV: *Northern Colorado*

Only part of this traverse has been selected for inclusion in the official CDT. It is one of the highest, hardest, gnarliest, windiest, most storm-whipped and lightning-prone sections of any of the three Triple Crown trails, but it is also glorious, with views of more mountains than you can count for as far as you can see. For strong, sure-footed hikers in good weather only.

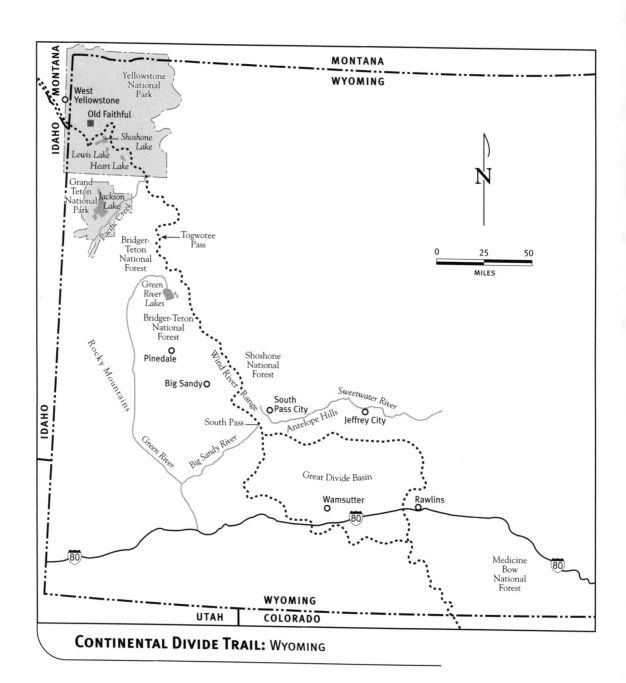

MONTANA
WYOMING

Yellowstone
National
Park

West
Yellowstone

Old Faithful

Shoshone Lake

Lewis Lake
Heart Lake

Grand
Teton
National
Park

Jackson Lake

Pacific Creek

Bridger-
Teton
National
Forest

← Togwotee
Pass

*Green
River
Lakes*

Bridger-Teton
National
Forest

Pinedale

Big Sandy

Wind River Range

Shoshone
National
Forest

Rocky Mountains

South
Pass City

Sweetwater River

Antelope Hills

Jeffrey City

South Pass

Green River

Big Sandy River

Great Divide Basin

Wamsutter

Rawlins

Medicine
Bow
National
Forest

IDAHO
MONTANA

IDAHO

WYOMING

UTAH | COLORADO

N

0   25   50
MILES

CONTINENTAL DIVIDE TRAIL: WYOMING

CHAPTER 18

Wyoming

Wyoming's CDT is divided into three major sections. Most of the southern part of the state is high desert. Next up is the Wind River Range, which stands out as one of the most scenic segments of any of the Triple Crown trails. And last, there is Yellowstone National Park, an American icon that, despite its fame, surprises and delights even the most jaded visitor.

While most of the trail in Wyoming is not complete, much of the route is easy to follow if you've done a little planning and marked it on your maps. In the south, you'll spend a fair amount of time on two-track roads.

THE TRAIL

Back at the New Mexico–Colorado border, the CDT headed uphill. At the Wyoming border, the trail heads back down. After a short passage through the Medicine Bow National Forest in southern Wyoming, the Continental Divide splits into two ridges, encircling 2.25 million acres of the Great Divide Basin.

Northbounders and southbounders both arrive here in August. North-bounders will find the terrain somewhat familiar. Like New Mexico, it is dry, hot, and largely waterless. This is a land of big, empty space and harsh winds; not everyone's idea of a beautiful landscape. Nor is it especially suited for towns and settlement. The Union Pacific Railroad came through here, giving life to Rawlins, a railroad town. (If you take a day off here, you can visit the pioneer jail.) Other than that, there are a few struggling towns and a lot of empty space in between. Along the route, you'll see evidence of sheep and cattle grazing, oil and gas drilling, mining for uranium—and now, hiking.

Faced with a largely unmarked route, limited water, and severe terrain, and aware that they are in a race with winter, many thru-hikers succumb to the temptation of roadwalking across the Great Divide Basin. Route planning then simply requires buying a road map (or better yet, ripping the pages out of your DeLorme atlas). One real downside to consider: the lack of water. If you roadwalk, you'll be depending on the kindness of passing motorists, who are few and far between. Another downside: sheer tedium.

The official route takes a long detour around the better-watered and more scenic eastern rim of the Basin. As in New Mexico, private land issues here have complicated the route, which combines paved roadwalking, dirt road walking, and some cross-country travel.

Hikers in southern Wyoming follow jeep tracks, which themselves follow the route of the Pony Express and the Oregon Trail.

The eastern route is historically interesting. Along the Sweetwater River, it follows in the tracks of the Pony Express, the Oregon Trail, and the Mormon Battalion. It is estimated that on the Oregon Trail, someone died every tenth of a mile. As you walk past the graves of seventy-seven Mormon pioneers, who died in an early-fall snowstorm more than a century ago, you may start to think about picking up your mileage. Like the settlers, thru-hikers are in a race with winter.

The two arms of the Continental Divide come together again near South Pass City. Pioneer wagon trains crossed the Divide at South Pass; South Pass City, an old gold-mining town, is today a historic site with a post office and a few exhibits. Don't send packages here without checking first; in some years, the post office has had limited services.

North of South Pass City, hikers traditionally get thoroughly lost as they make their way toward the Wind River Range. Once in the Winds, however, the trails are easy to follow. There are several alternate routes through the Wind River Range, each more scenic than the next. Jim Wolf's Wyoming guidebook and supplement lists a recommended route and several alternate routes which roughly parallel the Divide as it trends to the northwest through these beautiful mountains. The trail stays largely above 10,000 feet, but the grades are gentle and the walking is easy. Route decisions will largely be based on personal preference: How close do you want to get to the famous Cirque of the Towers? Will you need to resupply in Pinedale or Big Sandy Lodge? The map of the Bridger-Teton National Forest will help you quickly choose a route based on your answers to these questions.

Between the Winds and Yellowstone, the trail is incomplete, largely following confusing and poorly mapped roads as it crosses a section of multiple-use land. Next up is the Teton Wilderness and the beginning of grizzly country (see below). Here the trail passes a spot known as the Parting of the Waters, where the Divide splits a stream into two parts, one of which goes to the Atlantic and the other to the Pacific. It is the only place where you will actually see the Divide doing its heralded job as continental watershed.

In Yellowstone, the trail follows the Snake River to Heart Lake, Lewis Lake, Shoshone Lake, and the Shoshone Geyser Basin, before going right to Old Faithful, where you can watch the geyser erupt, regular as clockwork. The trail exits the park via the Madison Plateau, which was severely burned in the famous 1988 fires. Recovery is still decades away.

SEASONS

The Great Divide Basin is best hiked in spring and fall. Winter is cold, snowy, and above all, windy. Locals say that the snow doesn't melt—it just gets blown around until it's worn out.

The climate in the Wind River Range is alpine standard: Peak hiking season is mid-July through sometime in September. August can be crowded, especially near popular spots like Cirque of the Towers and Big Sandy Lake. As in Colorado, severe electrical storms are common.

Yellowstone is a high plateau. Snow lingers late in the spring. Summer is the peak hiking and tourist season. The hiking season extends into September and possibly early October, but temperatures can be cold. Yellowstone is open in winter for cross-country skiing and snowshoeing. Expect frigid temperatures, often well below zero.

PERMITS

For the first time on your trip (if you're going northbound), you'll need to get a permit and sleep in designated camping areas. Designated camping areas provide some measure of safety in numbers, as well as poles for hanging food out of the reach of bears. The rangers at Yellowstone will issue thru-hikers permits in advance by telephone. Coming northbound, you can call them from a lodge near Togwotee Pass, just south of the Teton Wilderness. Coming southbound, call them from the town of Macks Inn.

ALKALINE LAKES

If you've come north through New Mexico, you may think you know everything you need to know about dryland hiking. But there's one more thing: alkaline lakes. These salty lakes occur in dry areas where rapid evaporation leaves salts to accumulate.

The Great Divide Basin in southern Wyoming is a 2.25-million-acre desert.

There's nothing you can do to make water from an alkaline lake drinkable. As in seawater, the salts are dissolved and cannot be filtered. Alkaline lakes are identified as such on some maps, but not all. In the region of the Great Divide Basin, don't count on lakes as water sources—or even for bathing. Look instead for springs.

GRIZZLY BEARS

It is, suffice it to say, disconcerting for humans to realize that we are not at the top of the food chain.

On the CDT, grizzlies live primarily in Yellowstone National Park and in the Teton Wilderness, just south of Yellowstone in Wyoming, and in Glacier National Park and the Bob Marshall Wilderness, just south of Glacier National Park in Montana. It is far more likely that you will be struck by lightning or die from a bee sting than that you will be killed by a grizzly. Somehow that seems small comfort when in the middle of the night, protected only by a nylon tent, you hear something big snorting only feet (or is it inches?) away. There are a few things you can do to protect yourself.

First, hike in a group. It's anathema, I know, to the wilderness experience and minimum impact ethics to recommend making a lot of noise in wilderness, but in bear country, it's merely good sense. There has never been a documented fatal grizzly bear attack on a group of four or more people, and there has never been a documented mauling on a group of six or more. Park concessionaires even sell bells for the purpose of making noise.

Pay attention. Bears usually attack because they are surprised, defending a food source, or protecting cubs; attacks are not usually due to predatory behavior. Be especially careful in head-high huckleberry bushes, near running water (which may prevent the bear from hearing you), or near signs of carrion, which bears will defend as a food source. Don't go near cubs, and give them (and mama bear) plenty of space and an escape route.

If you see a bear, stay calm. Give it a moment; it may just move away from you. Do not get any closer (especially if you are within 100 yards or so; bears need a "personal space" zone of at least 60 yards). If possible, make a wide arc around the bear. Look carefully for cubs—they don't always stay right near mama and can be difficult to see.

A bear standing on its back legs is a terrifying sight, but most often, it's just near-sightedly checking you out. More ominous is a woofing sound (which means "Please go away"), shaking the head from side to side, or an expression where the lips are pulled back exposing the teeth. Avoid making eye contact, which may be interpreted as a challenge or a threat. Rangers advise looking for a tree to climb, but that's not easy in lodgepole country, and if you move too quickly toward one, it could trigger the bear's chase response. Above all,

"To deal with the isolation of the CDT, books are good, and so are partners. Unless you plan to hike with someone, it's likely you won't encounter many other people unless you go to town. Plan to hike with a partner if you do not do well with isolation. Otherwise, prepare mentally for the journey."

—David Patterson

do *not* run—even if charged. Bears frequently bluff charge, and if you run, you identify yourself as something to chase. If attacked, play dead, in a fetal position with your arms protecting your neck and your knees drawn up around your stomach.

In camp, cook and eat well away from your campsite (at least 200 feet) and hang all food, cooking utensils, and scented items (soap, toothpaste, sunscreen) on one of the bear poles provided. Some rangers and bear experts additionally recommend that you hang the clothes you were wearing when you ate dinner.

Finally, consider carrying pepper spray. This is a controversial subject. Some people feel that the spray does not give adequate protection and contributes to a false sense of security. Still, it's better than nothing, and there are plenty of reports of it stopping a bear attack. If you use pepper spray, wear it holstered on your hip so you can pull it out immediately when you need it. Aim for the bear's eyes, nose, and mouth.

There are several routes through the Wind River Range; all of them are scenic.

The Wind River Range is dotted with high lakes; the trail stays largely above 10,000 feet.

Highlight Hike
WIND RIVER RANGE

WHERE: Big Sandy Lake to Green River Lakes
DISTANCE: 73 miles
DIFFICULTY: Moderate
BEST TIME TO GO: Summer and early fall
GUIDES: Wolf, *Vol. III: Wyoming;* or Davis, *The Wyoming CDT Guidebook*

The Wind River Range ranks among the Triple Crown's best hikes. Numerous alternate routes give you lots of choices, all of which boast spectacular scenery, above-treeline travel, sparkling lakes, and, at the end, a descent along the well-named Green River, which carries glacial till from Wyoming's highest peaks.

In Yellowstone, the CDT
follows the Snake River.

Highlight Hike

Teton Wilderness and Yellowstone National Park

Where: Togwotee Pass to Old Faithful
Distance: 105 miles
Difficulty: Moderate
Best time to go: Summer
Guides: Wolf, *Vol. III: Wyoming;* or Davis, *The Wyoming CDT Guidebook*

On this stretch of trail you'll see the Parting of the Waters, where the Divide actually splits a stream and sends half to the Atlantic and half to the Pacific. You may also see grizzly bears, moose, and elk, along with a selection of Yellowstone's backcountry thermal basins, including fumaroles, mud pots, and at the end, Old Faithful itself.

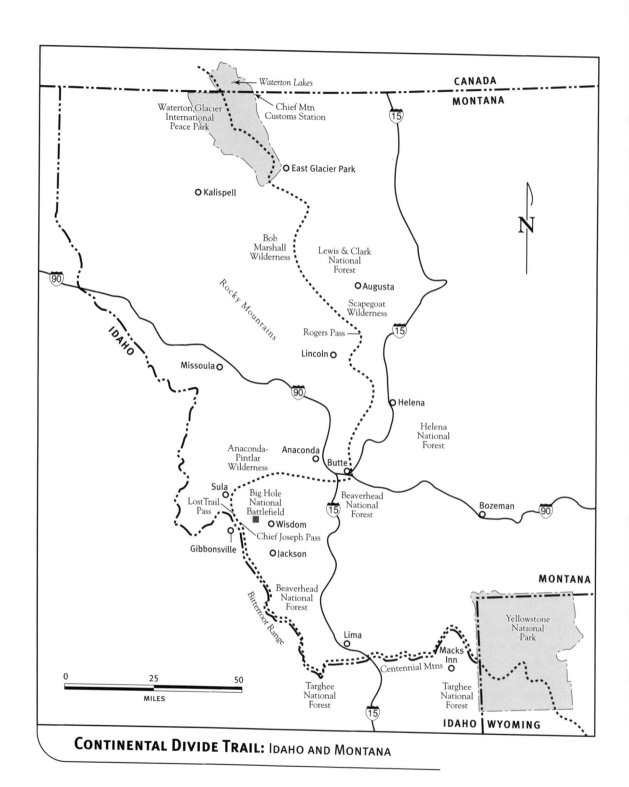

CONTINENTAL DIVIDE TRAIL: IDAHO AND MONTANA

CHAPTER 19

Idaho and Montana

With nearly 1000 miles of trail, the Idaho–Montana portion of the CDT is the longest. There's a great deal of variety: the alpine peaks of the Bitterroot Range, the Anaconda-Pintlar Wilderness, and Glacier National Park; the wild and remote Bob Marshall and Scapegoat Wildernesses; and the high dry peaks of the southwestern part of the state. There's also a fair amount of multiple-use land to cross, especially in central Montana and the Centennial Mountains. Much of the CDT in Montana is in good shape, but the hiking is remote and rugged, and you'll need a map and compass to find your way.

THE TRAIL

For the most part, the CDT in Idaho and Montana stays fairly close to the actual Continental Divide, often just to one side or the other of it.

From the Wyoming border, the Continental Divide defines the border between Idaho and Montana. Starting at the western border of Yellowstone National Park, the CDT climbs into the Centennial Mountains, where the route can be rough going. While new trail was built in this area, deadfall and storm damage have made parts of it impassable in recent years. You'll need to call the Forest Service for up-to-date info. Although the official route will stay atop the Divide just west of Yellowstone, most thru-hikers detour via Forest Service roads to the town of Macks Inn, where they can resupply for the long remote stretch ahead.

Continuing west, the CDT follows the Divide, which is open and grassy and surprisingly dry; the trail is often on the crest. It then swings north to follow the Bitterroot Range through a region of stunning alpine beauty. This is one of the most remote stretches of trail, with difficult resupplies. The two options involve hitchhiking either on Interstate 15 to the small town of Lima or on a barely traveled back road to Leadore. You'll pass near the headwaters of the Missouri River and cross the route of Lewis and Clark at Lost Trail Pass. At Lost Trail Pass, the Bitterroot Range continues north, but the Divide swings to the northeast, circles around the infamous Big Hole Battlefield, and climbs into the beautiful Anaconda-Pintlar Wilderness.

Central Montana is a sort of interlude between the more dramatic southern and northern ends of the state. Here the trail stays lower, passing through multiple-use forests that have seen a few too many chainsaws and miner's picks. The route here often follows Forest Service roads, which makes for fast

Crossing streams in Montana in late summer. Early in the season, be prepared for deeper water.

progress, if not especially scenic hiking. New trail construction is planned in the area around Butte. If you are hiking when snow is still on the ground, take care to stay on roads and trails, because the entrances to old mines may be impossible to detect under the snow.

North of Butte, approaching Helena, the trail is in good shape, but lower and more forested. Once north of Helena, the trail starts to rise again, often following the crest of the Divide, here a series of rounded mountains.

At Rogers Pass, the CDT enters the Scapegoat Wilderness, still recovering from an out-of-control fire that took place more than a decade ago. Still, this is a scenic high-country stretch of trail, and from here to Canada, the views improve with every step. Next up is the vast Bob Marshall Wilderness—grizzly country again (see the grizzly precautions in Chapter 18). The trail's Grand Finale takes place in Glacier National Park, a fitting end to this most dramatic of hikes.

Trail Conditions

Yeoman's work from Forest Service staff and management has given the Idaho–Montana CDT a route that is scenic and close to the Divide, although that doesn't mean that it is always marked on the ground. As they are throughout the CDT, maps and a compass are required, and GPS is useful.

A few notes:

Trail conditions vary wildly from year to year due to storm damage, wildfire damage, snow levels, runoff, and logging.

Trail is sporadically and unpredictably marked from ranger district to ranger district and even sometimes within a district.

Maps are also a problem. In a burst of enthusiasm, land managers published maps showing the route of the CDT before the trail was in place on the ground. Some of the route has since been relocated, and much of it is not marked. You'll need to inquire locally about the current status of both the trails and the maps that purport to show its route. As in New Mexico, there are two termini for the northern end of the trail. The official route ends at the Chief Mountain Customs Station on the east side of Glacier National Park rather than at the more scenic border monument at Waterton Lakes. Trail managers chose the Chief Mountain route to avoid complications from people crossing between the United States and Canada on foot (as they do, incidentally, without causing problems on the Pacific Crest Trail). The more scenic alternate route stays closer to the Divide and goes to Waterton Lakes on the Canadian side of Glacier–Waterton Lakes International Peace Park.

SEASONS

With high mountains and a northerly latitude, Montana's main hiking season is during the summer. Bug season depends on the snowmelt, but usually starts in late June and early July. Cold weather rolls in again in September, with the possibility of early-winter storms. While the first storms usually melt off, the snow starts sticking in October. In the mountains, accumulations can be several feet or more.

NORTHBOUND/SOUTHBOUND STRATEGIES

The problem with a southbound thru-hike generally begins the minute you arrive in Glacier National Park. In early season, park rangers may refuse to give permits due to the dangers of crossing the snow-choked high country and the

"When the trail disappears into a snowbank, follow the footprints if there's a consensus 'trail' over the snow. If not, make your own by following trail markers and other blazes or cairns, trimmed trees overhanging the trail, or trail cuts through buried blow-downs. When there's no sign of the trail, make a best guess based on the maps and where you think the trail might go. Then look for occasional markers or other signs. If there's an 'other side' to the snowbank, search along the perimeter for where the trail exits. Groups can search more quickly, so consider linking up with other hikers."
—Brian Robinson

Waterton Lakes on the U.S.–Canada border—a fitting ending to the scenic CDT.

swollen rivers down below. Even if you can demonstrate that you have got the skills and equipment to attempt the traverse, you'll soon realize that the rangers have good reason for their concern.

Each year the winter snow accumulation is different. Variable springtime conditions cause the rate of melt-off to differ considerably from year to year. In general, early-season hikers—those trying to start in early or mid-June, sometimes even later—will find that the CDT's high-country route through Glacier National Park is more difficult and dangerous than they had anticipated. Ice axes are a must, instep crampons are strongly recommended, and it should go without saying that hikers need the experience and judgment to use them both. Note: There are several routes through Glacier National Park. South of Swiftcurrent, the Highline Route closely follows the Divide but is not passable before the snow has melted because it is blasted into sheer rock.

Because of the difficulties of starting in Glacier, some southbound hikers in recent years have begun their thru-hike in central Montana to take advantage of the lower mountains and milder climate in the middle of the state. The way to do this is to hike the lower country between the Anaconda-Pintlar Wilderness (near Anaconda) and the Scapegoat Wilderness (near Lincoln) first. By the time you reach the Scapegoat Wilderness, the Bob Marshall Wilderness, and Glacier National Park, the snow will have had a few extra weeks to melt. Nonetheless, in a high-snow year, even this strategy can present hikers with some tough going. Once done with northern Montana, hikers would then head back down to tackle the Anaconda-Pintlar Wilderness, which is in an average year passable in early July.

Northbounders arriving early enough at Chief Joseph Pass or Anaconda could do a similar flip, skipping up to Glacier and then heading southbound. This strategy might buy you a couple of extra weeks, as northern Montana becomes snowbound earlier than central Montana.

If you want to do a one-season, one-direction thru-hike, the watchword for northbounders is *speed*. Winter usually comes to the high country in September or October. Lewis and Clark had the sense to stop exploring and make camp during a northern Rockies winter; hikers are best advised to do the same. Note that the northernmost part of the CDT goes through some of the wildest lands in the contiguous states. Once you're in, there may be no easy way out in case of storms. Bring extra food and good maps.

GLACIER'S GRIZZLIES

Most of Montana's grizzlies are found in the Bob Marshall Wilderness and Glacier National Park, although a few may stray into the Scapegoat Wilderness. Glacier's grizzlies have killed hikers on and near the CDT. The best defense against surprise encounters with grizzlies is a large group making lots of noise. Chapter 18 gives advice on hiking in grizzly country and bear-proofing a campsite.

> "Widen your perspective and look far beyond your current position when walking cross-country. You are no longer on a narrow trail, but rather on a broad corridor that offers numerous options to get from where you are to where you are going. Also, on open, steep slopes an altimeter helps you traverse at the desired elevation, especially in bad weather."
>
> —Roger Carpenter

Highlight Hike
ANACONDA-PINTLAR WILDERNESS

WHERE: Montana Highway 274 to Lost Trail Pass, Montana Highway 43
DISTANCE: 88 miles
DIFFICULTY: Moderate
BEST TIME TO GO: Mid-July through September
GUIDES: Wolf, *Vol. II: Southern Montana;* or Howard and Howard,
The Montana CDT Guidebook

This traverse follows the Continental Divide through classic alpine terrain. The earlier miles are more forested; the latter section is higher, wilder, rockier, and more difficult, but the views are well worth the work. Expect some steep ups and downs, along with some tricky footway. A highlight is the opportunity to camp near pristine alpine lakes.

Idaho and Montana   211

Twenty miles from the nearest road, the Chinese Wall is the Bob Marshall Wilderness's most famous landmark.

Highlight Hike
Bob Marshall Wilderness

WHERE: U.S. Highway 2 near East Glacier to Benchmark Work Station at Forest Road 235
DISTANCE: 108 miles
DIFFICULTY: Challenging
BEST TIME TO GO: Late summer
GUIDES: *Wolf, Vol. I: Northern Montana*; or Howard and Howard, *The Montana CDT Guidebook*

Just getting to the trailhead at Benchmark Wilderness Ranch, some 30 miles from the small town of Augusta, is an adventure in itself. From there follow the CDT to the Bob Marshall Wilderness's most famous feature, the aptly named Chinese Wall. Several interconnecting trails let you choose from among different options, handy in bad weather. The character of this rugged traverse is largely high country, with lots of climbing and descending. Note that frequent heavy horse traffic erodes the trails, especially in rainy weather and just after the snowmelt.

APPENDIX 1: **RECOMMENDED READING**

by Daniel R. Smith

APPALACHIAN TRAIL

The Appalachian Trail is the oldest and most popular of the Triple Crown trails, and it's been the subject of more than 100 books. Here's a selection to get you started.

Primary Planning Guides

The Appalachian Trail Guides are published by the Appalachian Trail Conference in Harpers Ferry, West Virginia. These eleven guides, periodically updated as needed, are the fundamental references for hiking all or part of the Appalachian Trail. Each describes the trail both northbound and southbound. Also included are cumulative distances for each section, maps with both topographical and elevation profiles, lists of shelters, campsites, location of trailheads, and information about local transportation and resupply opportunities.

The eleven guides are:

- *Maine*
- *New Hampshire and Vermont*
- *Massachusetts and Connecticut*
- *New York and New Jersey*
- *Pennsylvania*
- *Maryland and Northern Virginia*
- *Shenandoah National Park*
- *Central Virginia*
- *Southwest Virginia*
- *Tennessee and North Carolina*
- *North Carolina and Georgia*

The Exploring the Appalachian Trail series, edited by David Emblidge, is published by Stackpole Books (Mechanicsburg, Pa., 1999). This series divides the AT into day-hike and weekend-size chunks. These handsome books contain maps, profile maps, details about trailheads, and a host of other useful information, including history, natural history, camping know-how, and trail miscellany. This series is especially recommended for short-term hikers. It is arranged geographically as follows:

- *Hikes in the Southern Appalachians Deep South* (Georgia, North Carolina, and Tennessee)
- *Hikes in the Virginias* (Virginia and West Virginia)
- *Hikes in the Mid-Atlantic States* (Maryland, Pennsylvania, New Jersey, and New York)
- *Hikes in Southern New England* (Connecticut, Massachusetts, and Vermont)
- *Hikes in Northern New England* (New Hampshire and Maine)

For planning long-distance hikes, there are two other essential tools:

Chazin, Daniel D., ed., *Appalachian Trail Data Book* (Harpers Ferry, W. Va.: Appalachian Trail Conference, published annually). The data book lists the distances between key points of reference along the trail including shelters, water sources, and road crossings as well as distances off-trail to towns. It is of great help in planning a daily schedule.

Appalachian Trail Thru-Hiker's Companion (Harpers Ferry, W. Va.: Appalachian Trail Conference, published annually). This town guide lists motels, restaurants, grocery stores, hostels, and outfitters located on or near the trail, including distances and directions, maps of trail towns, and information about points of interest.

Other Planning Aids

Adkins, Leonard M., *The Appalachian Trail: A Visitor's Companion* (Birmingham, Ala.: Menasha Ridge Press, 1997). Provides information about the history of the AT, geology, plants, and animals. Also includes suggestions for short trips.

————, *Wildflowers of the Appalachian Trail* (Birmingham, Ala.: Menasha Ridge Press, 1999). Identifies wildflowers commonly found along the AT. Beautiful full-page photos by AT thru-hikers Joe and Monica Cook are combined with information about growing season and location along the trail, as well as the popular use of flowers by Appalachian residents and their role in local folklore.

Bruce, Dan, *The Thru-hikers Planning Guide* (Hot Springs, N. C.: Center for Appalachian Trail Studies, 1997). Some might call it overkill, but if you like to plan each campsite, dinner, food drop, and rest day, this workbook will help you do it.

Chase, Jim, *Backpacker Magazine's Guide to the Appalachian Trail* (Mechanicsburg, Pa.: Stackpole Books, 1989). Less a guide than an overview, this volume describes some of the historic sites, natural history, and geology along the way.

Chew, V. Collins, *Underfoot: A Geological Guide to the Appalachian Trail* (Harpers Ferry, W. Va.: Appalachian Trail Conference, 1988). Explains in layperson's terms the geological origins of the Appalachian Mountains as well as key geological features.

Curran, Jan D., *The Appalachian Trail: How to Prepare for and Hike It* (Harpers Ferry, W. Va.: Appalachian Trail Conference, 1997). A guide to getting your thru-hike off the ground.

Garvey, Edward B., *The New Appalachian Trail* (Birmingham, Ala.: Menasha Ridge Press, 1997). Ed Garvey, one of the legendary figures of the Appalachian Trail, completed a thru-hike in 1970. The resulting book was standard reading within the hiking community for decades. This updated version is both the story of his second thru-hike 25 years later and a commentary on the changing nature of the trail.

Hugo, Beverly, *Women and Thru-hiking on the Appalachian Trail* (Insight Publishing Company, 2000). To write this book, author and thru-hiker Beverly "Maine Rose" Hugo surveyed hundreds of women on everything from hiking partners to underwear. It's the only women's how-to book on thru-hiking—and it does a great job.

Logue, Victoria and Frank, *The Appalachian Trail Backpacker* (Birmingham, Ala.: Menasha Ridge Press, 1997). This book explains how to prepare for both short- and long-distance hikes on the Appalachian Trail. The authors relate the collective experiences of several dozen thru-hikers.

———, *The Best of the Appalachian Trail Overnight Hikes* (Birmingham, Ala.: Menasha Ridge Press, 1994). This work provides a detailed description of dozens of short hikes along the Appalachian Trail. Many of the suggested treks are loop hikes utilizing the AT and connecting trails. All hikes are rated according to difficulty. Directions by road to starting and ending points are included. Also check out *The Best of the Appalachian Trail Day Hikes*, by the same authors.

Mueser, Roland, *Long-Distance Hiking: Lessons from the Appalachian Trail* (Camden, Maine: Ragged Mountain Press, 1998). The author surveys a broad sampling of AT thru-hikers to collect and analyze data on gear, diet, daily mileage, and many other facets of long-distance hiking. A revealing insight into the long-distance community.

Whalen, Christopher, *Appalachian Trail: Workbook for Planning Thru-hikes* (Harpers Ferry, W. Va.: Appalachian Trail Conference, 1998). This workbook strips down the planning process to the essentials. Its forms are useful for food drops.

Journeys

Appalachian Adventure: From Georgia to Maine, A Spectacular Journey on the Great American Trail (Atlanta: Longstreet Press, 1995). A collection of stories and photographs by newspaper reporters from several East Coast newspapers, who hiked and wrote about the trail in 1994. Captures the thru-hiking experience and includes lots of trivia about everything from bears to trail building.

Brill, David, *As Far As the Eye Can See* (Nashville: Rutledge Hill Press, 1990). The humorous, sensitive, and engaging story of a 1970s thru-hiker.

Deeds, Jean, *There Are Mountains to Climb* (Indiana: Silverwood Press, 1996). When this middle-aged non-hiker decided to thru-hike the AT—for reasons even she did not fully understand—she brought along a keen sense of observation. One of the more inspiring narratives about the AT as a personal odyssey.

Eberhart, Eb, *10 Million Steps* (Helena, Mont.: Falcon Publishing, 2000). The AT isn't long enough for you? This account of the Eastern Continental Trail follows the author from Cap Gaspé to Key West.

Luxenberg, Larry, *Walking the Appalachian Trail* (Mechanicsburg, Pa.: Stackpole Books, 1994). The author shares the experiences of multiple thru-hikers along with those of trail maintainers, "trail angels," and other members of the AT community.

Ross, Cindy, *A Woman's Journey* (Harpers Ferry, W. Va.: Appalachian Trail Conference, 1990). This book, part text and part sketches, is a series of reflections by a woman who completed the AT in two long-distance hikes.

Setzer, Lynn, *A Season on the Appalachian Trail* (Birmingham, Ala.: Menasha Ridge Press, 1997). Writer and hiking enthusiast Lynn Setzer couldn't decide whether to thru-hike or write about it. She did a little of each. This book follows thru-hikers from Georgia to Maine.

Shaffer, Earl V., *Walking with Spring* (Harpers Ferry, W. Va.: The Appalachian Trail Conference, 1995). A "must" read. The first recognized AT thru-hiker tells his story. Beautifully written.

Inspirational

Emblidge, David, ed., *The Appalachian Trail Reader* (New York: Oxford University Press, 1996). Another "must" read. Emblidge combines the writings of long-distance hikers, active members of the trail community, and prestigious authors from Henry David Thoreau to Wallace Stegner to capture the spirit of the AT.

MacKaye, Benton, *The New Exploration: A Philosophy of Regional Planning* (Champaign-Urbana, Ill.: The University of Illinois Press, 1990). Offers insights into the philosophy and values of one of the dreamers who first envisioned an "endless" trail through the Appalachians.

Marshall, Ian, *Story Line: Exploring the Literature of the Appalachian Trail* (Charlottesville, Va.: University Press of Virginia, 1998). A unique and creative book. The author combines his own journeys on the AT with insights gleaned from famous travelers and writers such as William Bartram, Henry David Thoreau, and Annie Dillard, who themselves wrote about the Appalachian terrain and its residents.

Muench, David, *Uncommon Places* (Harpers Ferry, W. Va.: Appalachian Trail Conference, 1991). A beautiful coffee-table book with photographs of AT country taken by one of America's leading outdoor photographers.

PACIFIC CREST TRAIL
Primary Planning Guides

Five publications will help you plan a hike on any long stretch of the PCT:

Schaffer, Jeffrey P. et al., *The Pacific Crest Trail. Vol. I: California,* and *Vol. II: Oregon and Washington* (Berkeley, Calif.: Wilderness Press, 1996 and 2000). This two-volume work is the most important tool for anyone planning a long-distance hike on the PCT. The trail route is clearly drawn on 1:50,000-scale maps. Also included is a description of the official route and occasional suggestions for possible alternate routes. The author includes a great deal of information about geology, national and social history, as well as environmental issues. In Volume I, this is separated from the route description. In Volume II, it is integrated with the route description, which can be distracting.

Shaffer's guidebooks should be supplemented with the following references:

Berger, Karen, and Daniel R. Smith, *The Pacific Crest Trail: A Hiker's Companion* (Woodstock,

Vt.: Countryman Press, 2000). This interpretive guide breaks the trail into eighteen sections, describes the trail's route, then discusses what hikers will see, including plants, animals, historical sites, and geological features. It also contains practical information, including trailheads, nearby towns, gear needed, and best seasons to hike each section.

Croot, Leslie, *Pacific Crest Trail Town Guide* (Sacramento, Calif.: Pacific Crest Trail Association, 1998). This helpful booklet provides up-to-date information about most of the resupply points available to hikers from Mexico to Canada. Lists of accommodations, restaurants, banks, ATMs, grocery stores, etc., are included. Also contains maps of the more popular towns and descriptions of how to leave and return to the PCT route.

Go, Ben, *Pacific Crest Trail Data Book* (Sacramento, Calif.: Pacific Crest Trail Association, 1997). Lists cumulative mileage and elevation and greatly simplifies the job of calculating daily mileage, daily elevation changes, and distance between water sources.

Jardine, Ray, *The Pacific Crest Trail Handbook* (LaPine, Ore.: Adventurelore Press, 1997, out of print). Includes Jardine's controversial advice on health, hygiene, physical fitness, lightweight hiking techniques, and safety. Provides sample itineraries for thru-hikers. The book places major emphasis on traveling ultralight. Jardine's newer book, *Beyond Backpacking*, also discusses ultralight gear and techniques, but does not contain PCT-specific information.

Other Planning Aids

Skillman, Don and Lolly, *25 Hikes Along the Pacific Crest Trail* (Mechanicsburg, Pa.: Stackpole Press, 1994). Descriptions of the best short hikes along the PCT, especially those of 1 to 5 days.

Clarke, Clinton C., *The Pacific Crest Trailway* (Pasadena, Calif.: The Pacific Crest Trail System Conference, 1945, out of print). This hard-to-locate work is a must for anyone interested in the history of the PCT. Clarke was one of the early activists who started piecing together existing trails to establish a continuous footway from Mexico to Canada.

Journeys: The Classics

Fletcher, Colin, *The Thousand Mile Summer in the Desert and High Sierra* (Berkeley, Calif.: Howell North Books, 1965). One of the world's premier walkers hikes through southern and central California. Told with the humor and intense love of the outdoors that typify Fletcher's writing style.

Muir, John, My *First Summer in the Sierra* (New York: Penguin Books, 1987). Written in 1911, this book contains the recollections of one of America's most famous pioneer backcountry travelers. Muir speaks elegantly about the geology, plant and animal life, and above all, about the breathtaking beauty of the High Sierra.

Journeys: The Present Day

Berger, Karen, and Daniel R. Smith, *Along the Pacific Crest Trail* (Englewood, Colo.: Westcliffe Publishers, 1998). This coffee-table book tells the story of a 1997 PCT thru-hike. Includes beautiful full-page photographs by Bart Smith of the views along the Pacific Crest Trail.

Green, David, *The Trail North: A Solo Journey on the Pacific Crest* (Covelo, Calif.: Island Press, 1981). The story of a sixteen-year-old's summer-long solo horsepacking trip along the PCT. Fine insights into the author's growing pains and experiences as he learns to live in wilderness.

Hotel, Bob, *Soul, Sweat and Survival on the Pacific Crest Trail* (Livermore, Calif.: Bittersweet Publishing Company, 1994). The first person to run the PCT relates his three long-distance trips. Also contains a list of gear and a weekly summary of his distances and elevation gains.

Ross, Cindy, *Journey on the Crest: Walking 2600*

Miles from Mexico to Canada (Seattle: The Mountaineers Books, 1987). The story of a woman's two long-distance hikes along the PCT. Full of insights into the personal growth involved in a long-distance experience.

CONTINENTAL DIVIDE TRAIL

Primary Planning Guides

The most essential tool for planning a hike of any length along the Continental Divide Trail is the set of six guidebooks produced by the Continental Divide Trail Society, based in Baltimore, Maryland. The guides are broken into sections starting and ending at road crossings. Each section contains a description of the route, including cumulative distances between landmarks and elevation changes.

The guides are written in a north-to-south direction, which makes them much easier to use for southbound hikers than for northbounders. They do a remarkably good job of describing the route, especially when cross-country travel is required. At times they suggest alternative routes. The author of the guidebooks is Jim Wolf, founder of the Continental Divide Trail Society. Jim is the visionary who first conceived the idea of a border-to-border trail along the Divide.

The present series consists of six volumes, some of which have supplements containing updated information:

- *Volume I: Northern Montana* (1991)
- *Volume II: Southern Montana and Idaho* (1979, supplement published 1999)
- *Volume III: Wyoming* (1980, supplement published 1993)
- *Volume IV: Northern Colorado* (1982, supplement published 2000)
- *Volume V: Southern Colorado* (1997)
- *Volume VI: Northern New Mexico* (1998)

There is not yet a volume for southern New Mexico. Guidebooks can be purchased directly from the Continental Divide Trail Society, 3704 North Charles Street, Baltimore, MD 21218 (*cdtsociety@aol.com*). "Map-Paks" are available for Volumes I, II, III, IV, and V. They are an absolute must for anyone hiking any distance on the CDT.

In addition, Westcliffe Publishers of Englewood, Colorado, has published a series of guidebooks to the official route of the CDT as sanctioned by government agencies and the Continental Divide Trail Alliance:

- *The Montana/Idaho CDT Guidebook*, by Lynna and Leland Howard
- *The Wyoming CDT Guidebook*, by Lora Davis
- *The Colorado CDT Guidebook*, by Tom Lorang Jones
- *The New Mexico CDT Guidebook*, by Bob Julyan

Other Planning Aids

Continental Divide Trail: Long Distance Planning Guide (Pine, Colo.: Continental Divide Trail Association). This basic guide gives an overview of long-distance hiking on the CDT. It is available free to Continental Divide Trail Association members. Also available is a supplementary list of maps for the CDT.

Herrero, Stephen, *Bear Attacks: Their Causes and Avoidance* (New York: Lyons Press, 1985). Herrero is a recognized expert on grizzly bears. Here he tackles the frightening and important subject of bear attacks and what to do to prevent and survive them.

McNamee, Thomas, *The Grizzly Bear* (New York: Alfred A. Knoff, 1985). Hikers—especially folks who have never visited the northern Rockies—often wonder about what it's like to hike in grizzly country. This book gives answers.

Wendt, Clayton L., *Continental Divide GPS Companion: Montana, Wyoming, Colorado, and New Mexico* (Wendt Company, 1999). Because of the many sections of trailless cross-country travel on the CDT, this is a highly useful tool.

Schneider, Russ, ed., *Best Hikes Along the Continental Divide: From Northern Alberta, Canada to Mexico* (Helena, Montana: Falcon Press, 1998). Want to extend your CDT trip into Canada's Divide? This guide offers suggestions for both short- and long-distance hikers on both sides of the border.

Journeys

Berger, Karen, and Daniel R. Smith, *Where the Waters Divide: A 3,000 Mile Trek Along America's Continental Divide* (Woodstock, Vt.: Countryman Press, 1997). The story of a Mexico-to-Canada thru-hike. In addition to describing the journey, this book examines the history, culture, and geography of the Great Divide.

Robbins, Michael, *Along the Continental Divide* (Washington, D.C.: National Geographic Society, 1981). Beautiful images of the Divide's territory combined with vignettes about the people who inhabit the lands around America's backbone.

Westcliffe CDT Series (Englewood, Colo.: Westcliffe Publishers):

- *Along Montana and Idaho's CDT*, by Lynna and Leland Howard
- *Along Wyoming's CDT*, by Scott Smith
- *Along Colorado's Continental Divide*, by John Fayhee and John Fielder
- *Along New Mexico's CDT*, by David Peterson and Tom Till

You won't be able to stop dreaming of a CDT thru-hike after looking at these photos and reading about these journeys.

APPENDIX 2: **TRAIL ASSOCIATIONS**

T rail associations work with government agencies and marshal volunteer and corporate support to protect, manage, and maintain trails. Most of these organizations also provide hiker information, sell guidebooks, and answer questions. Membership in them helps to support the trails on which we hike. For more information, consult the following:

APPALACHIAN TRAIL CONFERENCE
P.O. Box 807
Washington and Jackson Streets
Harpers Ferry, WV 25425
304-535-6331
www.appalachiantrail.org

PACIFIC CREST TRAIL ASSOCIATION
5325 Elkhorn Boulevard, PMB 256
Sacramento, CA 95842
888-PCTRAIL
www.pcta.org

CONTINENTAL DIVIDE TRAIL ALLIANCE
P.O. Box 628
Pine, CO 80470
888-909-CDTA
www.cdtrail.org
cdnst@aol.com

CONTINENTAL DIVIDE TRAIL SOCIETY
3704 North Charles Street #601
Baltimore, MD 21218
410-235-9610
www.gorp.com/cdts
cdtsociety@aol.com

APPALACHIAN LONG DISTANCE HIKERS
ASSOCIATION (ALDHA)
10 Benning Street, PMB 224
West Lebanon, NH 03784
www.aldha.org

AMERICAN LONG-DISTANCE HIKING
ASSOCIATION: WESTERN STATES
(ALDHA-WEST)
P.O. Box 651
Vancouver, WA 98666
www.gorp.com/nonprof/aldhaw

APPENDIX 3: **MAIL DROPS**

No two hikers use exactly the same mail-drop schedule. The following mail drops, which are listed going northbound, are most commonly used by long-distance hikers. Many others offer services ranging from a post office in the back of a convenience store to a full-fledged town. Choose your mail drops based on what services you think you'll need (laundry, hotels, shops, outfitters). You'll find current information on trail town services on the AT and PCT in both the *Pacific Crest Trail Town Guide* and the *Appalachian Trail Thru-Hiker's Companion* (see Appendix 1). The CDTA (see Appendix 2) provides a list of mail drops and services prepared by recent hikers. The PCTA website (Appendix 2) has detailed instructions on how to resupply without mail drops (i.e., shopping en route).

Establishments with an asterisk (*) are private establishments. The private businesses included here are those that have accepted thru-hiker packages for a number of years. However, new hostels and lodges open regularly. The *Appalachian Trail Thru-Hiker's Companion* lists a startling number of businesses that will accept packages and shuttle you to road crossings, enabling you to further cut down on your pack weight. Remember that private establishments are bought and sold or go out of business. Before sending a mail drop to a business, check (directly or in current thru-hiker guidebooks) to find out whether they are still accepting packages and whether they charge a fee, require you to write in advance, or require that you send a package via UPS.

APPALACHIAN TRAIL

*Walasi-yi Center, Neels Gap, 9710 Gainesville Highway, Blairsville, GA 30512

*Berry Patch (guests only), 5038 U.S. Highway 76, Hiawasee, GA 30546; or Hiawasee, GA 30546

*Nantahala Outdoor Center, 13077 Highway 19W, Bryson City, NC 28713

Fontana Dam, NC, 28734

Gatlinburg, TN 28733

*Mountain Momma's, 1981 Waterville Road, Newport, TN 37821

Hot Springs, NC 28743

Erwin, TN 37650

Roan Mountain, TN 37687; or Elk Park, NC 28622

Hampton, TN 37658

Damascus, VA 24236

Atkins, VA 24311

Bland, VA 24314

Pearisburg, VA 24134

Troutville, VA 24175; or Cloverdale, VA 24077

Tyro, VA 22976

Waynesboro, VA 24464

Front Royal, VA 22630

Harpers Ferry, WV 25425

Boiling Springs, PA 17007

Duncannon, PA 17020

Port Clinton, PA 19549

Delaware Water Gap, PA 18327

Unionville, NY 10988

Bear Mountain, NY 10911; or Fort Montgomery, NY 10922

Pawling, NY 12564

Kent, CT 96757

Cornwall Bridge, CT 06754

Salisbury, CT 06068

Tyringham, MA 01264

Dalton, MA 01226

Cheshire, MA 01225
North Adams, MA 01247
Bennington, VT 05201
Manchester Center, VT 05255
Killington, VT 05751; or *Inn at Long Trail,
     Sherburne Pass, U.S. Route 4, Killington, VT
     05751
West Hartford, VT 05084
Hanover, NH 03755
Glencliff, NH 03238
North Woodstock, NH 03262
Gorham, NH 03581
Andover, ME 04216
Rangeley, ME 04970
Stratton, ME 04982
Caratunk, ME 04925
Monson, ME 04464

PACIFIC CREST TRAIL

Mount Laguna, CA 91948
Julian, CA 92036
Warner Springs, CA 92086
*Kamp Anza Kampground, 41560 Terwilliger
     Road, Space 19, Anza, CA 92539; or Anza, CA
     92539
Idyllwild, CA 92547
Cabazon, CA 92230; or Banning, CA 92220
Big Bear City, CA 92314; or Big Bear Lake, CA
     92315
Wrightwood, CA, 92397
Agua Dulce, CA 91350
Lake Hughes, CA 93532
Mojave, CA 93501; or Tehachapi, CA 93561
Onyx, CA 93255
*Kennedy Meadows General Store: (via post
     office) P.O. Box 3A-5, Inyokern, CA 93527;
     (via UPS) 1445 Kennedy Meadows Road,
     Inyokern, CA 93527
Lone Pine, CA 93545
Independence, CA 93526
*Vermilion Valley Resort, c/o Rancheria Garage,
     Huntington Lake Road, Lakeshore, CA
     93634; or *Muir Trail Ranch, Box 176,

Lakeshore, CA 93634
Mammoth Lakes, CA 93546; or Reds Meadow
     Resort, P.O. Box 395, Mammoth Lakes, CA
     93546
Tuolumne Meadows, Yosemite National Park, CA
     95389
Echo Lake, CA 95721; or South Lake Tahoe, CA
     96150
Sierra City, CA 96125
Belden, CA 95915; or *Belden Town Store, 14785
     Belden Town Road, Belden, CA 95915 (UPS
     only)
Old Station, CA 96071
Burney, CA 96013
Castella, CA 96017
Seiad Valley, CA 96086
Ashland, OR 97520
*Crater Lake Lodge, 400 Rim Village, Crater
     Lake, OR 97604; or Crater Lake, OR 97604
*Diamond Lake Lodge, OR 97731
*Shelter Cove Resort, W. Odell Lake Access,
     Highway 58, Crescent Lake, OR 97425
*Elk Lake Resort, Century Drive, P.O. Box 789,
     Bend, OR 97709; or Bend, OR 97701
Sisters, OR 97759
*Ollalie Lake Resort, c/o Clakamas Ranger
     District, 595 N.W. Industrial Way, Estacada,
     OR 97023
*Timberline Ski Area, WY'East Store, Timberline
     Lodge, OR 97028
Cascade Locks, OR 97014
Stevenson, WA 98648 (alternate route only)
White Pass Rural Branch P.O., 48851 U.S.
     Highway 12, Naches, WA 98937
P.O. at Time Wise Grocery, 771 State Route 906,
     Snoqualmie Pass, WA 98068
Skykomish, WA 98288
Stehekin, WA 98852

CONTINENTAL DIVIDE TRAIL

Deming, NM (Columbus terminus only), 88030
Hachita, NM 88040
Silver City, NM 88061

Mimbres, NM 88049
Reserve, NM (alternate route), 87830
Pie Town, NM (official route) 87827
Continental Divide, NM (alternate route), 87312
Grants, NM (official route) 87020
Cuba, NM 87013
*Ghost Ranch Conference Center, Abiquiu, NM 87510
Chama, NM 87520
Pagosa Springs, CO 81147
Creede, CO 81130; or Lake City, CO 81235
*Monarch Lodge, Garfield, CO 81227
Twin Lakes, CO 81251
Silverthorne, CO 80498
Grand Lake, CO 80447
Steamboat Springs, CO 80477
Encampment, WY 82325

Rawlins, WY 82301
South Pass City, WY 82520
*Big Sandy Lodge, #8 Spotted Tail Circle, Rock Springs, WY 82901 (inquire first)
*Togwotee Lodge, Moran, WY 83013
Old Faithful Station, WY 82190
Macks Inn, ID 83433
Lima, MT 59739
Leadore, ID 83464
Wisdom, MT 59761; Salmon, ID 83467; or Sula, MT 59871
Anaconda, MT 59711
Helena, MT 59601
Butte, MT 59701
Lincoln, MT 59639
*Benchmark Ranch, Augusta, MT 59410
East Glacier, MT 50434

Index

ABOUT THE AUTHOR

Karen Berger is a full-time writer specializing in travel, the outdoors, the environment, and—especially—backpacking. She is one of approximately twenty people who have thru-hiked the AT, the PCT, and the CDT. She is an accomplished and enthusiastic public speaker, a well-known and active member of the long-distance hiking community, and a successful magazine and book author. Her published books include *Along the Pacific Crest Trail* (Westcliffe), *Where the Waters Divide* (Harmony and Countryman), *Everyday Wisdom* (Mountaineers Books), *Advanced Backpacking: A Trailside Guide* (Norton), *Hiking and Backpacking* (Norton), *SCUBA Diving: A Trailside Guide* (Norton), and *The PCT: A Hiker's Companion* (Countryman).

ABOUT THE MOUNTAINEERS

THE MOUNTAINEERS, founded in 1906, is a nonprofit outdoor activity and conservation club, whose mission is "to explore, study, preserve, and enjoy the natural beauty of the outdoors . . . . " Based in Seattle, Washington, the club is now the third-largest such organization in the United States, with 15,000 members and five branches throughout Washington State.

The Mountaineers sponsors both classes and year-round outdoor activities in the Pacific Northwest, which include hiking, mountain climbing, ski-touring, snowshoeing, bicycling, camping, kayaking and canoeing, nature study, sailing, and adventure travel. The club's conservation division supports environmental causes through educational activities, sponsoring legislation, and presenting informational programs. All club activities are led by skilled, experienced volunteers, who are dedicated to promoting safe and responsible enjoyment and preservation of the outdoors.

If you would like to participate in these organized outdoor activities or the club's programs, consider a membership in The Mountaineers. For information and an application, write or call The Mountaineers, Club Headquarters, 300 Third Avenue West, Seattle, WA 98119; 206-284-6310.

The Mountaineers Books, an active, nonprofit publishing program of the club, produces guidebooks, instructional texts, historical works, natural history guides, and works on environmental conservation. All books produced by The Mountaineers fulfill the club's mission.

Send or call for our catalog of more than 450 outdoor titles:

The Mountaineers Books
1001 SW Klickitat Way, Suite 201
Seattle, WA 98134
800-553-4453
mbooks@mountaineers.org
www.mountaineersbooks.org